VIEWING CHILD PORNOGRAPHY ON THE INTERNET

Understanding the Offence, Managing the Offender, Helping the Victims

Edited by
Ethel Quayle and Max Taylor

Russell House Publishing

First published in 2005 by:
Russell House Publishing Ltd.
4 St. George's House
Uplyme Road
Lyme Regis
Dorset DT7 3LS
Tel: 01297-443948
Fax: 01297-442722
e-mail: help@russellhouse.co.uk
www.russellhouse.co.uk

British Library Cataloguing-in-publication Data:

A catalogue record for this book is available from the British Library.

ISBN: 1-903855-69-1

Typeset by TW Typesetting, Plymouth, Devon
Printed and bound by Antony Rowe, Chippenham

About Russell House Publishing

RHP is a group of social work, probation, education and youth and community work practitioners and academics working in collaboration with a professional publishing team.

Our aim is to work closely with the field to produce innovative and valuable materials to help managers, trainers, practitioners and students.

We are keen to receive feedback on publications and new ideas for future projects.

For details of our other publications please visit our website or ask us for a catalogue. Contact details are on this page.

Contents

Preface

The new technologies, especially the Internet, present society with a number of dilemmas. On the one hand, the Internet has revolutionised our capacity to communicate with other people, and in so doing it has in a sense effectively eliminated the national boundaries that formerly reduced and hindered contact between people. Indeed it could be argued that it has even abolished some of the constraints that distance binds us with, and travel and distance are now no longer the impediments they were to the development of relationships. Information exchange and the dissemination of knowledge can no longer be controlled and limited by Government, and whole new areas of ecommerce and trade have become possible.

On the other hand, the freedom that the Internet has given us also allows less benign activity to flourish. Amongst the array of problematic activity on the Internet, of particular concern to this book is the availability and distribution of abuse images of children. Abuse images (a more appropriate term to use than child pornography) are at their worst pictures of children being sexually assaulted. They are readily available on the Internet and they are traded and collected by an unknown, but probably large, number of people.

Collecting and distributing abuse images

Collecting and distributing abuse images of children is not a new phenomenon. Contemporary media coverage of this issue tends to stress the relationship between the Internet and abuse images as if it were something new, but in reality abuse images have probably always been produced in whatever the contemporary medium for visual representation was. In Victorian times, for example, abuse images of children seem to have been a part of the broader trade in pornography. There is some evidence that the preferred medium seems to have been postcards and some estimates suggest that the ratio of children to adult images was 5:1. Indeed, in as early as 1847 J.T. Wythe produced a postcard album containing erotic scenes some of which involved children. These activities were essentially commercial in character, and clearly the sales of such postcards justified their production. We can only presume that there was a parallel non-commercial production of abuse images, produced for private retention, or perhaps distributed to like-minded people.

Even in Victorian times, the size of collections of erotic images was very large. In what was one of the first recorded formal police actions against someone possessing pornography (including abuse images of children), the London Police in 1874 raided the studio of Henry Hayler and confiscated some 130,000 photographs; given that many of these images were on glass plates, the physical size of this collection was considerable. It is of course interesting to note that 125 years on, similar police actions are still taking place.

However now, instead of images being seized on postcards or glass photographic plates (as in Hayler's case) that must have probably filled a room, that same number of images (and many more) can be contained within a computer hard drive, or a small portable digital memory stick measuring 2 inches by 1 inch. This is of course one significant difference the Internet has made. But other changes have also come with the Internet: not only has it never been easier to collect and store (and perhaps hide) abuse images, but it has also never been so easy to make them (using digital cameras), and so easy to distribute them. Furthermore the breaking down of national borders that the Internet so effectively does serves to make detection, tracking and identification of child victims and perpetrators much more difficult than ever before.

This represents the challenge of the Internet – it is not responsible for the 'invention' of abuse images, nor has it created a demand that wasn't already there. Children were being sexually exploited before the Internet, and no doubt when we have solved the problems of the Internet, other forms of exploitation will emerge. What the Internet does is to make abuse images of children relatively easily available, at little or no cost, in circumstances of perceived anonymity. The challenge we face is to reduce and control the amount of abuse images available, without loosing the valuable qualities of the Internet; to retain its open and critical (and at time anarchic) qualities, without generating a surveillance and control regime that destroys the many positive qualities.

Crime on the Internet

The challenge of abuse images is part of the broader challenge that crime on the Internet presents to society. From a slightly different but relevant perspective, Pease suggests that 'Criminal careers will bifurcate into the confrontational and the clever. Those able to do so will learn criminal methods through the Internet . . . The Internet is the real university of crime . . . The speed at which innovation in crime takes place will increase, as a result of method of diffusion via the NET' (Pease, 1997: 242). The policing strategies developed to address the problems of abuse images have undoubtedly pushed forward techniques of surveillance, monitoring and crime control on the Internet, and have also greatly contributed to improvements in police liaison and co-operation, at both national and international levels. There is a balance to be struck, however, between legitimate oversight, and intrusive monitoring; between a right to privacy and the legitimate wish to protect children from exploitation. It is likely that the resolution to these issues will not be driven by a primary concern with abuse images, but reflect more commercial pressures related to ecommerce. However, the resolution to the problems of privacy and oversight will profoundly affect our lives.

Working with offenders

A further and different challenge relates to what to do with individuals who have been caught in possession of abuse images of children, or have been involved in their production.

We are beginning to better understand the dynamics of involvement with abuse images, and to take a more differentiated view of the kinds of offenders involved. The numbers that seem to be potentially at risk of arrest and involvement with the criminal justice system seem to be very large (judging from recent police actions). How are programmes to be developed to address the needs of these offenders? Are they the same as other forms of sex offender, or do they justify the development of different therapeutic interventions? And are we sufficiently addressing preventative measures, rather than responding to events as they arise?

Responding to these challenges calls upon the resources of a range of disciplines and professions. In focusing on the problem of abuse images, professional boundaries necessarily become permeable as the realisation emerges that no single profession or approach can on its own address the problem. To face this problem, we need to focus on shared responsibilities, sharing skills and learning from each other.

It is from this sense of sharing that this book has its origins. In May 2004 a Conference was held by the COPINE Project in Cork, Ireland, that sought to explore and learn from different disciplines and professional experiences dealing with the problem of abuse images of children. This was the 5th COPINE Conference to be held, and its agenda was to explore new legal, psychological and social perspectives on the problems of abuse images of children. The Conference was partially funded by the European Union Daphne Program, and the Government of Ireland, and this support enabled some of the foremost experts in the world to come together to discuss these issues; this book presents enhanced and developed versions of a number of the papers presented at the Conference, developing further the themes of legal, psychological and social issues.

Within the broader context of child sexual exploitation, four broad areas of concern can be identified from the chapters presented in this book – a concern with the empirical evidence, a concern with legal and law enforcement provision, a concern with conceptual and practical understanding of the offending process and the management of offenders, and a concern with victim issues. In an area that often attracts unthinking and uncritical media comment, it is important to develop both empirical knowledge and conceptual understanding of the problems presented by abuse images and the Internet. From different perspectives, the chapters presented in this book provide the foundations for systematic and critical development of knowledge and understanding, and represent a major step forward in an understanding of the problems that face us.

The chapters presented here do not necessarily all address the conference themes in the same way. Diverse participants from a wide range of professional backgrounds means that the topic is addressed from a number of perspectives. But taken together, this collection of chapters presents a challenging and comprehensive overview of the current situation, with clear relevance to professionals having legal, social welfare or therapeutic contact with abuse images, Internet offenders and their context. Alisdair Gillespie presents an account of some of the legal difficulties in the UK facing prosecution for possession of abuse images. Unlike other jurisdictions, the UK has approached this problem in a piece-meal way, and this is reflected in the problems faced in identifying offences, and relating legal provision to the need to control and manage the problem. In a sense, Janis Wolak (with David Finkelhor and Kimberley Mitchell) take some of these issues further by presenting new data about the nature of the problem. Given the often intemperate media coverage of offences related to abuse images, this paper offers a sound empirical base on which to base and extend our understanding.

John Hunter, Tony Krone, Kenneth Lanning, Lars Lööf and Hamish McCulloch offer international perspectives on the problems of abuse images and abusive youth. Whilst these papers address different aspects of the problem, they help to place into perspective both the range and nature of victimisation, and the international context. Whilst each author comes from different backgrounds, the commonalities in their papers help us to bring the problem of sexual offending and abuse images much more sharply into focus.

David Middleton (with Tony Beech and Rebecca Mandeville-Nordon) and Ethel Quayle address issues related to the management of offenders, and offer new and imaginative directions for therapeutic interventions for Internet offenders. In a very demanding and challenging chapter, Bryan Roche (with Maria Ruiz, Martina O'Riordan and Karen-Anne Hand) also raise issues related to offenders, but from a research background, presenting and developing a novel way of addressing assessment, as well as offering a new conceptual framework for understanding sexual offending. Victim issues are addressed by Tink Palmer and Gemma Holland, who draw on their experience in different contexts to extend our knowledge of the adverse consequences of the engagement for the child in the production of abuse images.

Helping victims

We are aware that these chapters are going to engage the reader in different ways, and may impact on knowledge, practice, process, policy and future research. As editors, we gave considerable thought to some of the material being presented, knowing that conceptually it may seem difficult and at times obscure. Calder (2004) talked about child sexual abuse and the Internet as being a new frontier, and that the contribution made by that book was 'a small building block as we endeavour to construct a larger and safer platform for effective and informed developments'. We are optimistic that these chapters add to the building blocks and will help inform our future strivings.

References

Calder, M.C. (Ed.) (2004) *Child Sexual Abuse and the Internet: Tackling the New Frontier.* Lyme Regis: Russell House Publishing.

Pease, K. (1997) Predicting the Future: The Roles of Routine Activity and Rational Choice Theory, in Newman, G., Clarke, R.V. and Soham, S.G. (Eds.) *Rational Choice and Situational Crime Prevention.* Aldershot: Dartmouth Publishing.

About the Authors

Anthony Beech is a reader in Criminological Psychology at the University of Birmingham, UK and a Fellow of the British Psychological Society. He has written and researched widely in the area of sexual offending.

David Finkelhor is Director of Crimes Against Children Research Center, Co-Director of the Family Research Laboratory and Professor of Sociology at the University of New Hampshire. He has been studying the problems of child victimisation, child maltreatment and family violence since 1977. He is well known for his conceptual and empirical work on the problem of child sexual abuse, reflected in publications such as *Sourcebook on Child Sexual Abuse* (Sage, 1986) and *Nursery Crimes* (Sage, 1988). He is editor and author of 10 books and over 75 journal articles and book chapters.

Alisdair A. Gillespie is a Reader in Law at De Montfort University and a member of the Home Secretary's Internet Task Force on Child Protection. Alisdair is qualified as a barrister (Middle Temple) but works as a full-time academic. He publishes regularly on the area of child abuse in the law, particularly in respect of abusive images of children and other abuse facilitated through modern communication technologies (e.g. child grooming, child procurement).

Karen-Anne Hand is a research student at the Department of Psychology, National University of Ireland, Maynooth.

Gemma Holland is a doctoral student in Forensic Psychology in University College Cork. She was a researcher and Project Manager with the COPINE Project since it was established in 1997 until 2004. She created the COPINE Database of Child Abuse Images which was among the first in the world. The database was developed with a victim focus in order to highlight the child protection issue. She also managed and conducted research for two EU funded projects. One of these projects, the Victim Identification Project (VIP) was carried out over a three year period. It examined investigations where children were identified from abuse images and the support those victims received. Ms Holland has presented at numerous conferences at an international level.

John A. Hunter is a newly appointed Professor of Public Health at Louisiana State University Health Sciences Center in New Orleans, Louisiana and Director of Mental Health for the School of Public Health's Juvenile Justice Program. Dr Hunter's research focuses on identifying differential subtypes and developmental trajectories in youth sexual aggression.

Dr Tony Krone is a research analyst at the Australian Institute of Criminology and works with the Australian High Tech Crime Centre to research high tech criminal offences. Tony taught law at the University of New South Wales and the University of Technology, Sydney and has extensive practical experience as a lawyer in the field of criminal law.

Kenneth Lanning is currently a private consultant in the area of crimes against children. Before retiring in 2000, he was a special agent with the FBI for more than 30 years. He was assigned to the FBI Behavioral Science Unit and the National Center for the Analysis of Violent Crime at the FBI Academy in Quantico, Virginia for 20 of those years. He is a founding member of the Board of Directors of the American Professional Society on the Abuse of Children (APSAC) and is a former member of the APSAC Advisory Board. He is a current member of the Advisory Board of the Association for the Treatment of Sexual Abusers (ATSA). Mr Lanning is the 1996 recipient of the Outstanding Professional Award from APSAC for outstanding contributions to the field of child maltreatment and the 1997 recipient of the FBI Director's Annual Award for Special Achievement for his career accomplishments in connection with missing and exploited children. He has lectured before and trained thousands of police officers and criminal justice professionals.

Lars Lööf is a clinical psychologist and psychotherapist with specialisation in the fields of assessment and treatment of children and adolescents. He has worked mainly with children and adolescents with extreme and abusive experiences from exploitation, war and torture. Since June 2002 he has been Head of the Children's Unit within the intergovernmental organisation, the Council of the Baltic Sea States.

Rebecca Mandeville-Norden is employed by Devon and Cornwall Probation Area as a research officer, and is also seconded to the National Probation Directorate, working as a forensic research psychologist. Rebecca is currently undertaking a PhD at Birmingham University, where she is evaluating the effectiveness of the current sex offender treatment programmes within the Probation Service.

Hamish McCulloch is a Detective Chief Inspector from the United Kingdom, seconded to the Interpol General Secretariat, situated in Lyon, France, by the National Crime Intelligence Service since February 1999. He has over 31 years police service, 25 years of which have been spent attached to Criminal Investigation Departments involved in the investigation of national and international crime, including drug trafficking, serious sexual assaults and homicide. Mr McCulloch has represented Interpol at many international fora, including the United Nations in New York, the European Parliament, the G8 Law Enforcement Project Sub Group, the Inter American Children's Institute, the Asia European Meeting (ASEM) and the 2nd World Congress against the Commercial Sexual Exploitation of Children. In total he has undertaken over 80 official missions to more than 30 different countries in North, South and Central America, Africa, Europe and Asia, at the request of governments, law enforcement and other organisations involved in combating the smuggling of people and crimes against women and children.

David Middleton is Head of Sex Offender Strategy and Programmes for the National Probation Directorate, in the Home Office. He is the UK representative on the Committee of Experts on Sex Offender Treatment at the Council of Europe.

Kimberly Mitchell is a Research Assistant Professor of Psychology at the Crimes against Children Research Center located at the University of New Hampshire. She has a PhD in Experimental Psychology and has written numerous articles about Internet-related sexual victimisation and the incidence, risk, and impact of child victimisation.

Martina O'Riordan is a forensic psychologist currently working as a researcher in the Department of Applied Psychology, at University College Cork. She has also worked on research projects for the Irish Mental Health Commission and the Southern Health Board.

Tink Palmer is the Director of Stop it Now! UK and Ireland. She has worked in the field of child care for 33 years and specialised in the field of child protection for the past 20 years. She is experienced in working with children in both a therapeutic and forensic capacity. Tink has written widely on aspects of the sexual abuse of children, including children with sexually harmful behaviours and is frequently requested to present at national and international conferences on these issues. She is a member of a number of government committees including the Home Office Taskforce for Safety on the Internet. Tink is a member of the Board of the Internet Watch Foundation.

Ethel Quayle is a lecturer in the Department of Applied Psychology, University College Cork and a researcher with the COPINE project. She trained as a clinical psychologist with a special interest in sexual offending. She is co-author of *Child Pornography: An Internet Crime* (Brunner–Routledge, 2003) and has published in academic and professional journals.

Bryan Roche is a lecturer in psychology at the National University of Ireland, Maynooth. He has published numerous scientific papers and book chapters on the experimental analysis of behaviour, with a particular emphasis on behavioural approaches to understanding sexual deviation.

Maria R. Ruiz is Professor of Psychology at Rollins College, Florida. She has worked as a consultant in the field of developmental disabilities for over twenty years. Dr Ruiz has conducted laboratory research on animal models of Attention Deficit Hyperactivity Disorders (ADHD) and publishes articles on feminist theory and issues related to social justice.

Max Taylor is Professor of Applied Psychology at University College Cork. His research interests include crime and the new technologies, and he is founder and director of the COPINE Project. The work in this book was undertaken whilst he held a Senior Research Fellowship for the Irish Research Council for the Humanities and Social Sciences.

Janis Wolak is a Research Assistant Professor at the Crimes Against Children Research Center of the University of New Hampshire. She has a law degree and an MA in sociology. She is the author and co-author of several articles about Internet-related child victimisation and is the Director of the Youth Internet Safety Survey and the National Juvenile Online Victimization Study.

Chapter 1

Tackling Child Pornography: The Approach in England and Wales

Alisdair A. Gillespie

Introduction

There is no single offence of 'child pornography' and indeed it is arguable that there is no single definition of what constitutes 'child pornography'. During the 2004 COPINE conference a discussion ensued as to what images of child abuse should be called, and this ranged from the term 'child pornography' to 'abusive images of children'. Within England and Wales it had, since 1978, been usual to refer to 'child pornography' as 'indecent images of children' (see s.1, Protection of Children Act 1978 and s.160, Criminal Justice Act 1988) but lately there is some doubt as to whether that remains the case. Sections 48 to 50 of the Sexual Offences Act 2003 refer to a child involved in pornography. Whilst, therefore, the precise term 'child pornography' is not used, it would appear that the nexus is present and the statute is clearly considering indecent images to be considered pornography involving children or, therefore, child pornography. Taylor and Quayle (2003: 7) note that the term 'child pornography' can be unhelpful because it tends to invite comparisons to be made to adult pornography, arguably minimising the nature of the material. Edwards (2000: 1) goes further by arguing that the term is, in fact, an oxymoron as it is actually about the 'systematic rape, abuse and torture of children'. Whilst this point is undoubtedly correct, and true, Taylor and Quayle (2004) somewhat reluctantly agreed that the term is readily understood and carries with it an international meaning. On that basis they continued to use the term and I adopt this convention with similar reservations. I have argued elsewhere (see Gillespie, 2004: 361) that the use of the term within the Sexual Offences Act 2003 (albeit by conjecture rather than through literal use) is unhelpful and, arguably, counter productive and I stand by that remark.

Identifying the relevant offences

What then is the law relating to child pornography in England and Wales? The law cannot be found in a single place, not least because the criminal law in England and Wales is not codified but, rather, is to be found in a collection of statutes and cases (Lord Bingham, the Senior Law Lord and sometime Lord Chief Justice of England and Wales has previously called for codification and there is no doubt that this would help streamline the position about to be highlighted here, see Bingham, 1998). The law is spread across five statutes and, whilst it is not intended to critically examine each of these statutes, it would appear prudent to rehearse them in, at least, basic form.

The first offence is a summary-only offence created by s.43 of the Telecommunications Act 1983. This section makes it an offence to send a message or other matter that is grossly offensive. However, there are some difficulties in that it requires the use of a public communications system and thus portals such as satellite-broadband or 'wi-fi' are unlikely to be covered. The second statute is the Obscene Publications Act 1959 (as amended). This is not a statute that is specific to child pornography and covers any obscene publication. There are difficulties with this legislation, however, not least the fact that the definition of obscene can be considered somewhat problematic and accordingly the definition has tended to fall into disuse somewhat. However it remains useful for material that does not fall within the indecent images legislation (discussed below).

The principal legislation is to be found in s.1 of the Protection of Children Act 1978 (as amended) which, inter alia, makes it an offence to make, take, distribute, show an indecent image of a child, or be in possession of an indecent image with intention to distribute or show the image. The legislation was amended by the Criminal Justice and Public Order Act 1994 which, amongst other amendments, inserted the verb 'to make' into the legislation in order to take account of the advances in modern technology; the effect of this will be considered below. Prior to 1988, however, it was not an offence to possess indecent images of a child but s.160 of the Criminal Justice Act 1988 created an offence of possessing indecent images of a child, all relevant definitions being cross-referenced to the 1978 legislation.

The final piece of legislation, and most up to date, is contained within s.48 to 50 of the Sexual Offences Act 2003 and, to a lesser extent, s.12 of that Act. These will be discussed later and, in effect, build upon the foundations laid down by the 1978 Act and, arguably, overlap with the existing offences to the extent that it could be unhelpful to law enforcement agencies (see Gillespie, 2004: 366–7).

Indecent images of a child

The main legislation is, therefore, concerned with the indecent images of a child, but what is an indecent image of a child? Section 7(2) of the Act states:

> References to an indecent photograph include an indecent film, a copy of an indecent photograph or film, and an indecent photograph comprised in a film.

Thus it can be seen that we often refer to 'images'. This, in fact, means photograph-based images. Therefore, as will be seen, cartoons, drawings etc. are outside the remit of this legislation because it cannot be said to be film-based. However the 1994 Act took this further by including 'pseudo-photographs' which are defined under the Act as:

> 'Pseudo-photograph' means an image, whether made by computer-graphics or otherwise howsoever, which appears to be a photograph. (s.7:(7))

In other words, an image can be manipulated or, arguably, created by a computer and still come within the 1978 Act. However, it is important to note that the image must still be photograph-based. Akdeniz (2001: 253) argues that a pseudo-photograph is when a photograph or collage of photographs is altered by a graphics manipulation package. It is also important to note that s.7(7) and 7(8) require a pseudo-photograph to look like a photograph and this was confirmed in *Goodland* [2000] 1 W.L.R. 1427 where the Divisional Court of the Queen's Bench Division quashed a conviction for possession of a pseudo-image when the defendant had what the Court considered to be a 'pathetic' image consisting of a 'hinged' picture of an adult pornographic picture and a separate picture of a child's head. When the 'hinge' was closed the child's head was superimposed onto the adult's body. It was held that this was obviously not a pseudo-photograph but two separate photographs, neither of which were ostensibly indecent. The Court did state, however, that if the image had been photocopied (or, presumably, scanned) a different result may have arisen because there it would be a single image.

The offences are, since the 21st January 2001, serious in that a conviction under s.1 of the 1978 Act is punishable by up to ten years imprisonment and under s.160 of the 1988 Act by up to five years imprisonment. A recent Court of Appeal decision, *Oliver* [2002] EWCA Crim 2766 (and for a commentary on the sentencing decisions see Gillespie, 2003) has laid down guidance for the sentencing of offenders caught by these provisions and this guidance also carries with it interesting features for the definitional aspects of the offences.

The place of the Internet

The Internet is a useful resource but, as Taylor and Quayle (2003) note, it is also an invaluable resource for the child pornographer (see Chapter 4). It is known that most collections are now accessed and downloaded from the Internet. The courts, within England and Wales, have been called upon to decide what this amounts to. It may be thought that an offender who has downloaded an image from the Internet would be considered to be in possession of that image but in a landmark decision from the Court of Appeal in *Bowden* [2000] 1 Cr App R (S) 26 it was held that this was actually an offence of 'making' an indecent image of a child contrary to s.1 of the 1978 Act. The justification for this is that when one downloads from the Internet then a new file is created (the image downloaded) and this did not previously exist on the machine, accordingly, an image has been made. This was extended in the later case of *Smith; Jayson* [2003] 1 Cr App R 13 where it was held that merely viewing an image on the Internet would be 'making' an indecent image on the basis that a duplicate image is automatically created in the computer cache and so, once more, an image that previously did not exist on a particular medium has been created.

Ormerod (2000) argued that this should not have occurred because the presence of the possession offence would have covered this mischief. Arguably this is correct and it is difficult to see why, for example, the storage of a computer image should be treated differently from the storage of the actual physical image but, of course, if someone were to photocopy or otherwise duplicate an original image they would be undoubtedly guilty of an offence under s.1 and so there is perhaps consistency in that approach. In any event, the Court of Appeal in *Oliver* ([2002] EWCA Crim 2766) argued that someone who accessed or downloaded an image should be sentenced as though guilty of possession (i.e. maximum penalty of five years imprisonment) rather than for making an image (paras 12 and 15 of the judgment). This led to some prosecutors simply charging offenders with the possession offence arguing that it was easier to prove (no need to show that the offender was the one who made, took, showed etc.) but in *White* [2003] EWCA Crim 2035 this practice was shown to be dangerous in that there are other differences between the sentencing regime in respect of s.1 and 160, most notably the fact that an offender convicted of possession cannot have his or her licence period extended (see below for the implications of this). It would seem, therefore, that it is important to charge s.1 where possible as this has the most versatile sentencing arrangements.

Meaning of indecent image of a child?

It was noted above that child pornography, within England and Wales, is principally to be found in the law relating to indecent images of a child. What, however, is an indecent image? And what is the definition of a child?

Until 2004, the indecent image had to be of a child under the age of 16. The 1978 Act made clear that it was not necessary for the actual age of a child to be proved:

> *In proceedings under this Act relating to indecent photographs of children a person is to be taken as having been a child at any material time if it appears from the evidence as a whole that he was then under the age of [16].* (s.2(3)).

In other words the relevance is not what the age of the child is but whether the subject of the photograph appears to be a child (subject, of course, to the fact that if it can be proved that the subject is not a child then it cannot, by its very nature, be an indecent image of a child). It has been held that the apparent age of the child is a question of fact solely for the jury and that expert evidence on age is not normally admissible (see *Land* [1998] 1 Cr App R 301), but where the age of a child is known then age can be relevant (see *Owen* [1986] 86 Cr App R 291). Smith (1988) argued that the implication of this case was that criminality would thus depend on age and not the pictures: that identical images may have a different legal status because of the age, not because of what has been depicted. Arguably, of course, this is not necessarily a bad thing as the mischief behind the 1978 Act was to stop indecent images of children, and thus to stop people photographing children in indecent poses.

In 2003, however, the government decided to raise the age of 'a child' within the meaning of the 1978 legislation from 16 to 18, ostensibly to comply with a European framework decision (see [2001] OJ C26E). There are arguments both for and against the decision to raise the age of a child to 18 but given that the age of consent in this country is 16 it does appear somewhat strange that a child can consent to having sexual intercourse with his or her partner but if they decide to take intimate pictures of each other they are potentially guilty of an offence punishable by up to ten years imprisonment (for more details on the competing argument surrounding the age of a child see Gillespie (2004) pp. 361–6).

Irrespective of the age (subject to the point in *Owen* above), the meaning of indecency was considered in *Stanford* [1972] 2 QB 391 where Mr Justice Ashworth stated that indecency and obscenity are at opposite ends of the same scale (p. 398 of the judgment), the argument being that indecency is a lesser form of obscenity. The learned judge argued that recognised standards of propriety needed to be observed but this, in effect, means asking the jury to decide whether the matter is indecent. In practice, however, very few defendants ever contest a charge on the basis that the image is not indecent, although this could be, in part, due to the fact that the police normally charge in respect of pre-pubescent children and, accordingly, it is unlikely that a jury would acquit on these matters.

In *Oliver* ([2001] EWCA Crim 2766), the Court of Appeal, prompted by the Sentencing Advisory Panel, decided that it would be useful to classify images in types of indecency. To do this they adapted the COPINE scale created by Taylor et al., (2001). It is interesting to note that one of the purposes put forward by Taylor et al., was to help law enforcement agencies categorise images (p. 100) but arguably the Court of Appeal has misrepresented the use of the scale in that it was never intended to be a scale of severity, but rather it was a way of describing the material (p. 98). The original scale had 10 levels to it although Taylor et al. recognised that not all levels were necessarily going to be illegal in all jurisdictions. The Court of Appeal has purported to compress the scale to a five-point scale (although later it will be argued that in fact it has compressed it into a four-point scale).

It achieved this by removing COPINE levels 1 to 4 from the scale (actually the position of level 4 is unclear as the Court of Appeal expressly removed levels 1 to 3 and then said the first stage was level

4 which appears to leave level 4 in the ether somewhere (see Gillespie, 2003: 85), making COPINE levels 5 and 6 the new level 1 and COPINE levels 7 to 10, levels 2 to 5 respectively. Arguably the removal of the first four levels could be considered accurate (although the position of level 4, deliberate posing suggesting sexual content, is perhaps more questionable) but the Court of Appeal does not appear that confident in its own decisions because in *Carr* [2003] EWCA Crim 2416, the appellant had 12,000 pictures of women and children's bottoms, including a number of 'upskirt' images. Applying the COPINE scale to these images would appear to suggest that the majority would be within levels 1 to 3 and thus, according to *Oliver*, outside the scope of the 1978 legislation. The appellant had been sentenced to nine months imprisonment in respect of these images and whilst the Court of Appeal quashed this sentence without imposing any punishment, it did not quash the conviction (para 27 of the judgment). The implication of this would appear to be that the Court of Appeal has, albeit implicitly, accepted that COPINE levels 1 to 3 may be within the remit of the indecent legislation although if this is the case then it is unclear what punishment should be handed down to the offender. It is unfortunate that the Court is not clear as to what amounts to indecency because it is difficult to see how a jury could be expected to know if senior members of the appellate courts do not.

Sexual Offences Act 2003

The 2003 Act introduced three new offences specifically relating to child pornography and a separate offence that relates, inter alia, to showing a minor pornography. The new offences are somewhat controversial in that they arguably duplicate existing liability (see Gillespie, 2004: 366–8) but they do, perhaps, make inchoate, or preparatory, behaviour substantive.

The three offences are:

- Causing or inciting a child to become involved in pornography (s.48).
- Controlling a child involved in pornography (s.49).
- Arranging or facilitating child pornography (s.50).

All three offences are punishable by up to fourteen years imprisonment which is four years longer than the 1978 legislation although, for reasons not immediately clear, an offender convicted under this legislation is not subject to the Part 2 notification requirements. The UK operates a sex offenders notification system whereby relevant offenders are required to notify the police of their personal details. The original scheme operated under Part 1 of the Sex Offenders Act 1997 (see Cobley, 1997) but the system has now been transferred to Part 2 of the Sexual Offences Act 2003. The logic of this appears to be that it was originally the intention for these offences to relate to commercial child pornography (see Home Office, 2000) but given that the Act does not require this, it appears a startling omission to withdraw notification from these offences and it may be, therefore, that prosecutors will have to consider using the 1978 legislation to ensure that offenders are appropriately monitored, even though the sentence is reduced.

As noted by their titles, it can be seen that the primary purpose of the new offences is to tackle those who are responsible for assisting in the production of child pornography rather than, for example, those who actually make the images. The crime under s.48 (causing or inciting) would be used when someone seeks to encourage, or force, a child into being involved with pornography. A literal interpretation of this offence does, however, show a difficulty in respect of its relationship with the 1978 legislation. Inciting a child to become involved in pornography must include asking a child to pose for an indecent image. Thus this creates a situation whereby if A asks B, a fourteen-year-girl, to pose for an indecent image, A would be liable for up to fourteen years imprisonment yet if A were to actually take an indecent image he would be liable only for ten (the maximum sentence under s.1 of the 1978 legislation). This appears somewhat illogical and perhaps demonstrates that the new offences were not particularly well thought out.

The offence under s.49 (controlling) applies to conduct whereby a person acts as the controlling influence over the child and is, therefore, somewhat analogous to the situation of a 'pimp' in prostitution circumstances. The final offence, s.50, applies where a person arranges or facilitates the involvement of a child in prostitution. This could include, therefore, the owner of premises where child pornography is made (if the owner knows this), or the person who brings the child to the location where the indecent images are to be created. An argument must exist, however, that such behaviour could also be tackled by using the principles of complicity in respect of the 1978 legislation.

The more interesting part of the 2003 Act however is contained within s.12 of the Act. Section 12(1)(a) states a person comes within the section if, inter alia:

> . . . for the purposes of sexual gratification, he intentionally causes another person [under the age of 16] to . . . look at an image of any person engaging in [a sexual] activity.

This would appear, at first sight, to duplicate s.1 of the 1978 Act by making it an offence to show an indecent image to a child but s.12 offence goes much further. Section 79(4) states:

> An image means a moving or still image and includes an image produced by any means and, where the context permits, a three-dimensional image.

The implication of this section is that the context of s.12 is, unlike s.1 of the 1978 Act, not a photograph, but an image in its wider definition. Whilst, therefore, pictures, drawings, cartoons etc. are outside the scope of the 1978 legislation, they would be within the scope of s.12 if they were to be shown to a minor and were indecent. Whilst this is not an offence relating to child pornography per se, it could be useful in the 'grooming' relationships that we know occurs. Taylor and Quayle (2003) note that use of pornography, including child pornography, can be a part of the grooming cycle (2003: 25) and accordingly the wider definition could perhaps be justified in that it stops adults using sexually-explicit material for the purpose of befriending children. The width of the section (effectively including any image-based material) can be justified because of the nexus of harm from such use, and the fact that there is a requirement for the offender to act for the purpose of sexual gratification, thus removing some instances of showing/distribution to the child. It is very interesting, however, that the Act should go this far as it includes material that would be otherwise legal (if *Stanford* is correct and obscenity and indecency are at opposite ends of the scale, then non-photograph-based images that were indecent but not obscene would not be caught by the 1959 Act through showing or distributing) and it may well act as the catalyst for reform of the other legislation.

Sentencing

There has not, at the time of writing, been any reported case where the new 2003 Act has been used, and accordingly the focus of this section of the chapter returns to the 1978 legislation and attempts to identify how the courts dispose of cases.

An initial comment that can be made in respect of sentencing is in respect of the appeals mechanism. Whilst defendants have the right to appeal against sentences where they believe the sentence is manifestly excessive, the prosecution only have a limited right of appeal where an offence is prescribed and they believe it to be unduly lenient (s.36, Criminal Justice Act 1988). The difficulty is that few offences have been prescribed under this section and thus many cases cannot be the subject of a prosecution appeal (see Shute, 1999: 605). Neither s.1 nor s.160 is currently prescribed even though other offences relating to children have been (see Shute, 1999: 607). It could be argued that this is somewhat unhelpful as whilst there has never been a precise study of sentencing practice in this area, some concern has been raised about the sentencing of those convicted in this area and perhaps, therefore, prescription would be useful in allowing the prosecution to take action in respect of unduly lenient sentences.

The sentencing framework

It is important to note the Criminal Justice Act 2003 makes significant changes to the sentencing framework. However at the time of writing the Act is not yet in force and accordingly reference is made to the current framework under the Criminal Justice Act 1991 and Powers of Criminal Courts (Sentencing) Act 2000.

The Sentencing Advisory Panel is an independent body charged by Parliament to provide advice to the Court of Appeal, when requested, on relevant offences. The Panel produced advice for sentencing of offences under the 1978 and 1988 legislation (see SAP, 2002) and in *Oliver* ([2002] EWCA Crim 2766) the Court of Appeal accepted most of the recommendations of the Panel and set down guidelines for these offences.

The guidance set out in *Oliver* is quite extensive and so it will not be possible to analyse all aspects of this decision, but it is possible to concentrate on some of the key issues within the sentencing framework.

Quantity and nature of the material

According to the Court of Appeal, the nature of the material, rather than its quantity, should be the key factor in the sentencing decision. It was noted above that the Court adapted the COPINE scale to help categorise the nature of the images and the theme running through *Oliver*, is that this should be relevant to the sentence. However quantity is certainly not irrelevant, not least because of the way that the law has restricted the way in which charges are to be brought.

The Thresholds

Oliver set out a series of thresholds that govern which sentence should normally be passed. The convention is that these thresholds are suitable for a not-guilty plea without any aggravating factors (see below). *Oliver* argued that where someone was in possession of a small number of level 1 images or the collection was wholly consisting of pseudo-photographs then a fine, or if the offender has no previous convictions, then possibly a conditional discharge may be appropriate.

A community penalty is, according to the Court, appropriate for a large quantity of level 1 or a small quantity of level 2 images (para 16). Arguably there is little within this to question but the Court then continues by stating that a custodial sentence of up to six months imprisonment will be justified for the distribution of a small quantity of level 1 or 2 images, possession of a large quantity of level 2 images or a small quantity of level 3 images. A custodial sentence of up to twelve months imprisonment would be justified for the distribution of level 2 or 3 images, or the possession of a large quantity of level 3 images or small quantity of level 4 or 5 images (para 16). There are two issues within this paragraph. Firstly, it is notable that levels 4 and 5 are dealt with together and it will be noted that this occurs in other places within the judgment too. This appears to compress the scale to a four-point rather than five-point scale which is unfortunate given that the scale actually consists of ten points. Also there is a difference between levels 4 and 5, with level 5 images amounting to torture. It seems incredible that the courts do not consider that there is a significant distinction (although later cases do appear to show that the courts will consider level 5 images slightly more serious). The second point is in respect of the custody threshold. Within England and Wales, where an offender is sentenced to less than twelve months imprisonment, they are released at the half-way point irrespective of their behaviour. There is no licence period, the remaining half of the sentence is waived on condition that the offender does not reoffend (s.33(1)(a) of the Criminal Justice Act 1991 – if the offender does reoffend then he is liable to be asked to serve the remaining period of his licence in custody although this is quite rare).

The implication of this is twofold. Firstly, it means that an offender is not under the supervision of any agency other than the police and even then only for the notification requirements under Part 2 of the 2003 Act which does not prevent the offender from doing anything. Secondly, it is recognised that short custodial sentences are of little use for sex offenders in that they will get no opportunity to join a sex offender treatment programme (see Halliday, 2001, para 3.2). Cobley, (2000: 254–5) notes that a significant custodial sentence has to be passed before a treatment programme is normally offered to an offender. A community penalty, in contrast, normally requires an offender to co-operate with the Probation Service for a period of time and can include conditions being placed on the order requiring, for example, attendance at a sex offender treatment programme (s.42, PCC(S) Act 2000). On that basis it could legitimately be questioned whether using a short custodial sentence is of any real use in these circumstances, and whether it would not be better to use a community penalty instead, allowing authorities to work with offenders to ensure that there is no repeat offending. Where a short custodial sentence is to be used then it would appear prudent to consider using the additional powers available to a court (see below) in order to help with the supervision and rehabilitation of an offender.

The Court of Appeal, accepting the advice of the Sentencing Advisory Panel, decided that the next band would be a sentence of between one and three years imprisonment. Such a sentence would be where an offender is in possession of large quantities of levels 4 and 5 material or has distributed level 3 material. The final threshold is for sentences over three years imprisonment. This should be used where an offender has distributed or produced images at levels 4 and 5, especially where it involves a breach of trust, or where an offender has commissioned or encouraged the production of images. This final aspect of the threshold illustrates the potential overlap between s.1 and the new offences contained within the 2003 Act as the idea of commissioning or encouraging the production of images must be considered to be mischief behind the new offences contained within sections 48 to 50 of the 2003 Act.

Quantity revisited

An alert reader will notice a slight contradiction within *Oliver*. In one breath the Court of Appeal is stating that quantity is not to be the primary factor in sentencing, but in the next they talk about 'small' and 'large' quantities. Of course it can be argued that this remains a secondary issue but it appears a very important secondary issue and, of course, the Court was completely silent as to what constitutes a 'small' or 'large' quantity. Indeed there was no mention as to even what yardstick should be used. *Oliver* is arguably not restricted to Internet child pornography, it applies to all relevant convictions. If an offender is in possession of a magazine that displays child pornography is this to be counted as one image or several? An analogy could arguably be drawn between a magazine and a folder on a computer, but it is more likely that the magazine would be considered one item.

What of moving images? The Court of Appeal in *Oliver* was completely silent as to the type of images but is a thirty-second movie clip to be considered for sentencing purposes as a single item even though it is known that a significant proportion of still images are actually 'captures' from the moving image (see Taylor et al., 2001: 104)? Is it just to consider someone who has 200 images from the film to be in possession of a large quantity of images, but the person who has only the moving image to be in possession of a small quantity of the same material? In *Feather* [2003] EWCA Crim 3433 the Court of Appeal expressly referred to the fact that moving images were contained within the section but they did not say what the significance of this was, i.e. how this altered the thresholds. It would, it is submitted, make more sense to consider moving images separately from quantities and it is submitted that where the term 'large quantity' is used in the thresholds, it may be appropriate to add the words 'or a moving image portraying this activity'. Of course the additional difficulty this may cause is whether issues such as length and quality should be considered relevant.

The Court of Appeal has not, perhaps unsurprisingly, adopted a particularly consistent line as to what 'large' and 'small' means. In *Brooks* [2004] EWCA Crim 579 the appellant had been convicted of the possession of 563 images at levels 4 and 5 (533 at level 4, 30 at level 5). The judge at first instance passed a sentence of three years imprisonment but this was reduced on appeal by nine months. In *Fillary* [2003] EWCA Crim 2682 the Court was asked to review a sentence in respect of 1,061 images at level 4 although reading the description of the material in paragraph 6 of the judgment it must be questioned whether this was necessarily the case where a sentence of thirty months imprisonment was reduced to twenty. The implication of this is, therefore, that someone who had almost twice the number of images received a sentence that was seven months shorter, which does not appear consistent. In *Senior* [2003] EWCA Crim 3331 the appellant was found to be in possession of 93 images at level 4 and 9 at level 5. The Court of Appeal, reducing his sentence to six months' imprisonment, said the number of images *'cannot be properly said to be small but they do not either fall into the category of a large quantity'* (para 11 of the judgment). This may appear somewhat self-evident but it does cause a difficulty in deciding an appropriate sentence where the Court only ever talks about 'large' and 'small' and not any other boundaries. Given that there is evidence that the size of collections is increasing (see Taylor and Quayle, 2003: 159–63) it must be seriously questioned how useful such benchmark statements are.

Aggravating factors

It was noted above that the thresholds exist for those offenders without any aggravating factors, but what are the aggravating factors? In *Oliver* the Court of Appeal argued that there were several:

- Showing or distribution to a child.
- Large number of images.
- The manner in which the collection is organised.
- Posting images in public areas where they could be found accidentally.

- Responsible for the actual production of images.
- The age of the child.

(para 2

Not all of these factors need to be discussed but it is interesting that a large number of images shou be considered to be both a threshold and an aggravating factor and this is undoubtedly a cause confusion. Taylor et al., (2001: 105) have previously argued that the organisation of a collection can be an indicator of seriousness and so it is welcome that the Court of Appeal has recognised this. Implicit within this (although perhaps it would have been better had it been explicit) must, it is submitted, be the fact that if an offender seeks to hide his collection (there are a variety of ways of doing this, including encryption) then this should be considered a significant aggravating factor.

The Court of Appeal sadly does not appear to have followed its own guidance on the fact that the age of a child should be relevant. In 28 Court of Appeal cases following *Oliver*, three cases expressly refer to penetrative acts against toddlers and nine mentioned 'very young children'. With the exception of one case, *Grosevenor* [2003] EWCA Crim 1627, age was never considered an aggravating factor in any of the cases, and it was simply referred to in the description of the images. It could be argued that the aggravation is implicit but the sentences (both at first instance and at appellate level) do not appear to demonstrate that age is being considered an aggravating factor. In *Grosevenor* the Court did refer to the age of the children (defining them as 'very young children') as an aggravating factor (para 12), although it did not explain the full impact of this.

The fact that courts do not, in general, appear to consider age to be an aggravating factor is something of a concern as Taylor et al., (2001: 105) argue that the age of children being depicted in child pornography is being reduced and state:

> *In these circumstances there is a greater imbalance in power between perpetrator and the victim, and the lack of language skills may reduce the child's capacity to disclose the assault. Pictures involving babies are particularly distasteful, in that they necessarily exploit situations of total dependency.*

Given these comments it does appear unfortunate that the courts are not considering age an aggravating factor and it is to be hoped that the Court of Appeal recognises this issue and corrects their approach.

Employment

One factor that the courts have not expressly mentioned is the employment of the offender but perhaps it could be relevant. The issue of employment has been a popular topic for the national media in respect of *Operation Ore* (the UK version of the international operation arising as a result of the investigation into the *Landslide Productions* website) where doctors, lawyers, police officers and even a judge have been arrested as a consequence.

One case where the employment of the offender could have been considered relevant was *Senior* [2003] EWCA Crim 3331 where the appellant worked at a nursery for three-year-old children and was also involved in running a theatre group for children between the ages of six and eleven. Should this be a relevant consideration? It would seem perfectly appropriate to take this into account where the activity involves the creation of child pornography rather than the acquisition of it, but should it be restricted to this? Ashworth (2000: 136–7) has argued that with some crimes the employment of an offender could be considered an aggravating factor because it involves a breach of trust, even if this trust is one in respect of society rather than to a specific individual. The paradigm example of this is where a law enforcement officer commits a crime, but perhaps the position could, and should, be extended to include people such as *Senior* where, at the very least, their conviction must raise concerns as to their employment.

One argument for treating employment as an aggravating factor is that public opinion would probably support such a move, yet Shute (1998: 476) makes the extremely powerful and important point that a judge is not a politician and so, arguably, should be above such matters. However, Shute also concludes that sentencing necessarily requires reference to public opinion but that the reference is dispassionate and not taking into account press campaigns or petitions (p. 476).

The position in respect of these crimes would be more sensible if Parliament legislated to remove the 'fear' part of these crimes. Arguably what makes the public concerned about cases such as *Senior* is that they fear that harm could occur to a child if a person who cares for the child is sexually attracted to children. The most contentious issue in this whole field is whether there is any link between the viewing of child pornography and contact offences. No specific research can be identified that says whether such a link exists and indeed the research is generally very confusing and contradictory. A solution is to ban offenders from working with children. Section 28 of the Criminal Justice and Court Services Act 2000 states there is a presumption in favour of making a banning order (making it a criminal offence to work, or seek work, with children) but only if a qualifying sentence is met. Currently the sentence must be at least twelve months imprisonment (s.30) and if an offender receives any lesser penalty, including a community penalty, then he cannot be banned from working with a child. It has already been noted that a short custodial sentence is of little use to sex offenders and it may seem an appropriate time to revisit the 2000 legislation and reduce the threshold to include non-custodial offences, for example community penalties.

Mitigation

In common with most crimes there would appear to be two potential principal mitigating factors, character and plea. In respect of character, the Court of Appeal said that, '*some, but not much, weight should be attached to character.*' (*Oliver*, para 21). It is not, however, clear that the Court is adhering to this principle as in many cases the Court expressly states that an offender is of good character or has no previous convictions, although in *Kopjas* [2003] EWCA Crim 20 the Court of Appeal did reaffirm the position and it is to be hoped that this becomes the consistent approach.

Arguably the most significant mitigating factor is that of the plea. This is a statutory mitigating factor in that s.152 of the Powers of Criminal Courts (Sentencing) Act 2000 states that a court must take into account, in sentencing, the stage and circumstances in which the plea was given. In *Hussein* [2002] EWCA Crim 67 the Court of Appeal confirmed that the statute did not require an automatic reduction in sentence, but that there were significant public policy reasons for granting a reduction unless the circumstances desired otherwise. The Sentencing Guidelines Council, who made the reduction in sentence the topic of their first sentencing guidelines, has extended this logic. (Section 170(9) of the Criminal Justice Act 2003 created the Sentencing Guidelines Council and s.172 of that Act requires courts to take the guidelines into account at the time of sentencing.)

Ashworth (2000: 142–3) argues that there are three potential justifications for discounting a sentence for plea:

- The saving of court time or investigation time.
- Saving the victim from having to testify.
- As an indicator of remorse.

The Sentencing Guidelines Council agree in part with these reasons, but argue that the issue of remorse should be dealt with separately (see SGC, 2004: 3). However it must be questioned whether any of these justifications apply to offences involving child pornography? It is very rare for a victim to testify in court, in that the majority of offences are in relation to the accessing and downloading of images rather than their creation. Whilst it may be thought that a plea may help save investigators time it is unlikely to do so. The Court of Appeal has said that images should be viewed, indexed and an accurate count for each level of images be presented (see *Thompson* [2004] EWCA Crim 669, para 11). On that basis the pre-trial work could be as intensive for a guilty plea as for a not-guilty plea, so why should a discount be offered?

Ashworth (2000: 144) argues that it is inappropriate to award a discount for saving time and expense at trial or investigation when an offender is caught 'red handed' and he quotes the decision in *Landy* [1995] 16 Cr App R (S) 908 where the circumstances surrounding the arrest of the defendant were such that it would be difficult to question the charges. The same argument could be made in respect of indecent images of children where there are few defences available although the Sexual Offences Act 2003 created a new substantive defence where the child is between the age of 16 and 18. It is not possible to discuss this defence in this chapter because of length constraints but for a critique of the defence see Gillespie (2004) pp. 363–365). This point was made, in a slightly different context, in *Pardue* ([2003] EWCA Crim 1562).

The courts do not appear to recognise Ashworth's point, or indeed to take account of *Landy*. A classic illustration of this is to be found in *Feather* ([2003] EWCA Crim 3433) where the Court said:

> [T]his man pleaded guilty to the earliest stage of the criminal proceedings in the magistrates' court and was entitled to a maximum credit of, it seems to us, at least a third to mark the amount of court time and preparation time which was thereby saved. (para 12)

It is submitted, however, that it is unlikely that very much preparation time was saved and, in any event, it completely misses Ashworth's point about being caught red-handed. It is highly likely that the appellant had no option but to plead guilty. The Sentencing Guidelines Council appears to decide that *Landy* is no longer good authority when it states that '*there is no reason why credit should be withheld or reduced*' on the grounds of the offender being caught red-handed (SGC, 2004: 5). This is a regrettable step backwards.

The other interesting phrase from the judgment of the Court of Appeal in *Feather* above, was its suggestion that the discount should be 'at least a third' which suggests that they could contemplate a greater discount. In *Senior* ([2003] EWCA Crim 331) this occurred when the appellant had his sentence of twelve months imprisonment reduced to six months in order to take account of the guilty pleas. Thus the discount was one-half and not one-third. Again, it is highly unlikely that the appellant had any option but to plead guilty. The Court did not explain why such a high discount was required but it is submitted that it is highly questionable whether it was, in fact, appropriate. Since the decision in *Oliver* there have only been two occasions when the Court of Appeal declined to provide the conventional discount, those being *Pardue* where a 15 per cent discount was given because, in the Court's opinion, the defendant had no choice but to plead and in *Hiscock* [2003] EWCA Crim 2079 the Court, under similar circumstances, awarded a discount of 25 per cent rather than the conventional one-third.

In an attempt to bring clarity to this area, the Sentencing Guidelines Council has decided to introduce a 'sliding scale' of discounts (see SGC, 2004: 4–5). The discount ranges from the one-third point for circumstances when the offender pleads guilty at the first available opportunity to a reduction of one-tenth when the plea was given at the door of the court or after the trial had started (SGC, 2004: 4–5). This consistency should be welcomed and it is to be hoped that the courts will implement it appropriately but the decision to depart from *Landy* is wrong, especially in this context, and unnecessarily rewards people for pleading guilty when they had no choice. It is unlikely that a plea in respect of abusive images would save much time in the preparation of the case and to provide the standard discount in these circumstances is regrettable.

Managing an offender

It was noted above that an offender who is sentenced to less than twelve months imprisonment will not be the subject of any supervision. However, whilst this is true in principle, it is possible that a court, when passing sentence, could seek to use additional powers to require an offender to co-operate with authorities in order to reduce the risk of harming a child. In this section I wish to focus on two areas, extended licences and Sexual Offences Prevention Orders (SOPOs).

Extended Licences

Section 85 of the Powers of Criminal Courts (Sentencing) Act 2000 allows a court to extend the licence period an offender is subjected to when it passes a custodial sentence. This power was first introduced under the Crime and Disorder Act 1998 (s.58 of that Act) and it is designed to cover those situations where it is considered that there would be a risk of serious harm if the traditional licence period was used. The notion of a licence was discussed briefly above but in summary it is a situation where an offender is released from prison early and is on licence for good behaviour. Conditions can be placed on licences (see s.37 of the Criminal Justice Act 1991) and this can include such matters as requiring an offender to attend a sex offender treatment programme or conditions as to where they may live etc.

A court may not extend a licence for more than ten years or beyond the statutory maximum for that offence (e.g. if an offence is punishable by up to five years imprisonment, then a licence could only be extended to the extent of taking it to a maximum period of five years), and in *Nelson* [2002] 1 Cr App R (S) 134 the Court of Appeal gave guidance on the use of extended licences and states expressly that a sentencing court should consider whether a longer than commensurate sentence would be more appropriate. A longer than commensurate sentence is where the actual time in custody is longer than an offender would normally be sentenced to but, because of the dangerousness of that particular offender, the sentence is increased (see s.80, Powers of the Criminal Courts (Sentencing) Act 2000). The difference between the sentences appears to be that a longer than commensurate sentence should be passed where there is a significant risk of the offender causing serious harm to the public, whereas an extended licence would be called for when there is a need to monitor the offender, assist his rehabilitation or prevent re-offending.

Extended licences have been used in child pornography offences although it is not really possible to identify any particular consistent approach to their use in this field. In *Oliver* ([2002] EWCA Crim 2766) the Court of Appeal accepted that an extended licence could help an offender address their offending (para 26) and in *Evans* [2004] EWCA Crim 632 the Court of Appeal followed this by suggesting that courts should consider the use of an extended sentence for these offences, but in *Oliver* the other appellants were not subjected to an extended licence even though their cases were not that different from the appellant *Oliver*. Other cases have led to the Court commending the use of s.85 (see, for example, *Kelly* [2004] EWCA Crim 256) and it is to be hoped that the courts will begin to understand that their use is appropriate.

The courts normally pass an extended licence on the basis that an offender may cross the boundary from possession of pornography to contact offending (see *Leonard* [2004] EWCA Crim 738, paras 8 and 12) but as will be seen below, the case of *Beaney* [2004] EWCA Crim 449, has perhaps altered this now to include re-offending of child pornography offences. If it has, and such an amendment would be commendable, then it is incumbent on courts to actively consider this power, as a very short custodial sentence (i.e. one that would not normally include a licence) has, in effect, no rehabilitative purpose. Taylor and Quayle (2003: 92–5) note that many offenders talk of a sort of collecting addiction and thus without any assistance, it would appear inevitable that a person will re-offend, thus leading to a spiral of liability. An appropriate use of s.85 may prevent this type of cycle occurring.

Sexual Offences Prevention Orders

The 2003 Act has introduced a new civil order known as a Sexual Offence Prevention Order (SOPO) (see s.104). In reality, however, the SOPO is a combination of two pre-existing orders, the sex offender order (introduced in s.2, Crime and Disorder Act 1998) and the restraining order (s.5A, Sex Offenders Act 1997). They are both, in essence, an injunction-type order in that they are an order of a court preventing an offender from doing anything named within the order. In this section of the chapter I am going to concentrate on the restraining-order part of a SOPO.

A court may, under s.104, make a SOPO at the time of sentencing an offender where 'it is necessary to make such an order, for the purposes of protecting the public . . . from serious sexual harm from the defendant'. The order lasts for the duration contained within the order or until further order (i.e. indefinitely) (s.107), although, inter alia, the defendant can apply to a court for its discharge (s.108). Breach of the order is an either-way offence carrying a maximum sentence of five years imprisonment (s.113).

The use of restraining orders in the context of child pornography became quite common, with judges at first instance preventing offenders from having access to the Internet etc. However in *Halloren* [2004] EWCA Crim 233 the Court of Appeal quashed such an order saying that it was not possible to make a restraining order because the fear of re-offending in terms of accessing indecent images of a child would not lead to 'serious harm' to the public (see para 16), and implied that only the fear of contact offences would suffice. Less than four weeks later, however, a differently constituted court reached a different decision in the case of *Beaney* ([2004] EWCA Crim 449). The Court held that it was possible to identify the public who would be at risk of harm, those being the children who were forced to pose, or participate, in sexual activity documented within the images (para 8 of the judgment). At first sight this would appear consistent with *Halloren* but the Court took it further and argued that serious harm includes psychological harm and there was a risk that re-offending would, therefore, cause serious harm because:

> The offences which they commit can properly be said to contribute to the psychological harm which the children in those images would suffer by virtue of the children's awareness that there were people out there getting a perverted thrill from watching them forced to pose and behave in this way. (para 9).

In other words there is psychological harm, that being the trauma suffered by a child not knowing who precisely has seen the images. Palmer (2004) demonstrates the reliability of this statement (see pp. 29–33) and provides examples of case-studies where children feel afraid walking down the street or meeting a new person because they are wondering whether the persons they are in contact with have seen the photograph.

Beaney is an important decision and its ramifications are beyond the confines of restraining orders because it shows that the courts have finally understood the seriousness of child pornography and the life-long impact it has on its victims. Notwithstanding *Beaney*, the Court of Appeal was asked to rule on a restraining order in respect of child pornography once again in the case of *Collard* [2004] EWCA Crim 1664. The Court of Appeal agreed with *Beaney* and said that such orders are apposite in child pornography cases (paras 9 and 10). However they emphasised that necessity does not just relate to either the offence or victim, but to the offender too. They noted that it was incumbent on a court to consider whether a restraining order (now SOPO) was required for the *offender*, and this meant looking at the history of the case, the defendant's antecedents, personal circumstances and risk of re-offending. *Collard* did, however, confirm that re-offending includes more downloading and not necessarily contact offences.

The decisions in *Beaney* and *Collard* are to be welcomed and it is to be hoped that courts carefully consider the use of SOPOs since, if they are used appropriately, they could be invaluable in managing offenders, including promoting and assisting the rehabilitation of offenders.

Conclusion

The law relating to child pornography has been transformed in recent years. There is no doubt that Parliament considers child pornography to be a serious crime and it has legislated to criminalise the production, distribution and viewing of photographs depicting the abuse of children. However, one cannot help but think that their focus has become somewhat blinkered in that they continue to be obsessed by photographs and do not consider other forms of child pornography, despite prompting from the police to consider alternatives. An ingenious sex offender could take an indecent photograph, place some tracing paper over the photograph and then trace the contents of that photograph. If they then coloured in this image and destroyed the photograph they would have a perfectly lawful image because it could no longer be said that the image is a photograph – it is quite plainly a drawing or a tracing. Has this minimised the abuse of a child? No. Could that image still be used to groom children for abuse? Yes. Whilst it is accepted that straying beyond photographs does raise competing interests in terms of balancing the right to protection against the freedom of expression, it would appear appropriate to extend liability in some circumstances. However, Parliament has simply adopted the approach of continuing to replicate and tinker with the law as regards photographs, potentially leading to confusion.

The courts have, arguably, been slightly slower than Parliament to recognise the importance of child pornography. There were traditionally quite light penalties passed, and a complete absence in recognition of the seriousness of such crime. However, it must be said that this is no longer the case and the courts do seem to be taking the problem more seriously. Whilst there are still areas of controversy, most notably in terms of the use of three years as a benchmark standard, and in the degree of discount awarded for mitigation, notwithstanding the overwhelming nature of a case, sentences have become more realistic. The case of *Beaney* also represented a significant step forward in the recognition of the repeated victimisation of those who are forced to be the subjects of child pornography.

In conclusion it can be said, therefore, that the UK does take child pornography seriously, and it has ensured that it has largely appropriate laws. However, it is important that the country does not rest on its laurels, but continues to consider ways in which the law can move forward, ensuring that children are protected from such exploitation.

References

Akdeniz, Y. (2001) Governing Pornography and Child Pornography on the Internet: The UK Approach. *UWLALR*. 32: 247.

Ashworth, A.A. (2000) (3rd edn), *Sentencing and Criminal Justice*. London: Butterworths.

Bingham, Lord (1998) A Criminal Code: Must we Wait for Ever? *Criminal Law Review*. 694.

Cobley, C. (1997) Keeping Track of Sex Offenders: Part 1 of the Sex Offenders Act 1997. *Modern Law Review*. 60: 691.

Cobley, C. (2000) *Sex Offenders: Law, Policy and Practice*. Bristol: Jordan Publishing.

Edwards, S.S.M. (2000) Prosecuting 'Child Pornography'. *Journal of Social Welfare and Family Law*. 1.

Gillespie, A.A. (2003) Sentences for Offences Involving Child Pornography. *Criminal Law Review*. 81.

Gillespie, A.A. (2004) Tinkering with 'Child Pornography'. *Criminal Law Review*. 361.

Halliday, R. (2001) *Making Punishment Work*. London: Home Office.

Home Office (2000) *Setting the Boundaries, Volume 1*. London: HMSO.

Ormerod, D.C. (2000) R v Bowden: Case Comment. *Criminal Law Review*. 381.

Palmer, T. (2004) *Just One Click*. London: Barnardo's.

Sentencing Advisory Panel (2002) *Sentences for Indecent Images of Children*. at www.sentencing-guidelines.gov.uk

Sentencing Guidelines Council (2004) *Reduction in Sentence for a Guilty Plea*. at www.sentencing-guidelines.gov.uk

Shute, S. (1998) The Place of Public Opinion in Sentencing Law. *Criminal Law Review*. 465.

Shute, S. (1999) Who Passes Unduly Lenient Sentences? *Criminal Law Review*. 603.

Smith, J.C. (1988) R v Owen: Case Comment. *Criminal Law Review*. 120.

Taylor, M. and Quayle, E. (2003) *Child Pornography: An Internet Crime*. London: Routledge.

Taylor, M. and Quayle, E. (2004) Abusive Images of Children, in Cooper, S., Giardino, A., Vieth, V. and Kellogg, N. (Eds.) *Medical and Legal Aspects of Child Sexual Exploitation*. Saint Louis: GW Medical Publishing.

Taylor, M., Holland, G. and Quayle, E. (2001) Typology of Paedophile Picture Collections. *Police Journal*. 74: 97.

Chapter 2

Combating Online Child Pornography in Australia

Tony Krone

This research paper does not necessarily reflect the policy position of the Australian Government.

Introduction

Child pornography existed before the creation of the Internet. It is not possible to say whether the advent of the Internet has fuelled the demand for child pornography and expanded an existing market or whether it simply satisfies in new ways a market that would have existed in any event. It is clear though that the Internet provides an environment for the proliferation of child pornography and the creation of an expanding market for its consumption. This paper explores three important questions. What is online child pornography? Is there a typology of offending online? And if so, what are the implications for law enforcement?

What is child pornography? – A non-legal definition

Taylor and Quayle (2003) point out that legal definitions of child pornography do not capture all the material that an adult with a sexual interest in children may consider sexualised or sexual. As they argue, understanding why child pornography is produced and collected requires us to think beyond the legal definition of child pornography. They identify ten categories of pictures that may be sexualised by an adult with a sexual interest in children based on a study of online content by Combating Paedophile Information Networks in Europe (COPINE). In the first category is non-erotic and non-sexualised pictures of children in their underwear or swimming costumes from commercial or private sources, in which the context or organisation by the collector indicates inappropriateness. The second category consists of pictures of naked or semi-naked children in appropriate nudist settings and the third category is of surreptitiously taken photographs of children in play areas or other safe environments showing underwear or varying degrees of nakedness.

Material in the first and second categories and some of the material in the third will not be caught by the legal definition of child pornography. However, all may be indicative of a sexual interest in children and are therefore potentially important in the investigation of child pornography offences.

The legal definition of child pornography

The Australian regime to regulate pornography (whether online or not) relies on state and territory laws (for convenience 'state laws'). Australian child pornography provisions as at 30 June 2004 are listed in Table 1. Generally, specific laws against child pornography were introduced in the 1990s as an addition to existing obscenity laws, which prohibited the sale of obscene material but not its possession. In this way, it became an offence to possess, as well as to sell, produce, or distribute child pornography. Child pornography is generally defined as material that describes or depicts a person under 16 years of age, or who appears to be less than 16, in a manner that would offend a reasonable adult. However, the legal definition can be difficult to apply especially because of jurisdictional differences (Grant et al., 1997). For example, in some states there must also be the depiction of sexual activity by the child or some other person in the presence of the child. Difficulty also arises from the fact that child pornography laws usually require a judgment to be made whether the material is offensive, or not, according to the standards of a 'reasonable person'.

These laws intersect with the censorship laws contained in the Classification (Publications, Films and Computer Games) Act 1995 (Cwlth) and in two states (NSW, NT), the definition of child pornography includes material that has been refused classification under the *Classification Act*. In addition, the Broadcasting Services Amendment (Online Services) Act 1999 (Cwlth) created a non-criminal process for reporting sites that host material that would be refused classification (or X and R rated material that is made available online without adult verification). The Australian Broadcasting Authority can issue a take-down notice to have hosts located in Australia remove such content from their site, or if the site is hosted overseas, to notify content filter developers to add it to their lists of offensive sites (Chalmers, 2002).

Children actually or apparently under 16

The state laws cover the depiction of any child up until the age of 16 years. Child pornography collections in Australia have been found to include images of infants and young children. An analysis of child pornography obtained openly over the Internet indicated that the majority of images were of children between the age ranges of 7–8 to 10–11 (Taylor and Quayle, 2003). It is also reported that the ages of children depicted appears to be falling (Taylor and Quayle, 2003).

There is no requirement however, to prove that a child depicted was less than 16 years of age at the time the image was created. It is enough that they appear to be under that age. Child pornography therefore includes images where a person over the age of 16 is made to appear less than 16. An account of the assessment of the age of a person depicted is given in the Review Board decision 'Computer image depicting young blond male with hand on soccer ball' of 20 October 2000.

What if a child depicted is under 16 but looks older than 16?

- If the child depicted is actually under 16 years but appears to be over that age, it is possible for a user to be convicted on proof of the child being under 16.

- In the ACT however, there is a defence available of reasonable belief that the child depicted was over 16, in NSW a defence is provided where an accused did not know, or could not reasonably be expected to have known, that an item is pornographic material involving a child under 16.

- In the remaining states, where it cannot be proved that a user knew that the child depicted was under 16, a prosecution would have to be able to show that the user intended to possess material depicting someone less than 16. Indeed, some states refer to being knowingly in possession of child pornography. An example of this would be where such an image was provided in answer to the accused's request for pictures of children under 16.

Table 2.1 State and territory child pornography possession offences

Offence	ACT	NSW	NT	QLD	SA	TAS	VIC	WA
Child pornography	s. 92NB Crimes Act 1900	s. 578B Crimes Act 1900	s. 125B Criminal Code	s. 14 Classification of Publications Act*	s. 33 Summary Offences Act	s. 72–74 Classification (Publications, Films and Computer Games) Enforcement Act 1995	s. 67A Crimes Act	s. 60 Censorship Act
Max. penalty	5 years	$11,000/ 2 years	2 years/ $20,000 corporate penalty	$22,500/ 1 year	$5,000/ 1 year	$5,000/1 year	10 years	5 years

*See also s. 228 Criminal Codes Act 1899 (Qld) (obscene publications and exhibitions including 'any obscene computer generated image').

However, it is not necessary to prove that a child depicted was less than 16 years of age at the time the image was created. It is enough that they appear to be under that age, thus including images of a person over the age of 16 who is made to appear less than 16. Standard medical indicators of the physical developmental stages of children may be used to assess whether an image depicts a child under the age of 16 (Censorship Review Board, 2000).

Morphed images of children

The definition of child pornography may include *morphed* pictures. Taylor (1999) refers to such images as pseudo-photographs and they are classified according to three types:

- Digitally altered and sexualised images of bodies, such as a photograph of a child in a swimming costume where the costume has been digitally removed.

- Separate images in one picture, such as a child's hand superimposed onto an adult penis.

- A montage of pictures, some of which are sexual.

How readily a morphed collection may be put together, even without the capacity to digitally alter images is shown in the case of convicted double murderer and serial rapist Lenny Lawson who was one of the longest serving prisoners in Australia. He died in custody at the age of 76, three days after being transferred to a maximum-security unit. The transfer followed the discovery in his cell of a collection of video tapes which in part contained images from Sesame Street spliced with other program material to produce what was described by the prison psychologist as a collection of 'voyeuristic sexual fantasies and sexual perversion, often associated with children' (Mitchell, 2004).

Creating fictitious children under 16

Sometimes pornography is created without directly involving a child. The offence provisions do not require a real person to be described or depicted and they include fictional characters or digitally created characters. The words 'describing or depicting' are capable of including text, images, and three-dimensional objects. While these laws were initially framed in relation to physical objects, the language extends to cover the development of online pornography.

  'Child pornography' in all but Queensland, extends beyond pictures and visual images to variously include 'any other thing', 'other goods', 'material', 'an article', or a 'publication'. Drawings and text are thus included and in some states the use of the words 'thing', 'goods', and 'material' could catch recorded aural material. General inclusive terms used are:

- A photograph or any other image (Qld).

- Any other thing (ACT).

- A document or other goods (Cwlth).

- Material (SA).

- An article (WA).

- In the other states the laws refer to a 'film, publication or computer game' where publication means any written or pictorial matter, but not a film or computer game. Publication in this sense then, does not mean made available to others. In this scheme 'computer generated images' are specifically defined as film.

In *Dodge v R* [2002] A Crim R 435 a prisoner in Western Australia was serving a long sentence for sexual offences against children. Dodge wrote 17 sexually explicit stories about adult males involved in sexual acts with young children (mostly boys less than 10 years of age). Dodge pleaded guilty and was convicted of child pornography charges for supplying another prisoner with these stories and of possessing the stories himself. Dodge appealed the sentence and the appeal court noted that a prison sentence was required because the law sought to prevent access to child pornography. The fact that no child was involved in producing the material was allowed for on appeal to reduce the sentence from 18 months to 12.

In contrast to the law in Australia, the Child Pornography Prevention Act 1996 (US) was a US Federal law that sought to prohibit virtual child pornography but the relevant provision was struck down for being too widely drafted.

In *Ashcroft v Free Speech Coalition* [00–795] 535 US 234 (2002) the United States Supreme Court held that the section infringed the First Amendment right to free speech. The provision defined child pornography widely using the words 'appears to be' and 'conveys the impression' in relation to depicting a person under the age of 18. The Court found this wording too broad in the absence of any requirement in the same provision for the prosecution to prove that the material is obscene.

Special provisions

Consideration of surrounding circumstances

In each state there is a threshold question whether the material is offensive to a reasonable adult. This ordinarily would require consideration of the surrounding circumstances. The South Australian law was changed to expressly state that the circumstances of production, sale, exhibition, delivery or possession of material can be considered in the assessment whether that material is indecent or offensive. The law prior to that stated that indecency or offensiveness had to be considered without regard to context. In the case of *Phillips v SA Police* the court pointed to the difficulty of considering the nature of material without taking into account the context in which it appears.

The case of *Phillips v SA Police* [1994] A Crim R 480 concerned a collection of videos showing men and boys in public toilets and change rooms. Images of the genitalia of boys less than 16 years of age urinating and undressing constituted a small percentage of the entire footage of several hours. The videos were taken surreptitiously by Phillips and kept by him. The South Australian Supreme Court found that the images of boys were not inherently indecent or offensive for the purposes of proving the charge that they were child pornography. The then wording of the section did not allow the circumstances of production to be taken into account, as the convicting magistrate had found in order to convict the defendant, and the conviction was overturned.

Artistic merit, or scientific or other purpose

In South Australia, a work of artistic merit is exempted if there is not 'undue emphasis on its indecent or offensive aspects'. Elsewhere, the question of artistic merit must be considered in relation to the question whether or not material is 'offensive' for the purposes of the definition of child pornography.

The Classification Board and the Classification Review Board are responsible for the classification of films and deals regularly with issues of artistic merit. A recent example where both refused the classification of a film portraying teenage sex was *Ken Park* in 2003. The film was arguably on the borderline of the definition of child pornography in that it depicted children in the age range of 15–17 years and included a number of explicit sex scenes some of which were between the teenagers and others with older adult characters. The film was refused classification and effectively banned on the basis of its prolonged and gratuitous depictions of fetishes (auto-erotic asphyxiation), violence, sexualised violence and child sexual abuse (on the basis of the child being under 18 years of age, which is the relevant age for classification purposes). These features were found to outweigh its claim to artistic or educational merit (Classification Review Board, 2003).

In some states, material may also be exempted if it is held in 'good faith and for the advancement or dissemination of legal, medical or scientific knowledge'. An example of the evaluation of the claimed educative benefit of material is shown in the Classification Review Board decision concerning a CD-ROM interactive film *The sexualisation of girl children and adolescents on the Internet*. A retired social worker and registered psychologist made this as a 'training aid for child protection professionals'. The CD-ROM was refused classification for the following reasons:

- It depicted child pornography involving girls between 4 and 16.
- The text could be used by those seeking instruction in paedophile grooming.
- The extensive referencing of child pornography websites could facilitate paedophile activity.
- There was a lack of academic rigour.
- There was no ethics approval.

In the end, the CRB held that 'the harm caused by the extensive and detailed depictions of child pornography involving children and young people would not be outweighed by the expected benefits to knowledge'.

In the Tasmanian case of *Knight v McDonald* [2002] TASSC 81, the defence claimed that as an art teacher the defendant kept images of naked young girls for artistic purposes. This was rejected on the basis that the images concerned were kept together with a more extensive range of adult pornographic material organised into pornographic themes.

Law enforcement purposes

In NSW, Victoria, WA and the NT the possession of child pornography by an officer of a law enforcement agency in the exercise or performance of a power, function or duty imposed by or under any Act or law is specifically exempted. Where not specifically exempted in the same legislative package, law enforcement officers would have to rely on general powers of investigation and for the keeping of evidentiary material to retain child pornography for law enforcement purposes.

Forfeiture and destruction

In NSW, and the NT the court is specifically empowered to order the destruction or disposal of offending material. In South Australia, the court may order forfeiture. In Victoria, the court may order forfeiture, and once a forfeiture order is made, destruction is authorised by the Minister.

Towards a national approach

In Australia there have been a number of investigations into the extent of organised paedophile criminal activity. Not surprisingly, before the widespread availability of personal computers, the

Parliamentary Joint Committee on the National Crime Authority (1995) found little evidence of the use of computers to transmit child pornography (at 3.69) or of organisation of paedophiles over the Internet (at 3.39). With the uptake of computer technology and expanding access to the Internet, the situation had changed over the next five years. Forde and Patterson (1998) drew attention to increasingly sophisticated paedophile Internet activity based on observations of online activity for a one-year period. By 2000 it was reported that the Internet was increasingly being used by child sex offenders to facilitate networking mainly for the purpose of the distribution and exchange of child pornography (Queensland Crime Commission, 2000: 107).

Indeed, international police investigations including Australian police have demonstrated the development of a virtual community of offenders and have resulted in a number of high profile law enforcement actions that cross many borders. The Australian government proposed a new federal law, tied to the power to regulate telecommunications, covering child pornography and grooming (Attorney-General's Department, 2004). The Bill defines child pornography in terms of the depiction of a child under 18 years of age and provides for a penalty of 10 years for accessing child pornography and 15 years for on-line grooming. There are separate proposals to reform the NSW, SA and WA legislation.

Categorising child pornography

In practice, police in Australia distinguish between five categories of child pornographic images. There is no legislation or case law mandating the use of these categories which were originally developed for law enforcement in the United Kingdom based on the ten-point typology of images developed by COPINE. The categories are shown in Table 2. While it may be beneficial for police to prioritise their investigations by reference to the seriousness of the images involved, the full extent of an offender's collection may not be known until an investigation is well under way.

When it comes to assessing the severity of an offence of possessing child pornography, attention is often given in sentencing proceedings to the number of images in a collection as in the case of *R v Jones* [1999] WASCA 24. In a Western Australian case of *R v Jones*, the court considered the size of a collection as an aggravating feature on sentence as 'the degradation of the children is more serious because there is a much larger number of images involved'. The court took into account both the number of children involved and the number of images of each child as aggravating features. The defendant had a collection of approximately 162,000 images kept on CD Rom. A full-time custodial sentence of 18 months was ordered in lieu of the original suspended sentence of two years. It is not enough to measure the number of images of various types involved. There are other indicators of seriousness, such as the offender's engagement with the material including how long it has been held, the degree to which it is organised by the offender, how it was acquired, and whether it is a trophy of the offender's own sexual abuse of a child (Taylor and Quayle, 2003).

How are offences committed online? – A typology of offending

Taylor and Quayle (2003) suggest that the Internet has created the social, individual and technological circumstances in which an interest in child pornography flourishes:

Table 2.2   Categories of child pornography

Level	Description	COPINE typology
1	Images depicting posing and erotic posing, with no sexual activity	*Posing* (deliberate posing suggesting sexual content) and *Explicit erotic posing* (emphasis on genital area)
2	Sexual activity between children, or solo masturbation by a child	Explicit sexual activity not involving an adult
3	Non-penetrative sexual activity between adults and children	Assault (sexual assault involving an adult)
4	Penetrative sexual activity between children and adults	Gross assault (penetrative assault involving an adult)
5	Sadism or bestiality	Sadistic/bestiality (sexual images involving pain or animals

Sentencing Advisory Panel, 2002.

- **Social** – The creation of a self-justifying online community for child pornography users.
- **Individual** – Individuals can access material and communicate with others through a computer terminal providing an apparently private sphere for the expression of sexual fantasy.
- **Technological** – The Internet makes it possible for child pornography consumers to become obsessive collectors so that the collection of images becomes an end in itself. The Internet also provides a ready means to access material supporting increasingly extreme sexual fantasies and then to act out those fantasies either through online interactions or physical meetings with children arranged through facilities such as chat rooms.

Knowing the differences in how online child pornography offences are committed is vitally important to understanding and combating the problem of the sexual exploitation of children. The following typology of offending is summarised in Table 3. There is an increasing seriousness of offending, from offences that do not directly involve a child, to offences that involve direct contact with children, and from online grooming to physical abuse.

Accident

Whether a person is an accidental browser or not is a question of fact. In a prosecution it must be proven that the offender had an intention to possess child pornography. In the absence of a confession, this may be shown by the surrounding circumstances such as repeat visits to a site.

Private fantasy

If a person has a private fantasy involving sex with a child no offence is committed. If that fantasy is preserved as something more than thought, then an offence may be involved. The representation of that fantasy in text or digital format on a computer may be sufficient to constitute the possession of child pornography even if the offender has no intention of sharing it with any other person. The case of Lenny Lawson, referred to above, is an example of a private fantasy collection in video format.

Of course, for the offender engaged in private fantasy the risk of exposure is low but it could occur in a number of ways: by tip-off from someone else with access to the computer or data storage device; in the course of searching a computer for evidence of other offences; when a computer is being serviced; when a computer is stolen, or even when a computer has been accessed remotely by a third party.

Trawlers

Among trawlers there is little or no security employed and minimal networking of offenders. Taylor (1999) lists three motivations. The sexually omnivorous user is oriented to a range of sexually explicit material of which child pornography is simply a part but not the focus. The sexually curious user has experimented with child pornographic material but has not pursued it. The libertarian is driven to assert a claim to be free to access whatever material they wish.

Non-secure collectors

The non-secure collector purchases, downloads or exchanges child pornography from openly available sources on the Internet or in chat rooms that do not impose security barriers, such as a password, minimum trade in images, or encryption. There is a higher degree of networking among collectors in this category than for trawlers.

Secure collectors

In contrast, the secure collector uses security barriers in collecting child pornography. In addition to encryption, some groups of secure collectors have an entry requirement that locked its members into protecting each other in that each member is required to submit child pornography images to join. The Wonderland Club was one such international child pornography ring exposed in 1998 and it had an entry requirement of 10,000 child pornography images. Both open and private collectors may be driven by the desire to amass a collection. As a result, extremely large numbers of images can be involved.

Online groomer

The online groomer is a person who has initiated online contact with a child with the intention of establishing a sexual relationship involving cyber sex or physical sex. Child pornography may be used to groom a child where it is shown to the child to lower that child's inhibitions concerning sexual activity. The new Commonwealth law covers indecent material as well as pornographic pictures and text when communicated to a child for the purpose of making it easier to procure that child for sexual activity, or to make it more likely that the child will engage in sexual activity. The same law includes specific offences of procuring a child for sexual purposes and refers to sending communications with the intent of facilitating a meeting for sexual activity.

The Queensland legislation contains an anti-grooming provision. This became law in 2003. Up until May 2004 there had been 18 arrests, including offenders from Victoria and the Northern Territory (Rouse, 2004). In the first successful prosecution under this law in February 2004, the offender was sentenced to two and a half years imprisonment with a minimum of nine months to serve. The 26-year-old had tried to procure a 13-year-old girl for sex using an Internet chat room. The girl was in fact a police officer involved in a sting operation (Townsend, 2004).

Physical abuser

Physical abusers are actively involved in the abuse of children and use child pornography to supplement their sexual craving. The physical abuse may be recorded for the personal use of the abuser but is not intended to be further distributed. In cases of this type a charge of making or possessing child pornography will usually be incidental to a charge for the physical abuse that has taken place.

Producer

The producer of child pornography is involved in the physical abuse of children and provides images of that abuse to other users of child pornography.

Distributor

The distributor of child pornography may or may not have a sexual interest in child pornography.

The Western Australian case of *R v W* [2000] 27 SR (WA) 148 involved a child prosecuted for possessing child pornography with intent to sell it. The offender had set up a website offshore to make money from advertisers. The content of the website included child pornography images and textual references to child pornography. The appeal court held he was properly convicted.

To the categories listed above might be added the child user or the youthful user who pursues material reflecting their own level of sexual maturity or exposure by adults to child pornography. It has been reported that children under 10 who have been exposed to sexually exploitative material have themselves become users of pornography (including child pornography) and abusers of other children (Stanley et al., 2003). Research in the United States, shows that the typical person arrested for child pornography offences is a Caucasian male over the age of 26 years (Wolak et al., 2003). Little is known however, about the characteristics of offenders in Australia. Even if there were consistent patterns of gender and age among offenders, it would be wrong to assume that offending fits a homogenous profile. The typology presented above shows that there are at least eight different ways of offending, with four of these having no direct contact with children, three either online or in physical contact with children, and one where there may or may not be contact with children. There are also significant differences in the level of security applied and the degree of networking engaged in. More research is required to explore the ways in which these different ways of offending are interlinked. A few of the most important research issues to address are:

- Is there any causal link between use of child pornography and the physical abuse of children?
- What is the extent of recidivism among child pornography offenders?
- What are the most effective ways of rehabilitating a child pornography offender?
- Does the use of child pornography follow a typical progress from the marginally pornographic to the most extreme images?

Table 2.3   A typology of online child pornography offending

Type of involvement	Features	Level of networking by offender	Security	Nature of abuse
Accidental browser – non offending conduct	Response to spam, accidental hit on suspect site – material deleted and not saved	Nil	Nil	Indirect
Private fantasy	Conscious creation of online text or digital images for private use	Nil	Nil	Indirect
Trawler	Actively seeking child pornography using openly available browsers	Low	Nil	Indirect
Non-secure collector	Actively seeking material often through peer to peer networks	High	Nil	Indirect
Secure collector	Actively seeking material but only through secure networks. Collector syndrome and exchange as an entry barrier	High	Secure	Indirect
Groomer	Cultivating an online relationship with one or more children. The offender may or may not seek material in any of the above ways	Varies – online contact with individual children	Security depends on child	Direct
Physical abuser	Abusing a child who may have been introduced to the offender online. The offender may or may not seek material in any of the above ways. Pornography may be used to facilitate abuse	Varies – physical contact with individual children	Security depends on child	Direct
Producer	Records own abuse or that of others (or induces children to submit images of themselves)	Varies – may depend on whether becomes a distributor.	Security depends on child	Direct
Distributor	May distribute at any one of the above levels	Varies	Tends to be secure	Indirect

Implications for law enforcement

Police are devoting increasing attention and resources to combat child pornography and online sex offences. Investigations are necessarily complex and time consuming because they are often co-ordinated across jurisdictions, they involve networks of offenders using varying levels of security, and an individual offender must be linked to the misuse of a computer. Despite this, the reliance of offenders on networks to commit their offences may be a key to effective law enforcement. Concentrating on linkages is likely to help address the problem of the proliferation of child pornography. Stopping the physical abuse of children requires an intensive investigation effort, concentrating on new material and on cracking into the more secretive world of individual and networked producers.

Police may use stings to locate individual offenders. The greater long-term value in any sting operation may lie in exploding the view that the Internet is an anonymous domain in which it is safe to offend. Such sting operations may need to operate on a number of levels to capture the various ways in which offences may be committed online:

- Police stings using false websites target unsophisticated users (Cyberspace Research Unit, 2003). By catching trawlers and deterring those who may be thinking of experimenting with child pornography an admittedly low level of offending will be disrupted. The Australian High Tech Crime Centre has joined the Virtual Global Taskforce of police from the UK, USA and Canada to run such sting operations and other co-ordinated activities (*The Guardian*, 2003).

- Sting operations aimed at groomers are more finely targeted at those who represent a real threat in terms of contacting children and acting out their sexual impulses with them. Queensland police have been able to operate with an anti-grooming law in that state to locate and prosecute groomers. We do not know how prevalent grooming is and stings of this type may rely on the police officer and the offender drawing on a 'shared fantasy' of the 'compliant and sexualised child' (Taylor and Quayle, 2003).

Much more needs to be done to understand the problem of child pornography online. Taylor and Quayle (2003) point out that the literature on adults with a sexual interest in children 'fails to accommodate behaviour that relates to the new technologies'. Not only does this failure impede the treatment of offenders, it also hampers the ability to prioritise matters for investigation and for prosecution. At this stage, we can speak of associations between risk factors and models of offending behaviour. Drawing on the work by Taylor and Quayle (2003), the following are markers of serious online offending: new or recent images, extreme images, images associated with text, participation in an online community of offenders, trading in images, cataloguing of images. Investigators need to consider the extent to which an offender found with child pornography may be involved in other levels of offending. The development of predictive indicators of involvement would therefore be an important advance in battling child pornography.

In the meantime, law enforcement agencies need to prioritise their investigation efforts. A useful scale of priorities has been developed in the UK in response to the flood of cases from Operation Ore. The top priority is given to cases involving convicted paedophiles and those with access to children, such as teachers and social workers. The second priority is given to cases of those in positions of authority like police and magistrates and the third is for suspects not involved with children.

Conclusion

There is no doubting the importance of protecting children from abuse by combating online child pornography. More research is needed to properly understand the problem, to fully assess the nature and scale of offending, to identify and protect victims, and ultimately to ensure that our approach is both effective and just.

Postscript

Operation Auxin commenced in September 2004 and for the first time involved all Australian police forces joining together in a co-ordinated simultaneous enforcement operation against child pornography. This operation was the Australian counterpart to Operation Falcon in the United States. There were over 700 suspects and police executed over 400 search warrants across Australia leading to over 200 arrests. This Operation led to a significant tightening of child pornography laws in a number of states including, the Northern Territory, New South Wales and South Australia.

References

Attorney-General's Department (2004) *Internet Child Sex Offences Bill Tabled*. Canberra: Attorney-General's Department. http://www.ag.gov.au/www/justiceministerHome.nsf/Alldocs/RWPAC-DAC926C9F91374CA256EBE000670AD?OpenDocument

Chalmers, R. (2002) Regulating the Net in Australia: Firing Blanks or Silver Bullets? *Murdoch University Electronic Journal of Law*. 9: 3, http://www.murdoch.edu.au/elaw/issues/v9n3/chalmers93_text.html

Classification Review Board (2000) *Decision 19–20 October 2000: Untitled Computer Image (Young Blonde Male With Hand on Soccer Ball)*. Surry Hills: Classification Review Board.

Classification Review Board (2003) *Decision 6 June 2003: Ken Park*. Surry Hills: Classification Review Board.

Cyberspace Research Unit (2003) *Cyberspace Research Unit's response to the National Crime Squad's announcement regarding the launch of Operation Pin*. http://www.uclan.ac.uk/host/cru/docs/crupr18122003.doc

Forde, P. and Patterson, A. (1998) *Paedophile Internet Activity. Trends and Issues in Crime and Criminal Justice*. No. 97. Australian Institute of Criminology, ACT.

Gallop, G. (2004) *Covert Police Team to Hunt Online Predators*. Press release 21 June. http://www.mediastatements.wa.gov.au/media/media.nsf/news/2d47c8cd1e7cb53a48256eba00226b41?opendocument

Grant, A., David, F. and Grabosky, P. (1997) Child Pornography in the Digital Age. *Transnational Organised Crime*. 3: 4, 171–88.

Mitchell, A. (2004) Inside the Mind of a Killer. Sydney: *The Sun Herald*. 22 February: 55.

Queensland Crime Commission and Queensland Police Service (2000) *Child Sexual Abuse in Queensland: The Nature and Extent*. Volume 1. Project Axis, Queensland Crime Commission, Quensland.

Rouse, J. (2004) *Personal communication*. Queensland Police Service. 7 May.

Sentencing Advisory Panel (2002) *The Panel's Advice to the Court of Appeal on Offences Involving Child Pornography*. London: Sentencing Advisory Panel.

Stanley, J. and Kovacs, K. (2003) *Child Abuse and the Internet*. Ninth Australasian Conference on Child Abuse and Neglect. Sydney: 25 November.

Taylor, M. and Quayle, E. (2003) *Child Pornography: An Internet Crime*. Hove: Brunner Routledge.

Taylor, M. (1999) *The Nature and Dimensions of Child Pornography on the Internet*. Conference Introductory speech US/European Union Joint meeting on Combating Child Pornography on the Internet, Vienna: September.

The Age (2004) Five Years for UK Man Who Downloaded Child Porn. *The Age*. 3 March. http://theage.com.au/articles/2004/03/03/1078191360537.html

The Guardian (2003) Police Sting Targets Internet Paedophiles. *The Guardian*. 18 December. http://www.guardian.co.uk/child/story/0,7369,1109589,00.html

Townsend, I. (2004). *Qld Internet Sex Laws Reveal Disturbing Extent of Internet Predators*. ABC Transcripts. 14 February http://www.abc.net.au/am/content/2004/s1045034.htm

Wolak, J., Mitchell, K. and Finkelhor, D. (2003) *Internet Sex Crimes Against Minors: The Response of Law Enforcement*. New Hampshire: National Center for Missing and Exploited Children.

Internet resources

Australian High Tech Crime Centre, http://www.ahtcc.gov.au
Child Wise: ECPAT in Australia http://www.ecpat.org/index.html

All links accessed on 26 June 2004

Chapter 3

The Varieties of Child Pornography Production

Janis Wolak, David Finkelhor and Kimberly J. Mitchell

The findings are from the National Juvenile Online Victimization Study, which was conducted by the Crimes against Children Research Center at the University of New Hampshire and funded by the US Department of Justice and the National Center for Missing and Exploited Children.

Introduction

Before the Internet and video and digital photography, people thought of child pornography (CP) as being produced the same way as much adult pornography is produced, but more furtively. Some child advocates and law enforcement officials have begun calling child pornography 'images of abuse' to emphasise the criminal nature of the acts shown in many of the pictures. We have retained the term 'child pornography' because we are discussing a broader range of types of images and because, in the US, there is a history of court decisions and other writings that have used and developed the term 'child pornography.' A stereotype involved photographers with cameras and lights recording scenes using children who were coerced or seduced into performing sexual acts. This idea of CP production may have been accurate back in the days when photography demanded expensive cumbersome equipment, technical skill and special developing facilities. However, people who have studied the CP market in the past decade have noted that the days of commercial child pornography operations ended with the advent of video cameras, digital photography and computers. It takes no special skill and little in the way of equipment to take a sexually explicit picture of a child and post it on the Internet. What it takes is the desire and ability to find and exploit a victim.

Child advocates, law enforcement agents and others concerned about the sexual exploitation of children worry that growing numbers of children may be victimised by CP production if increasing numbers of images are being created to feed an expanding online market. However, we have little information about how many cases of CP production exist, who the offenders and victims are, what kinds of images are being produced and whether and how often images are distributed online. Further, because the Internet has played a large role in facilitating the distribution of child pornography, and the images found online have become so visible to law enforcement agencies, CP production has come to be seen as an 'Internet' crime. As a result, some law enforcement agencies that specialise in Internet crimes are focusing resources on tracing online CP from the Internet to its source. It seems that less attention is being paid to cases of CP production that may come to light in the context of child sexual abuse cases in local law enforcement agencies.

In this chapter, we examine a sample of US criminal cases in which offenders arrested for Internet-related sex crimes against minors took pictures of victims that ranged from sexually explicit to suggestive. Information about these cases was collected as part of the National Juvenile Online

Victimization Study (N-JOV Study), which gathered information from investigators in a national sample of US law enforcement agencies. For an overview of the N-JOV Study, see Wolak, J., Mitchell, K. and Finkelhor, D., (2003) *Internet Sex Crimes against Minors: The Response of Law Enforcement.* which can be downloaded from the website of the Crimes against Children Research Center at www.unh.edu/ccrc.

We asked a number of questions about CP production. How many offenders were arrested for Internet-related sex crimes that involved CP production? Who were the CP producers and victims? What types of images were produced? How often did CP production occur in concert with other sex crimes? How did CP producers manage to take pictures? How often were images distributed? How did CP production cases come to the attention of law enforcement?

Methods

Interviewers for the N-JOV Study gathered data from a US national sample of law enforcement agencies about cases involving Internet-related sex crimes against minors, including CP production. The study was designed to gain:

1. An overall picture of arrests for Internet-related sex crimes against minors in the US.
2. An understanding of how these arrests emerged as cases and were handled in a diverse group of agencies.
3. Detailed data about the characteristics of the crimes, offenders and victims.

We used a two-phase process to collect data from a national sample of 2,574 local, county, state and federal law enforcement agencies. In Phase 1, we sent mail surveys to the agencies asking if they had made arrests in Internet-related child pornography or sexual exploitation cases between 1 July 2000 and 30 June 2001. In Phase 2, interviewers conducted detailed telephone interviews with law enforcement investigators about a sample of the cases reported in the mail surveys. The interviewers also recorded a narrative description of each case. The final data set, weighted to account for sampling procedures and other factors, included data from 612 completed interviews, 122 of which involved offenders who produced child pornography.

To be eligible for the study, a case had to:

- Be a sex crime.
- Have a victim who was younger than 18.
- Involve an arrest that occurred between 1 July 2000 and 30 June 2001.
- Be Internet-related.

Cases were Internet-related if an offender-victim relationship was initiated online (online meeting cases); an offender used the Internet to communicate with a victim to further a sexual victimisation or otherwise exploit the victim; a case involved an Internet-related undercover investigation; child pornography was received or distributed online, or arrangements for receiving or distributing were made online; or child pornography was found on a computer or removable media (disks, CDs, etc.), as computer printouts or in a digital format.

The study was limited to cases that ended in arrests rather than crime reports or open investigations because cases ending in arrests were more likely to involve actual crimes and have more complete information about the crimes, offenders, and victims. We interviewed law-enforcement investigators because investigators have been in the forefront of identifying and combating these crimes and were the best sources of accessible, in-depth information about them. More details about instrumentation and sampling and weighting procedures are available in the N-JOV Study Methodology Report, available online at www.unh.edu/ccrc.

Subsample used in this paper

Internet sex crimes against minors include a diverse range of offences. The subsample examined in this paper comprises crimes against identified victims that involved CP production (n = 122, weighted n = 402). In 22 per cent of these crimes, offenders met identified victims online (n = 26, weighted n = 89). In 73 per cent, offenders used the Internet to facilitate sex crimes against victims who were family members or face-to-face acquaintances of the offenders (n = 93, weighted n = 291). Offenders who were strangers to their victims committed a small number of the crimes (5 per cent, n = 3, weighted n = 22). All of the offenders produced CP, and many of them committed other sexual offences as well.

We refer to the alleged perpetrators as 'offenders,' however, not all were convicted. At the time of data collection, 83 per cent of offenders had pled guilty or been convicted; charges had been dropped for 1 per cent, 2 per cent were dead or missing and case outcomes were pending or unknown for 13 per cent.

How we defined child pornography and CP production

In the United States, there is no simple, straightforward definition of child pornography. Statutes defining CP differ among states and between state and federal jurisdictions. Federal statutes define 'child' as a youth age 17 or younger, and child pornography as the 'visual depiction . . . of sexually explicit conduct' (18 USCS 2256). The statute describes sexually explicit conduct as including sexual acts such as intercourse, bestiality, and masturbation, as well as 'lascivious exhibition of the genitals or pubic area'.

The US Supreme Court has defined 'lascivious exhibition of the genitals or pubic area' broadly to include images of minors that focus on the genitals of children even when wearing clothing (US v. Knox, 1994). For example, sexually suggestive pictures that focus on the genitals of minors wearing swim suits or leotards can be child pornography. At the same time, photos of nude minors that show their genitals, but do not focus on them are not child pornography if the images do not constitute a 'lascivious exhibition'. Many state laws are modelled after the federal statutes and have 'lascivious exhibition' provisions, but some states have different standards. Also, some state laws define 'child' as a youth younger than 16 or 17. These legal decisions and statutory proscriptions mean that images do not have to depict sexual activity, child sexual abuse, nudity or children under the age of consent to qualify as child pornography, so in the United States, child pornography is not synonymous with child sexual abuse.

For the N-JOV Study, we wanted to collect data on the full range of picture taking that might constitute CP production, so we defined CP production broadly to encompass any picture taking of a person younger than 18 that was at least sexually suggestive.

Results

About 402 offenders were arrested for Internet-related sex crimes that involved CP production during the year covered by the N-JOV Study.

We estimate that there were 402 arrests in the US for Internet-related sex crimes against minors that involved CP production in the 12 months beginning 1 July 2000. (This estimate has a 2.5 per cent margin of error in either direction, which means that the true number is between 329 and 474 arrests.)

This estimate of 402 CP production cases ending in arrest is by no means a full measure of the number of Internet-related CP producers. It is only an estimate of the number of *arrests* involving CP production during the year covered by the N-JOV Study. To give some perspective on this number, we estimate from the FBI's National Incident Based Reporting System that there were approximately 65,000 arrests in 2000 for all types of sexual assaults against minors. Clearly, the number of arrests for Internet-related CP production is quite small in comparison. However, arrests for CP production may be growing due to the spread of the Internet and the related trade in child pornography.

The CP producers were diverse

In some ways, the arrested CP producers were homogenous. They were almost all male (98 per cent), with most older than 26 (89 per cent) and 44 per cent aged 40 or older. (See Table 1) Only 3 per cent were minors, younger than 18. Ninety-three per cent were White. Most were employed fulltime (81 per cent). Most possessed child pornography that was produced by others, in addition to producing their own (73 per cent).

In other ways, the CP producers were highly diverse. Some were well educated and some were not. Over a third had never married (36 per cent), but many were married or living with a partner at the time of the crime (37 per cent) and many were divorced, separated or widowed (27 per cent). Close to half lived with a minor child at the time of the offence (46 per cent), but most did not. A few were mentally ill (1 per cent) or had sexual disorders (3 per cent), but the great majority did not. Some were engaged in deviant sexual behaviour that did not involve children, like bestiality or sadism (16 per cent), or had problems with drugs or alcohol (20 per cent), but most did not. Most had never been violent as far as investigators knew, but some had (16 per cent). Some had prior arrests for non-sexual offending (26 per cent), and 12 per cent had been arrested previously for sex offences against minors, but most had never been in trouble with the law.

Few cases involved multiple offenders

One of the pre-Internet stereotypes about CP production is that many CP producers were part of organised groups. That was not the case with the CP producers in the N-JOV Study. Almost all of them acted alone (91 per cent). A few operated with one other offender and sexually victimised youth who were family members or acquaintances (8 per cent). Only 1 per cent of cases involved more organised sexual abuse, including small-scale prostitution rings and groups of offenders that produced and exchanged images among group members.

Almost half of the victims were teenagers

While most of the victims were aged 12 or younger (53 per cent), close to half were teenagers, ages 13 to 17. Overall, one in five victims were boys, and boys made up a quarter of victims younger than 13. As with offenders, almost all of the victims were White (91 per cent).

Offender-victim relationships varied based on the ages of victims

Most CP producers were family members (37 per cent) or acquaintances (36 per cent) of victims, although some met victims online (22 per cent) and a few were strangers (5 per cent). However, the contexts of CP production and the nature of the offender-victim relationships changed with the ages of the girls and boys who were photographed (see Figure 1).

Among the youngest victims, those aged 12 or younger, most CP producers were family members or caretakers. There were incest cases where men sexually victimised and photographed their daughters or step- or granddaughters over long periods of time; offenders who befriended and babysat for parents with children, then sexually abused and photographed the children; and a few families in which CP production was part of a pervasive atmosphere of sexual and physical abuse.

CP producers found ways to get access to school age victims outside of victims' households. Some ingratiated themselves with families by showing a special interest in children and taking them on outings and trips where they were abused and photographed. Some of these CP producers had legitimised their interest in children by affiliating themselves with youth organisations or schools. Some CP producers bypassed parents by targeting unsupervised children and young teens, giving them places to hang out and exploiting their natural interest in sex by talking about it, giving them pornography and allowing and encouraging sexual activity.

When victims were teenagers, the number of family member CP producers shrank, and the number that victims knew from outside of their homes, like teachers, coaches and neighbours grew. We also found a new group of CP producers, men who met victims online. The female victims in these Internet-initiated cases were often in love. For example, a 14-year-old girl met a man in his 40s in a chatroom. They communicated online for several months and then had several encounters at hotels. He took nude Polaroid photos of her and recorded a video of them having sex. Most of the boys who were photographed by men they met online were trying to understand their feelings of sexual attraction to men. A 13-year-old boy went to a chatroom geared toward gay men and asked if anyone lived near him. A 38-year-old man replied. They met face-to-face and spent the night in a hotel, where the man took pictures of their sexual activity with a digital camera.

Most CP producers had multiple victims and many victimised groups of children or adolescents

We tend to think of sexual activity as being between two people, however a surprisingly large number of offenders, over one-third, victimised children or adolescents in groups, apparently relying on group dynamics to 'normalise' the sexual activities and CP production. The groups ranged in size from two victims to ten, and included groups of siblings victimised by a family member or caretaker,

Table 3.1   CP production: Characteristics of offenders and victims*

Offender characteristics	CP production cases % (N = 122)
Offender gender	
Female	2% (3)
Male	98% (119)
Offender age	
Younger than 18	3% (2)
18 to 25	8% (9)
26 to 39	45% (59)
40 or older	44% (52)
Offender race	
Non-Hispanic White	93% (110)
Other group	4% (8)
Employed full-time	81% (95)
Possessed CP produced by others	73% (86)
Had some college education	46% (59)
Marital status	
Single, never married	36% (45)
Married or living with a partner	37% (45)
Separated, divorced, widowed	27% (32)
Lived with a minor at time of crime	46% (53)
Had a diagnosed mental illness	1% (2)
Diagnosed with a sexual disorder	3% (6)
Evidence of deviant sexual behaviour not involving children	16% (24)
Problems with drugs or alcohol	20% (24)
Any past violence, excludes current crime	16% (15)
Prior arrests for nonsexual offences (f35)	26% (27)
Prior arrests for sex crimes against minors	12% (20)
Number of offenders	
One	91% (108)
Two	8% (11)
Three to six	1% (3)
Victim characteristics	
Victim gender	
Girls	80% (94)
Boys	20% (28)
Victim age	
5 or younger	10% (15)
5 to 12 years	43% (52)
12 to 17 years	47% (55)
Victim race	
Non-Hispanic White	91% (108)
Other group	9% (13)

Table 3.1 *Continued*

Offender characteristics	CP production cases % (N = 122)
Offender-victim relationships	
Family members of victims	37% (46)
Face-to-face acquaintances	36% (47)
Offenders met victims online	22% (26)
Strangers	5% (3)
Multiple victim cases	
Numbers of victims	
One	37% (55)
Two	35% (26)
Three to five	17% (29)
Six or more	10% (11)
Don't know	1% (1)
Group victimisation	
Single victims	37% (56)
Group of victims	37% (44)
Multiple victims, not group	26% (22)

*If there was more than one victim or offender in a case, we picked a 'primary' victim or offender. The primary victim was the victim who used the Internet the most, or, if the victims were equal in that respect, the one who was the most seriously victimised. If there was no difference based on degree of victimisation, we picked the youngest. Similarly, the primary offender was the one who used the Internet the most, or who committed the most serious offence or the youngest. The victim and offender information presented here pertains to primary victims and offenders.

Note: Some categories may not add up to 100 per cent because of missing data or rounding. Also, percentages and numbers may not be proportionate because we used weighted data but unweighted counts to avoid any confusion about the number of cases upon which the findings are based.

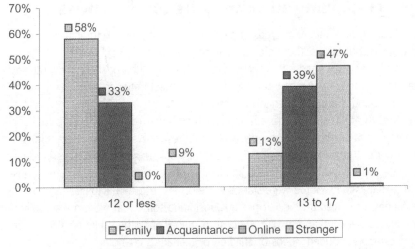

Figure 3.1 Type of offender-victim relationship based on whether victim was age 12 or younger or age 13 to 17

groups that included one or more children of an offender plus their friends, and groups of unrelated adolescent boys, girls or both that were organised around an adult.

The children in the sibling groups were sometimes quite young. For example, one man molested and filmed his girlfriend's three children, who were all younger than eight. Another offender offered to help a large family with childcare. He moved in with them and sexually assaulted and photographed several of the siblings, who ranged in age from four to ten. He made games of sexual activities and posing for pictures, and used the older siblings to introduce younger ones to the games.

Some offenders appeared to be using their children to recruit other victims. One young teenager who was being sexually abused and photographed by her uncle approached her friends on his behalf to recruit them for picture taking. A father took photos of his daughters and their friends.

There were also several of groups of unrelated adolescents, formed around individual adults, who got access to victims by inviting them into their homes, often offering the youths beer and marijuana and allowing and encouraging sexual activity. Some of these groups were all male, some were all female and some were mixed. Some of the CP producers were paedophiles who sought out boys from poverty stricken homes, gave them gifts, attention and emotional support, indoctrinated them into sexual activity and took photographs. One was looking for sexual contact with boys, but if boys resisted, he encouraged them to bring their girlfriends to his home for sex, which he watched and photographed. Some CP producers were focused on girls and formed groups of girls that were similar to the all boy groups. The girls had sex with the men and posed for pictures or took pictures of each other. The men gave the girls alcohol, drugs and cigarettes.

We can only speculate about why so much CP production happened in the context of groups. A photographer by nature is a third party observer to the action of others, so CP producers may have deliberately formed groups to create atmospheres where intimate activities like sex were observed. Once sex was observed, photography may have seemed acceptable. Also there may have been an 'I dare you' attitude among groups, particularly those involving adolescents that broke down inhibitions and made the youths more willing to pose.

Most CP producers took a variety of types of images that ranged widely in explicitness

The CP producers took a variety of types of pictures. Some of these pictures unequivocally depicted serious sex crimes, but others, though criminal in nature, did not (see Table 2).

Most CP producers took images that focused on a child's genitals or showed explicit sexual activity (71 per cent). Many took images that portrayed sexual contact between a child and an adult, defined as an adult touching the child's genitals (or breasts) or vice versa (43 per cent), and 30 per cent created pictures of adults sexually penetrating children. Some took photographs that showed other sexual penetration of children (15 per cent). These pictures showed sex between minors, penetration with objects or masturbation. Also, some CP producers took pictures that showed children enduring sexual violence, including sadism, bondage and beatings (6 per cent). These pictures showed a variety of types of sexual assaults. Some were staged while others recorded actual sadistic or violent acts.

Most offenders produced a range of pictures, including some that were not sexually explicit, but showed nudity (73 per cent) and sexually suggestive images of clothed children (40 per cent). Pictures in the nude category included videos of children or teenagers changing clothes or taking showers, snap shots of nude teenage girls or boys or, in some cases, more elaborate studio-type nude photographs. The suggestive category included photographs of sporting events that focused on glimpses of underwear, thighs, groins or cleavage and pictures of young children posed in skimpy bathing suits, filmy dresses or revealing outfits. These suggestive images may or may not have been treated as child pornography by law enforcement, depending upon the laws of the jurisdiction that handled the case and other circumstances of the crime.

Further, some offenders had also taken what most of us would consider ordinary photos of young people. We did not gather systematic information about this subject, but investigators told us about offenders who made videos of children walking back and forth to school, at beaches, sporting events and high school graduations in addition to the child pornography they produced. These images did not appear to have a sexual focus until they were seen in the context of other images created by the offenders.

In addition to determining the variety of images taken by CP producers, we looked at the most serious level of image produced by each offender, defining images that showed sexual assaults by adults as the most serious. Close to half of CP producers created images that showed contact sexual abuse (47 per cent), including those whose most serious image showed penetration by an adult (30 per cent), other sexual assault by an adult but not penetration (13 per cent) and penetration, but not by an adult (4 per cent). For over one-quarter of CP producers, the most serious image graphically showed genitals, but did not depict abuse (27 per cent). Finally, in 26 per cent of cases, investigators did not find any sexually explicit images, but did find images depicting nudity (23 per cent) or sexually suggestive poses (3 per cent).

Most CP producers sexually assaulted victims, but some did not

While we found that not all picture taking involved images showing sexual abuse, we expected that most CP production would occur in relationships that included contact sexual abuse or assault. We found that about two-thirds of the CP producers had sexually assaulted their victims, and the majority had committed sexual assaults that involved intercourse or other forms of sexual penetration (58 per cent). For example, a father who videotaped himself having sex with his young daughter coerced her into intercourse from the time she was seven until she told her mother at age 10. A 25-year-old man took in a 15-year-old boy from a deeply troubled home, seduced him and took photographs. Another man digitally penetrated and photographed a sleeping three-year-old girl who was spending the night in his home.

However, almost one-third of CP producers did not commit crimes that involved physical contact with their victims. Some used hidden cameras. Some convinced teenaged girls to pose for nude photos. Many of these images were not sexually explicit, but some producers created sexually explicit images without having sexual contact with victims. Two examples are a woman who took graphic nude photos of her nine-year-old daughter for her boyfriend, and a man who allowed teenagers to use his home for sexual encounters, which he recorded on video.

Most CP producers took pictures openly, but some used covert methods

Most CP producers took pictures openly (71 per cent), but one in five used covert methods that allowed them to capture images without having to gain the acquiescence of victims or, in some cases, interact with them at all. A few CP producers used both overt and covert methods (5 per cent).

Covert CP production

The most common covert method of CP production was *hidden cameras*. Examples include a father who hid a camera in a bathroom and took pictures of his daughters showering; a man who smuggled a camera into a locker room and took pictures of nude young boys; and a man who invited boys into his home, showed them pornography, and secretly filmed them masturbating. Many of these CP producers did not sexually assault their victims, but some did. For example, an offender in an Internet-initiated case pressured his 14-year-old victim into engaging in bondage and secretly filmed it.

A few offenders secretly used *sedatives or other drugs* to render victims compliant. One CP producer gave young girls mild sedatives, sexually assaulted them and recorded the assaults. Another man, who enticed teenage girls to his home by pretending to run a modelling agency, gave them soft drinks secretly laced with Ecstasy before he assaulted and photographed them. A third offender used both hidden cameras and sedatives. He was reported to police when a visiting boy saw a video camera hidden in the man's bathroom. This offender had taken the boy on a trip a few weeks previously, and police found a tape of the man molesting the boy during that trip. The boy remembered nothing. In the tape, he appeared drugged. Also, some offenders photographed and sometimes molested *sleeping* victims. Finally, *computer 'morphing'* was another form of covert CP production, although it was quite rare. One man produced an image that showed him sexually abusing his girlfriend's daughter. He acquired a simple photograph of the child and used computer graphics to 'morph' it into a sexual scene.

Overt CP production

While some CP producers used covert methods, most took pictures openly and used coercion, manipulation, and payment to gain the acquiescence of victims.

Coercion

Coercion took a variety of forms, ranging from minor use of force to pressure to threats. A small number of CP producers acquired pictures by using minor physical assaults such as ripping away towels and pulling down pants. Some used parental authority to coerce victims of incest into being photographed. Threats were also used. A man in his 40's allowed two teenage girls to use his home to have sex with their boyfriends, and then threatened to tell their parents if they did not provide sexual favours and pose for pictures. Another CP producer, a neighbour of two brothers, threatened them with violence if they revealed that he was assaulting and photographing them.

Manipulation

Many CP producers used ways other than coercion to gain victim co-operation in sexual activity and picture taking. Some offenders used play to seduce young children into posing. A CP producer, who sexually assaulted and took pictures of a four-year-old girl over a period of 18 months, used this tactic to introduce the child to sexual activity and photography. Some CP producers gave older victims alcohol and drugs to loosen inhibitions. The mother who produced sexually explicit photographs of her nine-year-old daughter gave the girl wine coolers and daiquiris. A man who met a 14-year-old boy in a gay chat room, gave the boy marijuana and beer, then seduced and photographed him. Romance was a popular tactic for men whose victims were teenage girls. A teacher who romanced, seduced and took pictures of a 13-year-old girl after he had been hired as her tutor was in this category, as were several of the offenders who met their victims online.

Payment

Finally, some offenders paid adolescent victims to pose. One commercial CP producer enticed boys to his home by giving them access to computers. He paid them per picture by creating accounts for each boy and giving them credits that could be used to buy things online. A man who created videos of teenage girls and sold them online paid the girls for posing. Another man convinced a group of girls to take pictures of each other, paying them with beer and cigarettes.

Three out of ten CP producers distributed the images they produced, but not always online

We expected that distribution to the Internet CP market would be a primary motive for CP production and that most produced pictures would be distributed online. However, we could not conclude this was true. Investigators were certain that images were distributed in less than one third of cases, and that distribution did not always occur via the Internet. In about half of the remaining cases, investigators did not know whether CP producers had distributed images and in the other cases the CP producers did not distribute. So it seemed that CP producers used images for a variety of purposes and that distribution, when it occurred, happened in a variety of ways, not just online. At the same time, one of the exacerbating circumstances of CP production as a crime is that any image can be easily circulated online, so that the potential harm of Internet distribution exists for victims long after the crime has ceased, if the images are in the hands of someone who might put them online.

CP producers had a variety of motives for distributing images

CP producers who distributed images had a variety of motives for doing so. Some were deeply involved in the Internet CP market or were running commercial enterprises. These CP producers distributed images broadly. But others distributed images in a limited manner.

The Internet CP market

Only about one-fifth of CP producers were clearly deeply involved in the Internet CP trade; they produced child pornography, distributed what they produced and possessed CP produced by others. Examples include an elementary school teacher who sexually abused several children, all of whom were younger than 10, and videotaped the abuse. He ran a file server through which he collected and distributed child pornography, including the videos he had made. His CP collection contained over 5,000 images. One CP producer, who had a CP collection of over 8,000 images, circulated images of himself abusing his infant daughter. He used photo-editing software to block her face in the images. Some fathers who abused their daughters for years were also traders and collectors of child pornography.

These CP producers were active participants in the CP market who posted images online or transmitted images directly to other traders. Many of the CP producers used the Internet to converse

Table 3.2 Characteristics of CP produced

Characteristics	CP production cases % (N = 122)
Offender produced CP depicting . . .	
Genitals or sexual activity	71% (95)
Sexual contact between adults and minors	43% (59)
Penetration of a child by an adult	30% (44)
Penetration of a child not by an adult	15% (27)
Violence	6% (9)
Nude or semi-nude, not graphic	73% (86)
Suggestive poses, clothed	40% (59)
Most serious image by offender showed	
Sexual penetration by an adult	30% (44)
Other sexual assault by an adult	13% (15)
Penetration, not by adult	4% (8)
Sexually explicit nudity	27% (30)
Simple nudity	23% (20)
Sexually suggestive poses, clothed	3% (4)
Communicated online with others involved with CP	39% (49)
Distributed produced images	
Yes	28% (39)
No	43% (55)
Don't know	29% (28)
How images were distributed	
Online	23% (32)
Offline (by mail or hand-to-hand)	10% (12)
Both on and offline	5% (6)
Offender produced, possessed and distributed produced images	19% (24)
Sexual abuse committed by offender against victim	
Photography only	27% (30)
Soliciting images	4% (4)
Sexual assault without penetration	11% (16)
Intercourse, oral sex or other penetration	58% (72)
Production method was . . .	
Covert	21% (22)
Overt	71% (97)
Both	5% (7)
Don't know	10% (9)

Note: Some categories may not add up to 100 per cent because of missing data or rounding. Also, percentages and numbers may not be proportionate because we used weighted data but unweighted counts to avoid any confusion about the number of cases upon which the findings are based.

with other offenders who were involved in child pornography. In the online CP market, newly produced images may serve as currency that allows CP producers to trade for other images and to achieve status in underground online groups devoted to child pornography and child sexual abuse (Jenkins, 2001; Taylor and Quayle, 2003). There is little doubt that many of the images created by these CP producers have permanently joined the eternally circulating stream of child pornography available online.

Commercial exploitation

CP images are a valuable commodity, but most CP producers who distributed were not selling images. A few, however, had established moneymaking businesses, including running websites for profit. According to investigators, one offender had a 'vast' computer business producing and selling sexually explicit pictures of boys, using a highly sophisticated encrypted computer system. Another offender maintained a website that featured girls ages 14–17. Members could order videos that featured specific girls and 'special requests' for $450 per video. Not all of the for-profit websites were sexually explicit. One man set up a paid membership website where people could view images of girls videotaped at sporting events.

A small number of the CP producers ran prostitution rings that featured children and adolescents. One man offered a run-away 13-year-old girl a place to stay, then forced her into prostitution. He posted sexually explicit pictures online to advertise her services. In two other cases, the offenders both pimped and produced CP videos that featured young teen girls. One of these pimps sent the videos through the US mail to a man who posted them online. The other distributed videos by showing them to groups of men. Two cases involved the prostitution of pre-pubescent children. A mother and her boyfriend used the Internet to offer her children for sex, and a man similarly offered a 12-year-old boy from his neighbourhood that he had seduced.

Limited distribution

Some CP producers engaged in more limited distribution; they distributed images to a small number of individuals with whom they had established relationships. We found three categories of limited distribution. The first included most female offenders, who were pandering to men they knew. They took pictures of their children and distributed the images to the men. The second included a small number of cases involving rings of offenders who produced and traded images among themselves. The third category included CP producers who used produced images to seduce other youth into sexual activity or persuade them to pose. For example, a man took pictures of himself having sex with a 16-year-old boy and sent the images via e-mail to two younger teen boys he met in chatrooms. While these CP producers may not have intended for the pictures go beyond the recipients, there was, of course, no guarantee images would remain out of the larger Internet CP market.

Other CP producers had motives for taking pictures that did not involve distribution

A considerable number of CP producers did not distribute the images they created (43 per cent). In many cases, the offenders may have wanted pictures as souvenirs of encounters with victims or for purposes of sexual fantasy. (Many CP producers who distributed images may have also had these motives.) While this was not something we could determine by interviewing law enforcement investigators, the case narratives did give insight into two common motives of CP producers who did not distribute images.

Seduction

Some CP producers appeared to use the process of picture taking to entice victims into sex. Some of these offenders were, or claimed to be, professional photographers. One man exemplified this group. He manipulated girls into posing by telling them they could become models. He started off taking 'glamour' shots, and then gradually moved them to sexual situations. These offenders appeared to use the role of photographer to flatter victims and acquire a level of intimacy that set the stage for seduction.

Voyeurism

Another group of offenders, especially the ones using hidden cameras, may have been voyeurs. Voyeurism is a sexual disorder characterised by 'recurrent, intense sexually arousing fantasies, sexual urges, or behaviours involving the act of observing an unsuspecting person who is naked in the process of disrobing, or engaging in sexual activity' (DSM IV, 1994). This probably explains the behaviour of many of the offenders who used hidden cameras to record victims in bathrooms, bedrooms and other places.

Most CP production cases come to the attention of law enforcement as child sexual abuse cases

Because child pornography is so associated with the Internet, a stereotype has developed that cases come to the attention of police because of Internet-related investigations or because people see images online that are traced back to specific CP producers.

We looked closely at how the CP production cases came to the attention of the criminal justice system. We found that the great majority came to light as conventional child sexual abuse cases (87 per cent). (See Table 3) Only 10 per cent came to the attention of law enforcement as a result of investigations of CP possession, while another 3 per cent became known because offenders solicited undercover investigators who were posing as minors online. Whether produced images were distributed did not have an impact on how CP production became known to law enforcement. Further, citizen reports to law enforcement generated the great majority of CP production cases (91 per cent), while less than 10 per cent arose through law enforcement activity like undercover investigations.

Implications

This paper examined a US national sample of cases in which offenders who were arrested for Internet-related crimes produced child pornography. We found the CP producers were a diverse group of offenders who committed a range of sex crimes and took pictures in a variety of contexts and for a variety of motives. There was no typical scenario for CP production. We also found that

Table 3.3   CP production cases: How cases became known to the criminal justice system

Characteristics	CP Production cases %(N = 122)
Case began as . . .	
Child sexual abuse case	87% (99)
Solicitation to undercover investigator	3% (6)
Possession or distribution of child pornography	10% (17)
Cases where produced CP was distributed began as . . . (n = 39)	
Child sexual abuse case	89% (32)
Solicitation to undercover investigator	2% (2)
Possession or distribution of child pornography	9% (5)
How case originated	
Citizen report	91% (103)
Law enforcement activity	9% (19)

Note: Some categories may not add up to 100 per cent because of missing data or rounding. Also, percentages and numbers may not be proportionate because we used weighted data but unweighted counts to avoid any confusion about the number of cases upon which the findings are based.

the pictures taken by CP producers varied considerably in terms of the sexual explicitness of the images, how CP producers used them and whether the images were distributed. Further, while in some cases the pictures explicitly recorded the sexual abuse committed by offenders, in other cases they did not. Some CP producers who committed incest or other penetrative sexual assaults took only nude or sexually suggestive pictures of victims. And some CP producers who did not commit sexual assaults produced pictures that were quite explicit.

Nonetheless, we did not find that CP production was a widespread crime. The estimated number of 402 arrests for CP production during the year covered by the study is small compared to overall arrests for sex crimes against minors, 65,000 during that same year. However, this estimate accounts only for arrests, and not for cases that were unknown to law enforcement or cases that were known but arrests were not made.

Implications for law enforcement

One important aspect of our findings is that the great majority of these cases came to the attention of law enforcement in the form of child sexual abuse cases that were reported to authorities by citizens. There has been much publicity and discussion about child pornography on the Internet and great concern about the children who are pictured in the images seen there. Law enforcement and child advocates are pushing to find ways to identify these children, primarily to rescue them from their situations, but also so that the law enforcement agencies that maintain databases of CP images in Europe and the US can maintain accurate records.

While efforts to find children whose pictures are seen online are important, our finding that most CP production cases began in local law enforcement agencies with complaints of child sexual abuse adds another dimension to these efforts. It is important to remember that, while CP images circulate globally on the Internet, the criminals that produce the images operate in local communities. Conventional child sexual abuse investigations should not be overlooked as a means of stopping CP producers and identifying victims.

We recommend that standard protocols for child sexual abuse cases prompt investigators always to consider the possibility that pictures were taken. Searchers should always look for pictures. Interviewers should routinely ask about pictures. Cases that involve CP possession or online meetings deserve heightened alert to the possibility that CP images were produced.

There are two reasons this is so important. First, the harm to and needs of victims cannot be fully assessed if the professionals involved in cases do not find out, or try to find out, if CP images were produced. Second, pictures can provide concrete evidence of crimes. In some cases images directly document the sexual abuse and provide disturbing and graphic evidence of what occurred between offenders and victims. Even if pictures are not explicit, they can corroborate victim testimony and provide evidence of inappropriate actions by offenders that can shed light on their motivations and actions.

In cases where CP production is established, it is particularly important to determine whether pictures were distributed and to recover images that could cause embarrassment to victims in the future if at all possible. Many of the investigators we interviewed did not know whether the images they found had been distributed. Training investigators in how to detect distribution would be beneficial. Also, policies need to be developed that are sensitive to the reactions of victims who may be reluctant to reveal that images were created or who may feel humiliated at their pictures being viewed as evidence.

Implications for prevention and education

Education and prevention programmes geared toward protecting children from sexual offenders should include age-appropriate, candid information about CP production and the contexts in which it can occur. With younger children, education programmes can bring up inappropriate picture taking when talking about inappropriate touching.

Adolescents need a different approach. In the N-JOV Study, many of the offenders who photographed teenagers victimised youth who felt attached to the offenders by ties of romance or friendship or sexual bonds. We need to be emphatic about why these relationships are illegal, wrong and unhealthy. Adolescents should know: adults who engage in sexual activity with underage youth are committing crimes and can go to jail. The youth in these relationships may feel appreciated and understood, but it's often because they are being manipulated to feel that way. Posing for sexy pictures may seem glamorous, but pictures are permanent and who sees them is rarely in the control of the person who posed. Pictures can end up circulating on the Internet forever. Further, when pictures are discovered, the youth involved are usually horribly embarrassed; their lives are disrupted and the pictures may end up as evidence in court. In the US, it is a federal crime to take sexually explicit pictures of persons younger than 18. Adults who take sexual pictures of children and young teens should be reported to the police to protect other youth from being victimised. If youth know that friends or acquaintances are involved in inappropriate relationships with adults, they need to protect their friends by disclosing what they know.

Limitations

The N-JOV Study is the first research that has gathered information about a national sample of arrested CP producers. Data from a national sample is the strength of the N-JOV Study, but like every scientific survey, the study also has limitations and defects. Readers should keep some of these important things in mind when considering the findings and conclusions of this study.

First, some errors and biases may have been introduced because we interviewed law enforcement investigators. We regarded these respondents as the best sources for in-depth information about the nature of Internet-related crimes because their professional responsibilities require them to gather extensive information about these cases. However, the information they provided could be biased by training, professional attitudes, or the adversarial nature of their roles in some of these cases.

In addition, the findings of the study apply only to CP producers who were arrested for Internet-related sex crimes against minors. We do not know if these arrested offenders were representative of CP producers who were undetected by law enforcement or those who were detected but not arrested. Because of this, our findings cannot be interpreted to apply to offenders who were not arrested or those who committed sex crimes that were not Internet-related.

Conclusion

We found that CP production is not unusual in the context of Internet-related sex crimes against minors, although we cannot say how common it is in crimes that have no Internet nexus. We are concerned that the advent of the Internet child pornography market may have increased the demand for images and that CP production may be increasing as a result. At the same time, many of the pictures that were taken in these cases were not distributed online.

The Internet supports the CP market by making it easily accessible. But the Internet and related technologies have contributed to the problem of CP production in other ways also. First, the online CP market may motivate some offenders to produce images for trade. Second, even though many of the offenders in our study did not distribute images online, the potential for distribution exists now in any case where an image is created. Any picture can be scanned and uploaded onto the Internet. Third, since the advent of computers, scanning and digital photography, CP production can be done easily and privately. Offenders who may have been inhibited in the past because film had to go through third parties for development may feel they can now take pictures with little risk. Fourth, new technology allows offenders to photograph victims easily without their knowing, so CP producers can pander to voyeuristic tendencies by hiding cameras and secretly filming victims.

The Internet is also the source of a large and, in the US, legal adult pornography market, which also may have an impact on CP production, particularly where adolescents are concerned. About half of the CP production cases involved teenagers younger than 18. We expect that most of these victims were sexually mature, and that the target audience for their images did not include paedophiles. Some of these teenagers posed willingly for pictures, sometimes out of misguided love for offenders, but sometimes in exchange for money, gifts, drugs or alcohol. The Internet may have contributed to a sense that posing for sexually explicit pictures is glamorous and exciting. Pornography sites are widely advertised online, and television shows have touted Internet pornography stars as celebrities. Offline sources also contribute. Videos of girls flashing their breasts and raising their skirts are promoted and sold on television and the extent of sexually provocative advertising, some involving models who appear to be young teens has been commented on widely. These social mores may make it easier for CP producers to convince teens to pose for pictures.

While not all of the cases we examined involved sexually explicit images or victims who were sexually assaulted, it is important to acknowledge the disturbing nature of many of the cases we described in this chapter. Many CP producers were taking pictures of acts that most people do not want to imagine, much less see. It is painful to know that children and teenagers are being used so callously. Child pornography is not new, just like child sexual abuse is not new. However, the Internet may be adding new dimensions to this crime by allowing illicit images to circulate widely via a medium that is easy to use, widely accessible and hard to police. These factors may promote the growth of the trade in child pornography, which in turn may promote a growth in production of images. More children may be at risk.

References

American Psychological Association (1994) (4th edn.) *Diagnostic and Statistical Manual on Mental Disorders: DSM-IV*. Washington DC: American Psychological Association.

Jenkins, P. (2001). *Beyond Tolerance: Child Pornography on the Internet*. New York: New York University Press.

Taylor, M., and Quayle, E. (2003) *Child Pornography: An Internet Crime*. Hove: Brunner Routledge.

United States of America v. Stephen A. Knox, 32 733 (United States Court of Appeals for the Third Circuit 1994).

Chapter 4

Compliant Child Victims: Confronting an Uncomfortable Reality

Kenneth V. Lanning

(**Note**: An earlier version of this chapter was published in the *APSAC Advisor*, Vol. 14, No. 2, Spring 2002)

In this discussion, the term *compliant* will be used to describe those children who co-operate in or 'consent' to their sexual victimisation. Because children cannot legally consent to having sex with adults, this compliance should not in any way alter the fact that they are victims of serious crimes. Some have suggested using terms such as *statutory, complicit, consensual, voluntary, cooperating*, or *participatory* to refer to such victims. Each of these terms may have perceptual advantages and disadvantages. The term compliant is being used, however, because at this time I cannot think of a better one. The term used is not as important as recognising and understanding the reality of the behavioural dynamics involved. For the sake of child victims and professional interveners, it is important to bring out into the open possible reasons for and the complexity and significance of this compliance.

The sexual victimisation of children involves varied and diverse dynamics. It can range from one-on-one intrafamilial abuse to multioffender/multivictim extrafamilial sex rings and from stranger abduction of toddlers to prostitution of teenagers. The often forgotten piece in the puzzle of the sexual victimisation of children is acquaintance molestation. This seems to be the most difficult manifestation of the problem for society and even professionals to face. People seem more willing to accept a sinister stranger from a different location or father/stepfather from a different socio-economic background as a child molester than a clergy member, next-door neighbour, law-enforcement officer, paediatrician, teacher, or volunteer with access to children. Society seems to have a problem dealing with any sexual-victimisation case in which the adult offender is not completely 'bad' or the child victim is not completely 'good'. The idea that child victims could simply behave like human beings and respond to the attention and affection of offenders by voluntarily and repeatedly returning to an offender's home is a troubling one. For example, it confuses us to see the victims in child pornography giggling or laughing.

Pitfalls in understanding the compliant child victim

The sexual victimisation of children by family members and by 'strangers' can, of course, involve compliant child victims. In my experience, however, this compliance occurs most often in cases involving children sexually victimised by adult acquaintances. In other words, stranger offenders can use trickery to initially lure their child victims, but they tend to control them more through confrontation, threats of force, and physical force. Likewise, intrafamilial offenders tend to control their victims more through their private access and family authority. The concept of child compliance is obviously much harder to define and evaluate when the offender is a parent.

In contrast, acquaintance child molesters, although sometimes violent, tend by necessity to control their victims through the grooming or seduction process. This process not only gains the victim's initial co-operation, but also decreases the likelihood of disclosure and increases the likelihood of ongoing, repeated access. An acquaintance molester who uses violence is likely to be quickly reported to law enforcement and easily identified, but an acquaintance molester who seduces his victims can sometimes go unreported for years if not indefinitely. For this discussion, the determination of who is an 'acquaintance' child molester will be based more on the process and dynamics of the child victimisation and less on the technical relationship between the offender and child victim. An offender who is a stepfather, for example, might be an acquaintance molester who used 'marriage' just to gain access to children.

One of the unfortunate outcomes of society's preference for the 'stranger-danger' concept has a direct impact on intervention into many acquaintance-sexual-exploitation cases. It is what I call, 'say no, yell, and tell' guilt. This is the result of societal attitudes and prevention programmes that focus only on 'unwanted' sexual activity and tell potential child victims to avoid sexual abuse by saying no, yelling, and telling. This technique might work better with the stranger lurking behind a tree, but children who are seduced and actively participate in their victimisation, however, often feel guilty and blame themselves because they did not do what they were 'supposed' to do. These seduced and, therefore, compliant victims may sometimes feel a need to describe their victimisation in more socially acceptable but inaccurate ways that relieve them of this guilt.

The reality of this problem must be recognised, understood, and addressed if these cases are to 'nice guys' who typically sexually exploit children by befriending and seducing them. Equally important, we must also understand that the child victims are human beings with needs, wants, and desires. Child victims cannot be held to idealistic and superhuman standards of behaviour. Their frequent co-operation in their victimisation must be viewed as an understandable human characteristic that should have little or no criminal-justice significance.

In theory, the law recognises the developmental limitations of children and affords them with special protection. The repeated use, however, of terms such as *rape, sexual violence, assault, attack, sexually violent predator*, and *unwanted sexual activity*, when discussing or inquiring about the sexual exploitation of children assumes or implies in the minds of many that all child victims resist sexual advances by adults and are then overpowered by coercion, trickery, threats, weapons, or physical force. Although cases with these elements certainly exist, when adults and children have sex, lack of 'consent' can exist simply because the child is legally incapable of giving it. Whether or not the child resisted, said no, and was overpowered are, therefore, not necessarily elements in determining if a crime has occurred. Understanding this is especially problematic for the public (i.e., potential jurors) and professionals (i.e., physicians, therapists) who lack specialised training in criminal law and may not rely on strict legal analysis. The sad reality is, nonetheless, that such victim behaviour *does* have significance in the perception of society and in the 'real world' of the criminal justice system.

Society's lack of understanding and acceptance of the reality of compliant child victims often results in the following:

1. Victims failing to disclose and even denying their sexual victimisation.
2. Incomplete, inaccurate, distorted, even contradictory victim disclosures when they do happen.

3. Lifetime of victim shame, embarrassment, and guilt.
4. Offenders being able to have numerous victims over an extended period of time.
5. Ineffective prevention programmes that not only do not prevent victimisation, but also make the first four problems worse.

This discussion intends to cast some light on the issue and encourage dialogue to address and improve this situation for the benefit of the victims and interveners. Although society has become increasingly more aware of the problem of the acquaintance molester and related problems, such as child pornography and the use of computers, a voice still persists that calls the public to focus on 'stranger danger' and calls many child-abuse professionals to focus on intrafamilial sexual abuse. This narrow focus often leads to a misperception of the entire spectrum of the sexual victimisation of children.

Mixed definitions

Referring to the same thing by different names and different things by the same name frequently creates confusion. For example, the same 15-year-old individual can be referred to as a *baby, child, youth, juvenile, minor, adolescent, adult,* or (as in one forensic psychological evaluation) *underage adult*. A father who coerces, a violent abductor, an acquaintance who seduces, an online child-pornography collector, or an older boyfriend can all be referred to as a *child molester or pedophile/paedophile*. Terms such as *sexual exploitation of children and youth or sexual exploitation of children and adolescents* imply that a youth or an adolescent is not a child. At what age does a child become a youth or adolescent? If such a person is sexually victimised, is that considered youth molestation or sexual abuse of adolescents?

There clearly can be a conflict between the law and society's viewpoint when it comes to defining a *child*. Many people using the term *sexual abuse of* **children** have a mental image of children 12 or younger. The main problem, therefore, is often with the 13 to 17-year-old age group. Those are the child victims who most likely look, act, and have sex drives like adults, but who may or may not be considered children under some laws and by society. There can be national, cultural, and ethnic variations in attitudes about who is a child. Pubescent teenagers can be viable sexual targets of a much larger population of sex offenders. Unlike one-on-one intrafamilial sexual abuse in which the victim is most often a young female, in many acquaintance sexual-exploitation cases the victim is a boy between the ages of 10 and 16.

Legal definitions of who is considered a child or minor also vary from country to country, culture to culture, and even statute to statute when dealing with adolescent victims. During a prosecution, the definition can even vary from count to count in the same indictment. The age of the child may determine whether certain sexual activity is a misdemeanour or felony and what degree felony. To legally determine who is a child, investigators and prosecutors turn to the law. That is, the penal code will legally define who is a child or minor. But they must still deal with their own perceptions as well as those of other professionals, juries, and society as a whole.

In general, a child will be defined for this discussion as someone who has not yet reached his or her eighteenth birthday. One of the problems in using this broad, but sentimentally appealing, definition of a child is that it lumps together individuals who may be more unalike than alike. In fact 16-year-olds may be socially and physically more like 26-year-old young adults than like 6-year-old children. Adolescents are frequently considered and counted by child advocates as children in order to emphasise the large scope of the child-victimisation problem. But then, little or nothing said or done about addressing the problem seems to apply to the reality of adolescent victims. If adolescents are considered child victims of sexual exploitation, then their needs, interests, and desires must be realistically recognised and understood when addressing the problem.

Issues about age of consent

In the United States in the early 1980s, an infamous case involved a judge who sentenced an adult convicted of child molestation to a minimal sentence because the judge felt the five-year-old victim was 'sexually promiscuous.' Society and professionals were outraged and demanded that the judge be removed from the bench. The sad reality is that most people were outraged, but for the wrong reason. They thought it was impossible for a five-year-old child to be sexually promiscuous. Although not typical or probable, it is possible. Of course, this is more likely the **result** of some maltreatment, not the cause. Instead, we should have been outraged because it makes no difference whether or not the five-year-old child was sexually promiscuous, a fact that in no way lessens the offender's crime or responsibility. If you change the case slightly and make the victim nine years old, does that make a difference? Most people would probably say no. If you change it again and make the victim 12 years old, many people would still say it makes no difference, but might want to see a picture of the victim. If you change it again and make the victim 13, 14, 15, or 16 years old, the response of society and the law would vary greatly. For example, those interested in minimising such sexual activity might emphasise referring to the victims as *minors* rather than as *children*.

In sex crimes, the fundamental legal difference between victimisation of an adult and a child is the issue of **consent**. In cases of sexual activity between adults, with a few rare exceptions, a lack of consent must be established for there to be a crime. In sexual activity between children and adults, a crime can exist even if the child co-operates or 'consents'. But the reality of age of consent is not so simple.

Age of consent can vary depending on the type of sexual activity and individual involved. At what age can a child do the following: consent to get married; engage in sexual activity; appear in sexually explicit visual images; or leave home to have sex with an unrelated adult without parental permission? Federal case law in the United States seems to suggest that the consent of a 14-year-old to run off and have sex with a 40-year-old man she met on the Internet is a valid defence for the kidnapping charge, but not for the sexual assault charge. At what age can an adolescent consent to have sex with a relative, a teacher, a coach, an employer, or a 21-year-old boyfriend or girlfriend?

In the United States, society and criminal investigators and prosecutors seem to have a preference for sexual victimisation cases where the victim, adult or child, clearly does **not** consent. Among lack of consent cases, the **least** preferred are cases where the victim could not consent because of self-induced use of drugs or alcohol. Cases where the victim was just verbally threatened are next, followed by cases where a weapon was displayed. For purposes of ease of proof, the **most** preferred lack-of-consent cases are those where the victim has visible physical injuries or is, sad to say, dead. Many compliant child victims may inaccurately claim they were asleep, drunk, drugged, or abducted in part to meet these lack of consent criteria and in part to avoid embarrassment.

Sexual-victimisation cases in which the child victim is not forced or threatened and co-operates or 'consents', are more troubling and harder for society and investigators to deal with. If such victims were adults, there usually would not even be a crime. Although 'consent' is supposed to be irrelevant in child-sexual-victimisation cases, there are unspoken preferences in these cases as well. The **most** preferred are 'consent' cases where the victim can explain that the co-operation was due to some general fear or ignorance about the nature of the activity. That is, the child was afraid to tell or did not understand what was happening. The next most preferred are cases where the child was tricked, duped, or indoctrinated. If the offender was an authority figure, this 'brainwashing' concept is even more appealing. Next on this preference scale are the cases in which the victim was willing to trade 'sex' for attention, affection, and romance. Much less acceptable are cases in which the child willingly traded sex for material rewards (e.g., clothes, shoes, trips) or money (i.e., prostitution). Almost totally unacceptable are cases in which the child engaged in the sexual activity with an adult because the child enjoyed the sex. In fact, it is almost a sacrilege to even mention such a possibility.

These societal and criminal-justice preferences prevail in spite of the fact that almost all human beings trade sex for attention, affection, privileges, gifts, money or other benefits. Although any of these reasons for compliance are possible, many seduced child victims inaccurately claim they were afraid, ignorant, or indoctrinated in part to meet these societal preferences for this co-operation and in part to avoid embarrassment. Many victims are most concerned over disclosure of and therefore more likely to deny *engaging in sex for money, bizarre sex acts, homosexual acts in which they were the active participant*, and *sex with other children*.

Any of the above scenarios in various combinations are certainly possible. A child might co-operate in some sexual acts and be clearly threatened or forced into others. All are potential crimes. The offender, the victim, society, or the professional intervener may perceive what constitutes *compliance* differently. Investigators and prosecutors always need to attempt to determine what actually happened, not attempt to confirm their preconceived beliefs about sexual victimisation of children.

A young adolescent boy appearing on a television talk show focusing on the topic of sexual victimisation of child athletes by their adult coaches was asked by the host why the abuse went on for so long without him telling anyone. The boy, who had been non-violently seduced by his coach, answered that he was frightened of his coach. Although seemingly inconsistent with the facts, everyone gladly accepted and applauded his answer. What would have been the reaction of the television host and the audience had the boy provided more plausible answers, such as he did not tell because by having sex with the coach he got to play more or because he enjoyed the sex? Such answers are reasonable and perfectly understandable and should not change the fact that the boy was the victim of a crime. Maybe anticipation of society's response and not any threat of the molester is what most 'frightened' the boy into not telling sooner.

Most acquaintance-exploitation cases, including those involving computers, involve these seduced or compliant victims. Although applicable statutes and investigative or prosecutive priorities may vary, individuals investigating sexual-exploitation cases must generally start from the premise that the sexual activity is **not** the fault of the victim even if the child:

- Did not say 'no'.
- Did not fight.
- Actively co-operated.
- Initiated the contact.
- Did not tell.
- Accepted gifts or money.
- Enjoyed the sexual activity.

Investigators and prosecutors must also remember that many children, especially those victimised through the seduction process, often:

- Trade sex for attention, affection, or gifts.
- Are confused over their sexuality and feelings.
- Are embarrassed and guilt-ridden over their activity.
- Describe their victimisation in socially acceptable ways.
- Minimise their responsibility and maximise the offender's.
- Deny or exaggerate their victimisation.

All these things do not mean the child is not a victim. What they do mean is that children are human beings with human needs. Society, however, seems to prefer to believe that children are pure and innocent. Child abuse conferences often have subtitles such as 'Betrayal of Innocence.' Bags with children's endearing crayon drawings on them are distributed to attendees to carry handout material. The FBI's national initiative on computer exploitation of children is named 'Innocent Images'. This preference for idealistic innocence persists in spite of the fact that anyone who has spent time with children, even infants and toddlers, knows they quickly and necessarily learn to manipulate their environment to get what they want. Many children have only a vague or inaccurate concept of 'sex'. They are seduced and manipulated by clever offenders and usually do not fully understand or recognise what they were getting into. Even if they do seem to understand, the law is still supposed to protect them from adult sexual partners. This protection is based on the developmental immaturity of children, not their 'innocence'. Consent should **not** be an issue with child victims. Sympathy for victims is, however, inversely proportional to their age and sexual development.

If necessary, an education expert witness can explain the dynamics of these 'consenting' victim patterns of behaviour to the court. I have personally done so in several cases in the United States with the admissibility of my testimony upheld by appellate courts. The ability to make these explanations, however, is being undermined by the fact that children, at an age when they cannot legally choose to have sex with an adult partner, can choose to have an abortion without their parents' permission or be charged as adults when they commit certain crimes. Can the same 15-year-old be both a 'child' victim and an 'adult' offender in the criminal-justice system?

Offender-victim bond

The successful investigation and prosecution of sexual exploitation of children cases often hinges on being able to answer two questions:

1. Why didn't the victim disclose (fully or partially) when it happened?
2. Why is the victim disclosing (fully or partially) now?

For objective fact-finders, the answers to these questions should be what the evidence supports not what society prefers. Because victims of acquaintance exploitation usually have been carefully seduced and often do not realise or believe they are victims, they repeatedly and voluntarily return to the offender. Society and the criminal-justice system have a difficult time understanding this. If a neighbour, teacher, or clergy member molests a boy, why does he 'allow' it to continue and not immediately report it? Most likely he may not initially realise or believe he is a victim. Some victims are simply willing to trade sex for attention, affection, and gifts and do not believe they are victims. The sex itself might even be enjoyable, and the offender may be treating them better than anyone else ever has. But, they may come to realise they are victims when the offender ends the relationship.

Then they recognise that all the attention, affection, and gifts were just part of a plan to use and exploit them. This may be the final blow for a troubled child who has had a difficult life.

Many of these victims never disclose their victimisation. Younger children may believe they did something 'wrong' or 'bad' and are afraid of getting into trouble. Older children may be more ashamed and embarrassed. Victims not only do not disclose, but they often strongly deny it happened when confronted. In one case, several boys took the stand and testified concerning the high moral character of the accused molester. When the accused molester changed his plea to guilty, he admitted that the boys who testified on his behalf were also among his victims.

In my experience, some of the more common reasons that compliant victims do not disclose are:

- The stigma of homosexuality.
- Lack of societal understanding.
- Failure to tell when they should have done so.
- Presence of positive feelings for the offender.
- Embarrassment or fear over their victimisation.
- The belief they are not really victims.

Because most of the offenders are male, the stigma of homosexuality is a serious problem for male victims, especially if no threats or force were used prior to the sex. Although being seduced by a male child molester does not necessarily make a boy a homosexual, the victims do not understand this. If a victim does disclose, he risks significant ridicule by his peers and lack of acceptance by his family.

These seduced or compliant child victims obviously do sometimes disclose, often because the sexual activity is discovered (e.g., abduction by offender, recovered child pornography, overheard conversations, computer records located) or suspected (e.g., statements of other victims, association with known sex offender, proactive investigation), after which an intervener confronts them. Others disclose because the offender misjudged them, got too aggressive with them, or is seducing a younger sibling or their close friend. Compliant victims sometimes come forward and report because they are angry with the offender for 'dumping' them. They might be jealous that the offender found a new, younger victim. They sometimes disclose because the abuse has ended, not to end the abuse. Some compliant victims eventually disclose due to significant changes later in their lives such as marriage or the birth of a child.

In addition some compliant victims do not want the perpetrator prosecuted or sent to prison. At sentencing, they may even write a letter to the judge indicating their 'consent' in the sexual activity and expressing their love for the defendant. Should such a letter get the same consideration as a letter from a victim requesting harsh punishment?

Children never lie?

The available evidence suggests that children rarely lie about sexual victimisation, if a *lie* is defined as a statement deliberately and maliciously intended to deceive. If children in these cases do lie, it may be because factors such as shame or embarrassment over the nature of the victimisation increase the likelihood that they misrepresent the sexual activity. Seduced victims sometimes lie to make their victimisation more socially acceptable or to please an adult's concept of victimisation. Occasionally children lie because they are angry and want to get revenge on somebody. Some children, sadly, lie about sexual victimisation to get attention and forgiveness. A few children may even lie to get money or as part of a lawsuit. This can sometimes be influenced by pressure from their parents. Objective investigators must consider and evaluate all these possibilities. It is extremely important to recognise, however, that because children might lie about part of their victimisation does not mean that the entire allegation is necessarily a lie and they are not victims. Acquaintance-exploitation cases often involve complex dynamics and numerous incidents that often make it difficult to say an allegation is all true or all false.

An important part of the evaluation and assessment of allegations of sexual victimisation of children is comparing the consistency of allegations:

1. Among *what* multiple victims allege to have happened.
2. Between *what* is alleged and *who* is suspected of doing it is.

If a victim describes his or her victimisation as involving what clearly sound like the behaviour patterns of a certain type of sex offender, then the fact that the alleged offender fits that pattern is corroborative. If he does not, there is an inconsistency that needs to be resolved. For example, is it consistent for a victim to claim that they did not initially disclose the victimisation due to threats of violence or death when the 'nice guy' offender appears to have controlled his victims by grooming them with attention and affection? The inconsistency could be because the alleged *what* is inaccurate (e.g., distorted account from victim, insufficient details), the suspected *who* has been misevaluated (e.g., incomplete background, erroneous assessment), or the alleged *who* is innocent (e.g., suspect did not commit alleged crime). In my experience, distorted accounts from victims are frequently caused or influenced by various interveners (e.g., therapists, physicians, parents, law enforcement) who are unwilling to non-judgmentally accept the reality of the nature of the actual molestation of children. Instead, they influence, pressure, or lead the children to describe the victimisation in a way that fits their agenda or needs and in the process destroy the consistency and prosecutive potential of a valid case.

Understanding the seduction process

Most compliant child victims were courted, groomed, or seduced over time by an adult. True understanding of this process must be incorporated into the intervention of these cases. For example, paediatricians or therapists who only discuss forced or unwanted sexual activity with their patients are potentially missing a significant area of sexual victimisation of children. Because a child wanted to have sex with an adult, does not mean it is not abuse and a crime.

The seduction process usually begins with the offender identifying a preferred or acceptable child target. It continues with the gathering of information about the interests and vulnerabilities of the child. The acquaintance offender in particular must find a method of access to children. To gain such access, it is important that the offender be or perceived to be a 'nice guy' who cares about children. Acquaintance offenders with a preference for younger victims (younger than age 12) are more likely to also have to spend time seducing the potential victim's parents or caretakers to gain their trust and confidence. Acquaintance offenders may also encourage and exploit the targeted child's conflict with or alienation from parents. Offenders can gain access to children through a wide variety of activities (e.g., sports, religion, education, online computers). The offender must then fill the potential victim's needs with the most effective combination of attention, affection, privileges, gifts, money, etc. The offender must also lower any sexual inhibitions the child may have. This is most often done by combinations of varying techniques (i.e., games, 'back rubs', photography, talk about sex/ cybersex, pornography, drugs, alcohol, separation from support systems, and manipulation into changing clothing and spending overnight together). **Any** child is vulnerable to seduction by **any** adult, but troubled children from dysfunctional families targeted by adults who are authority figures seem to be at even greater risk of being seduced. The success of the seduction process of offenders is usually determined by how well they select their victim, their ability to identify and fill victim needs, how much time they have, and how proficient they are at relating to and seducing children.

After understanding the seduction process, the intervener must be able to communicate this understanding to the victim. This is the difficult part. Interveners need to be careful about asking questions that communicate a judgment about the nature of the victimisation (e.g., Tell me if you were scared? Tell me if he threatened you? Is it hard to remember such terrible things?). If *why* questions are asked (e.g., *Why* didn't you immediately tell? *Why* didn't you resist? *Why* did you return to the offender? *Why* are you smiling in this photograph?), every effort should be made to communicate to the victim that **any** truthful answer is acceptable, including 'because I enjoyed it'.

Interveners must understand and learn to deal with the incomplete and contradictory statements of seduced victims of acquaintance molesters. The dynamics of their victimisation must be considered. Any behaviour or claims of victims must be understood and evaluated in the context of the entire process. Compliant victims are often embarrassed and ashamed of their behaviour and correctly believe that society will not understand their victimisation. Many younger child victims are most concerned about the response of their parents and often describe their victimisation in ways they believe will please their parents. Adolescent victims are typically also concerned about the response of their peers. Victims and their families from higher socio-economic backgrounds may be even more concerned about the public embarrassment of any disclosure. Interveners who have a stereotyped concept of child-sexual-abuse victims or who are accustomed to interviewing younger children molested within their family will have a difficult time interviewing adolescents seduced by an acquaintance. Many of these victims will be street-wise, troubled, or even delinquent children from dysfunctional homes. Such victims should not be blindly believed, but should not be dismissed because the accused is a pillar of the community and they are delinquent or troubled. Such allegations should be objectively investigated and evaluated.

Some victims will continue to deny their victimisation no matter what the interviewer says or does. Some children even deny victimisation that the offender has admitted or other evidence clearly discloses. Some will make admissions but minimise the quality and quantity of the acts. They may minimise their compliance and maximise the offender's involvement by claiming he drugged them, threatened them, had a weapon, or had even abducted them. Of course some of these allegations may be accurate and should be investigated. They are, however, not typical of acquaintance-exploitation cases. Violence is most likely used to prevent disclosure. Sadistic offenders may also use violence during sex, but this is relatively rare in cases involving seduction. As previously mentioned, these potential inaccuracies in the details of the allegations of seduced victims may explain some of the inconsistencies between the alleged *what* and the suspected *who*.

The intervener must communicate to the victim that they are not at fault even though the victim did not say 'no,' did not fight, did not tell, initiated the sex, or even enjoyed it. When the victim comes to believe that the intervener understands what he experienced, they are more likely to talk. Victims often reveal the details little by little, testing the intervener's response. The intervener must recognise and sometimes allow the victim to use face-saving scenarios when disclosing victimisation. As stated, such victims might claim they were confused, tricked, asleep, drugged, drunk, or tied up when they were not. Adolescents, who pose special challenges for the interviewer, use these face-saving devices most often. The intervener must accept the fact that even if a victim discloses, the information is likely to be incomplete, minimising his or her involvement and acts. Some of these victims simply do not believe they were victims.

In the absence of some compelling special circumstance or requirement, the interview of a child possibly seduced by an acquaintance molester should **never** be conducted in the presence of parents. The presence of the parent increases the likelihood that the child will just deny or give the socially or parentally acceptable version of the victimisation. This is especially true of younger victims. Assuming a more accurate disclosure of compliant victimisation results, the issue of if, when, and how to then advise parents is a complex dilemma for interveners.

Some victims in acquaintance-child-exploitation cases disclose incomplete and minimised information about the sexual activity that is contradicted by further investigation. This creates significant problems for the investigation and prosecution of such cases. For instance, when the investigator finally gets a victim to disclose the exploitation and abuse, the victim furnishes a version of his victimisation that he or she swears is true. Subsequent investigation then uncovers additional victims, child pornography, recordings, or computer chat logs and other records–directly conflicting with the first victim's story. A common example of this is that the victim admits the offender sucked his penis, but denies that he sucked the offender's penis. The execution of a search warrant then leads to the seizure of photographs of the victim sucking the offender's penis. Some victims continue to deny the activity even when confronted with the visual images. Additional victims may also confirm this, but then lie when they vehemently deny that they did the same thing.

The allegations of multiple victims often conflict with each other. Each victim tends to minimise their behaviour and maximise the behaviour of other victims or the offender. Today, investigators must be especially careful in computer cases where easily recovered chat logs, records of communication, and visual images may directly contradict the socially acceptable version of events that the victim is now giving. In my experience, the primary reason compliant child victims furnish these false and misleading details about their victimisation is their correct recognition that society does not understand or accept the reality of their victimisation. This happens so often that distorted and varying details in such cases are almost corroboration for the validity of the victimisation.

Can we come to conclusions?

The typical adolescent, especially a boy, is **easily sexually aroused, sexually curious, sexually inexperienced**, and **somewhat rebellious**. All these traits combine to make the adolescent one of the easiest victims of sexual seduction. It takes almost nothing to get an adolescent boy sexually aroused. An adolescent boy with emotional and sexual needs is simply no match for an experienced 50-year-old man with an organised plan. Yet, adult offenders who seduce them, and the society that judges them, continue to claim that these victims 'consented'. The result is a victim who feels responsible for what happened and embarrassed about his actions. Once a victim is seduced, each successive sexual incident becomes easier and quicker. Eventually the child victim may even take the initiative in the seduction.

Some victims come to realise that the offender has a greater need for this sex than they do, and this gives them great leverage against the offender. The victims can use sex to manipulate the offender or temporarily withhold sex until they get things they want. A few victims even blackmail the offender especially if he is married or a pillar of the community. Although all of this is unpleasant and inconsistent with our idealistic views about children, when adults and children have 'consensual' sex the adult is always the offender, and the child is always the victim. Consent should be an issue only for adult victims.

As has been stated, sympathy for victims is inversely proportional to their age and sexual development. We often focus on adolescent victims when we want volume and impact, but we do little to address the nature of their victimisation. We want to view them as innocent children when they are sexually victimised, but then try them as fully accountable adults when they commit a violent crime. The greatest potential to worsen societal attitudes about child victims who comply in their sexual exploitation comes from societal attitudes about child offenders. If increasing numbers of ever younger children are held fully accountable for their criminal behaviour and tried in court as adults, it becomes harder and harder to argue that the 'consent' of children of the same ages is irrelevant when they engage in sexual activity with adults.

The reality of compliant child victims is subtly and discreetly dealt with everyday in the United States by investigators, prosecutors, judges, juries, and others. Some professionals feel that this controversy is best dealt with by overtly pretending that it really does not exist. They believe that to explicitly admit or discuss it is harmful to child victims. Many would certainly object to the use of a term or label like *compliant child victim*. I believe, however, that this reality must be openly recognised, discussed, and addressed. I have come to believe the best way to deal with the problem is to change, not fuel, people's unrealistic expectations about the sexual victimisation of children.

The criminal sexual assault of an adult is, by definition, almost always violent. The criminal sexual assault of a child may or may not be violent. In the United States, however, it is common to view or even legally define sexual victimisation of children as violent even if many cases do not meet common definitions of violence (i.e., threats, force). Although emotionally understandable, this often creates confusion and unrealistic evidentiary expectations. Many lay people and even professionals hearing terms such as *sexual assault* or rape in the sexual victimisation of children seek out or expect evidence of physical violence even when the law may not require it. Often in response to atypical, highly publicised, violent sexual assaults of children, laws requiring sex offender registration and community notification were passed in the United States to protect society from these 'sexually violent predators'. Only later is it 'discovered' that many of the most persistent and prolific child molesters typically use seduction (not violence) and are, therefore, not adequately covered by these laws.

In this discussion, I have focused primarily on the problems (i.e., false denials, delayed disclosures, incomplete and inaccurate details, unrealistic expectations, etc.) that compliant child victims present for the criminal justice system. I believe, however, such victims also present considerable problems and challenges for therapists, physicians, social workers, and other professionals. Awareness and prevention programmes that focus on recognising evil sexual 'predators' and 'paedophiles' and on advising victims to say 'no', 'yell, and tell' are not only ineffective in preventing compliant victimisation, but they make the problem worse. Such programmes decrease the likelihood of victim disclosure and increase the shame and guilt of such victims. In almost every case involving compliant child victims that I have evaluated, true victims have had to distort varying aspects of their victimisation in statements to parents, investigators, therapists, physicians, attorneys, and the court. Each subsequent statement often requires increasing deceptions to defend the previous ones. What are the long-term emotional and psychological consequences for child victims who are exposed to prevention and awareness programmes that seem to deny the reality of their victimisation or who must distort, misrepresent, and lie about what actually happened to them in order to have it accepted as 'real' victimisation?

Advice to prevent sexual exploitation of children by adult acquaintances is very complex and difficult to implement. Children less than 12 years of age tend to listen to prevention advice but often to not understand it. Children more than 12 years of age tend to understand it, but often no longer listen to it. How do you warn children about offenders who may be their teachers, coaches, clergy members, neighbours, or Internet 'friends' and whose only distinguishing characteristics are that they will treat the children better than most adults, listen to their problems and concerns, and fill their emotional, physical, and sexual needs? Will parents, society, and professionals understand when the victimisation is discovered or disclosed? Much prevention advice simply does not distinguish to which types of sexual victimisation it applies. The right to say 'no' and 'good touch/bad touch' would be applied differently to a stranger, parent, teacher, physician or Internet acquaintance.

Children at an early age learn to manipulate their environment to get what they want. Almost all children seek attention and affection. Children, especially adolescents, are often interested in and curious about sexuality and sexually explicit material. In today's world, they will sometimes use their computer and online access to actively seek out such material. They typically find pornography online because they are looking for it, not because they made a mistake. They are moving away from the total control of parents and trying to establish new relationships outside the family. Ask any adult what was the number one thing on their mind when they were adolescents and the answer is always the same: sex. Yet parents seem to want to believe their children are asexual and, I suppose, children want to believe their parents are asexual.

Prevention advice that does not recognise these realities is doomed to failure. Yet, prevention material dealing with online child safety continues to repeatedly warn only about not talking to strangers/predators and advise children to tell their parents if someone they meet online makes them feel uncomfortable. Is it realistic or even accurate to suggest that someone you regularly communicate with for weeks or months is a 'stranger' just because you have not met them in person? In most cases where an adolescent left home to personally meet with an adult they had first met online, they did so **voluntarily** in the hope they were going to have **sex** (not to get help with their homework) with someone they felt they **knew** and who cared about them. Unrealistic advice about putting the computer in the middle of the family room and using blocking software will have little effect on protecting children who are committed to overcoming their parents' efforts. How do you prevent something that parents and society may not want to happen, but the child does? Ongoing, loving communication is likely to be more effective than check-off lists and software. Surreptitious parental monitoring of children's computer activity is something that parents will have to decide for themselves based on knowledge of themselves and their children.

Summary

In valid cases, recognising, understanding, and documenting the behaviour patterns of compliant child victims may not specifically prove an accused offender's guilt, but may help refute claims of innocence. In addition to appropriate investigative responses, innovative and sensible prevention strategies and therapeutic approaches that recognise the realities of compliant child victims must be developed and implemented.

Chapter 5

Behind the Screen: Children who are the Subjects of Abusive Images

Tink Palmer

Introduction

Our understanding regarding the impacts of sexual abuse on children's emotional and psychological well-being has grown rapidly over the past twenty years (Bentovim et al., 1988; Briere, 1989; Finkelhor, 1986; Jehu, 1988; Sgroi, 1982; Barnardo's, 1998; Jones et al., 1999). We now have assessment and treatment programmes which can assist child victims in their recovery and help them make sense of what has happened to them. However, with the introduction of the internet and new mobile phone technology we are faced with a new conduit for those intent on sexually harming children. (Barnardo's, 2004; Taylor and Quayle, 2003)

This chapter will be dedicated to the impact of the phenomenon of abusive images on the child victims. In particular, it will be addressing the need to look at the disparity between current UK child protection practice, procedures and policies and the needs of children whose abuse becomes the subject of such images. Consideration will be given to the differential nature of this particular form of abusive activity, the impact of that difference on the child victims and the concomitant need for the child protection system and the policing of such matters to be re-addressed in a way that reflects its local, regional and international dimensions.

There are many ways in which the new technology has been identified as an instrument of abuse of children. The only study to date that has exclusively looked at this issue is that carried out by Barnardo's in 2003. All Barnardo's services (approximately 350 in number) were contacted with a view to establishing the extent that the abuse of children via the internet and mobile phones was impacting on the work of the organisation. The result of this survey was a report entitled *Just One Click!* (Barnardo's, 2004).This report outlines the differential ways in which the new technology may be used to abuse children, gives case examples and discusses the implications for practice.

There are ten areas of concern identified in the report and, at the time of writing (November, 2003) Barnardo's was able to confirm that staff in the organisation had worked with eighty three cases. The areas of concern are listed below:

- Children viewing adult pornography.
- Children sold online for sexual abuse offline.
- Children abused through prostitution.
- Adults/young people engaging in cyber-sex with children.
- Young people placing images of children online.
- Children of adults who download/distribute abuse images of children.

- Young people who download abuse images of children.
- Children groomed online for sexual abuse.
- Children sold online for sexual abuse online.
- Children made the subjects of child abuse images.

Children made the subjects of abuse images (28 cases) was the largest category and accounted for 33 per cent of the total sample. This chapter will be concentrating on this category and on the issues facing the children and the professionals attempting to assist them. Whilst doing this, one needs to be mindful of the fact that abusive activity may take more than one form and that the scenario facing children may frequently be more complex than being victim to only one type of abuse.

The scale and nature of the problem

It is impossible to quantify the number of children who are the subjects of abuse images. This is mainly due to the fact that the child victims rarely disclose what is happening to them and the matter is so difficult to police due to the hidden nature of the activity. In addition, there is currently no strategic approach in the UK which aims to actively seek out the child victims. Some ad hoc activity on the part of specific police forces has revealed some positive results but, to date, we do not have the necessary guidelines or structures embedded within our child protection system which encourages a pro-active approach to this matter. However, we are able to evidence that children are currently being abused and that their abuse is being photographed and distributed via the world wide web in numbers that are increasing in a way which causes concern.

Historically, those people who wished to make, obtain or distribute abusive images of children had a serious dilemma on their hands. If they photographed the abuse of a child they would have had the greatest difficulty in getting the picture developed – taking it to a shop to be developed would have resulted in their detection as an abuser. If they wanted access to such photographs they would have to act with extreme caution in trying to find a source. Similarly, if they wished to distribute such images they would not be able to overtly advertise the fact without running the risk of being found out.

The introduction of the Polaroid camera made it a little easier to actually make the photographs but did not solve the problems associated with obtaining or distributing images. Thus, until about four years ago most of the online abusive images seized by law enforcement agencies were scans of old hard copy images. The one technological development which has changed the whole game plan is the introduction of the digital camera which occurred in the latter part of the 1990s. No longer does an abuser have to rely on outside sources to distribute the abusive images he makes. He merely has to transfer the images from his camera to his computer, click the button and send the images anywhere in the world. (Jones, T. Conference presentation, February 2004)

Until May 2004, the COPINE Project (Combating Paedophile Information Networks in Europe), based at the University of Cork, monitored the online behaviour of sexual abusers within newsgroups. In 1999 COPINE identified an average of four new children a month appearing in child sex newsgroups. In August 2002 the situation was beginning to change quite considerably. Over a six week period the COPINE staff identified 20 new children in child sex newsgroups. Thus over a three year period, there was a 300 per cent increase in the number of new children identified by the project staff. During the same period over 140,000 child sex images were posted to newsgroups, of which 35,000 were images of new children. 30,000 of these images depicted children posing erotically, often in an explicit way. However, 1,000 images depicted highly abusive sexual behaviour towards children, including explicit sexual activity, assault and gross assault. (Taylor and Quayle, 2003)

In practice, the above statistics mean that many children are currently being systematically sexually abused, their abuse is recorded through digital technology and distributed. Police forces, worldwide, have tens of thousands of images of children being sexually abused – the UK's Childbase has 450,000 images on its records alone – but they don't know where the vast majority of the children in the images may be living, in fact, the generally accepted estimate of the number of child victims who have been traced throughout the world is between 250 and 400. Interpol state they know of 261 specific cases. (Hamish McCulloch, Interpol. COPINE Conference, May 2004)

To bring the matter closer to home, following an investigation by the US Postal Inspection Service into the activities of Landslide Productions in Texas, thousands of suspects worldwide were identified as having paid for access to websites displaying a wide variety of graphic images of child abuse. Approximately 7,000 of those suspects were believed to be UK citizens. The subsequent investigation within the UK, named Operation Ore, has identified 102 children to date (the investigation is not yet completed) that required protection. However, whilst this figure includes children found in the abusive images, the majority requiring protection were those living in households where they were deemed to be at risk of or were currently being sexually abused.

The most worrying trend noted by the COPINE staff in 2003 was not only a huge increase in the numbers of new images but also a change in the nature of the images. They were able to report that the children in the new images appeared younger in age – some of very tender years – the abuse perpetrated against them was of a more serious nature and many of the venues for the abuse appeared to be domestic in nature. What we have is an irrefutable truth – increasing numbers of incidents of children being sexually abused are being photographically recorded and these records are being distributed worldwide. (Taylor. Presentation, Just One Click Conference, February 2004)

The impact of photography of their abuse on child victims – an added dimension to silencing

Although very little has been written regarding the impact of photography on child victims who are the subjects of abusive images, (Burgess et al., 1984; Silbert, 1989; Scott, 2001), Svedin and Back (1996) published an account of the impact of such abuse on a group of Swedish children. In particular they noted how difficult it was for the children concerned to talk about or even admit what had happened to them. Similarly, in 2003 the Swedish authorities were faced with an investigation of a number of children whose images had been traced elsewhere in the world and were eventually identified as coming from Sweden. When interviewing the children the same resistance to acknowledging that they were the subject of the images was found.

A similar phenomenon has been observed in England during the on-going investigations of Operation Ore. Some children who were interviewed categorically denied they had been abused and even continued to do so when the interviewing police officers explained that they knew they had been abused because they had seen the photographs/video recordings of the children's abuse. Thus there seems to be an element of silencing which is over and above that of the perpetrator/victim dynamic when photography is not involved – another dimension is introduced to the sexually abusive equation.

It would seem that there are a number of reasons for this:

- The children feel that they are being seen to let the abuse happen.
- They might, quite frequently, be smiling and therefore appear to be 'enjoying' the activity (in reality they are forced to do so by the perpetrator).
- They may have been encouraged to introduce other children to the perpetrator and thus feel responsible for letting it happen to others.
- They may have been encouraged to be pro-active in either their own sexual abuse or that of other children.
- They may have been shown their own abuse images by the perpetrator with threats that he will tell of, or even show, the pictures to their parents or carers or other significant people in their lives if they do not co-operate and they may carry the shame of not stopping the abuse.

All of the above factors are, of course, not the responsibility of the child but reflect the modus operandi of the abuser. Probably the greatest inhibitors to disclosing what has occurred is the humiliation that the children feel regarding who may have seen their images and their fear of being recognised. They feel they have literally been 'caught in the act'.

The replacement of disclosure by discovery

Our current system in the UK for protecting child victims of sexual abuse involves five stages which begins with a disclosure and the process continues with an investigation, assessment of the child's recovery needs, therapeutic intervention and preparation and support should the child be required to give evidence during criminal proceedings regarding the perpetrator. We know that, due to the grooming behaviours of the abusers, it is rare for children to disclose sexual abuse. There are many reasons for not disclosing the main ones of which include belief in the threats that are made by the abuser, believing they are responsible for the abuse, thinking they won't be believed, trying to drop hints to an adult or friend but finding that the hints are not 'taken up' and children abused when very young don't know that there is anything wrong with what has happened to them. In addition, the abuser is often someone of personal and emotional significance to the child and to whom the child feels a strong attachment.

Disclosure may take the form of a child telling an adult or a confidant, the abuse may have been witnessed by someone who discloses this information or the child may display concerning behaviours, the aetiology of which is unknown but, after investigation, the source is discovered. However, disclosure can come in a different guise when the internet and use of digital technology are introduced to the equation. Before disclosure, we have two earlier stages of the process before protection of the child is ensured. Firstly, there is the discovery of the abusive images taken of the child which are evidence of sexually abusive behaviours having taken place, and therefore a crime scene, and secondly, there is the need to identify the child in the images. For the first time in the history of child protection we are faced with the dilemma of having foolproof evidence that children are being sexually abused, as well as proof of the activities that take place and evidence of the children's distress, but not knowing who they are, where they are and who their abusers may be.

The implications of such a development for the professional bodies charged with safeguarding children are legion. The costs in time and personnel required to identify and trace the child victims, let alone the perpetrators of their abuse, are phenomenal – particularly when we consider the tens of thousands of images that law enforcement agencies have worldwide which represent unprotected child abuse victims. Ethically we must pro-actively seek out the children in the images. Sexual abuse is, by its very nature, a hidden and secretive activity which has lasting impacts on the victims (Palmer, 2001). Children rarely disclose sexual abuse and, as mentioned above, those who have also been subjected to the photographic recording of their abuse are doubly silenced.

The emergence of the phenomenon of pictorial evidence, on a scale which is unprecedented, is of critical relevance. Since the phenomenon of the sexual abuse of children has been part of our national agenda for safeguarding children – the introduction of the category of 'sexual abuse' for registration on the Child Protection Register only occurred following the Cleveland crisis in the late 1980s – children's revelations of sexual abuse have not been given the validity they deserved. Myths still abound, particularly amongst certain members of the judiciary, the legal profession and some members of law enforcement agencies that children are more likely to tell lies, what they are saying must be fantasy – 'they're making it up' – or they must have been coached by an adult (Palmer, 2001). If children have been able to disclose their abuse, the manner of their disclosure has been haphazard and, for judicial purposes, sufficiently muddled for the matter not to be pursued within the criminal justice system. In many of these latter cases, the interviewing officers had no doubt that 'something' had happened to the child but were unable to proceed with the case because the evidence would not stand up in court and, frequently, the child was of too tender years to be able to withstand cross examination in the way that it currently occurs within our system. The fact that we now have the evidence in the images – evidence that is irrefutably that of a child being sexually abused – is a pivotal time in the history of our understanding of child sexual abuse. We are now able to see the children's faces, hear their cries and witness their abuse, we can do no other than to actively seek them out and protect them.

However, before going boldly forward in this enterprise there is an important caveat to be considered. Although there is evidence of increasing numbers of new abusive images of children being made, distributed and collected, the majority of the earlier images which were gathered in the mid to late 1990s were old images, many of which had been scanned into the internet system and were taken from old magazines, still photographs and videos. These images represent children who are now adults and who may be living a life in which they have not disclosed their abuse – perhaps due to blocking out the memory, not knowing of the existence of the images or choosing not to do so. Careful thought needs to be given about why it might be necessary to seek out and inform such adults that the images have been found. We know little about the impact of such a revelation on the now adult 'child victim' and need to think strategically about why and when such a disclosure may be necessary. There is also the added dimension of the individuals' rights to know about information relating to them. What criteria should be used in deciding when and when not to tell someone? Who will be charged with making this decision? Similarly, we need to consider how and when, if at all, we tell children and young people that images of their abuse have been discovered. The trauma of such disclosure should never be underestimated.

Changes to current professional practice

The new technology has introduced some challenging dilemmas for professionals working in the field of child protection. It is going to be necessary for police officers, social workers and counsellors to re-evaluate their working practices in the light of what we have learnt to date. The three key areas which need to be addressed are managing the discovery/disclosure process and the investigative interview of the child victim, assessment of the therapuetic/recovery needs of the child and the nature and content of the ensuing therapeutic process with the child. The following observations highlight the issues and will raise questions to which we need to endeavour to find answers.

Policing

Management of discovery of the images by the police forces throughout the UK and the entire world poses a new and complex policing challenge. The image may be discovered in Taiwan but the child depicted may be living in Tewkesbury. The reality of what we have is a local crime (the photographic recording of the abuse in Tewkesbury) which becomes an international issue (the distribution to, viewing, and discovery of the abusive images in Taiwan). Such a scenario has implications for the nature of the co-operation required between national and international police forces.

Co-operation between the police forces in the UK is essential if we are really going to endeavour to take a pro-active stance to discovering the children in the images. This is unlikely to happen, however, until the importance of protecting our children is given recognition in the National Policing Plan and made one of the national policing priorities. In addition, the work, so far, has been carried out on a shoe string. The new skills that are required will cost money and require extra resources – particularly personnel for forensic examination of equipment. We have a good infrastructure in place for protecting children in the UK, this needs to be built upon and adapted to meet the demands that abuse via the new technology is placing upon professionals working in this area. This is the time for considering innovative ways in which the police and social workers and child care specialists from the children's NGOs can work together in a collaborative way to review their current practices to ensure that the protection strategies that are put in place meet the needs of the victims.

Due to the international nature of this form of criminality, co-operation between all countries and their respective police forces will also be necessary if we are to tackle this problem head on. There are some positive movements already on the international scene with increased co-operation by the G8 countries via such initiatives as the Virtual Global Summits and through the activities of Interpol of which 187 countries are members. However, a clear systemic model to ensure co-operation on a Global scale has still to be developed. The model needs to be such that there is genuine co-operation and a willingness by all countries to ensure that information flows freely and in a timely fashion between the police forces of every country.

Discovery/disclosure

We need to rethink how we approach child victims of abusive images once they have been identified and their whereabouts discovered. The impact of disclosure on the child should never be underestimated. Knowledge of the discovery of the images can be emotionally devastating due to the 'double silencing' described above and we need to think carefully about how we deal with such matters to ensure that the professional system itself doesn't become an agent of abuse. The key to understanding the trauma to child victims when being informed that the images of them have been discovered lies with the fact that they have no control whatsoever of the disclosure process. They can't choose when to disclose, what to disclose, how to disclose and who they want to disclose to. They are left impotent and knowing that police officers and social workers will be aware of intimate details of what has happened to them. What they believed to be a 'secret' becomes a most open secret and they are left feeling humiliation, shame and fear.

Investigation

The investigation process regarding this specific area of abuse is in need of review and adaptation. The main thrust of this chapter is to raise awareness about the needs of the child victims but there are also other aspects of the investigation process which need mention in order to draw attention to the overall scenario that has to be managed.

When police officers enter a home where they believe a child is living who has been the subject of abusive images, they will, initially, be wanting to establish whether this is the case. Having carried out this process, there are various other lines of inquiry that will need to be carried out. They will want to know:

- Who the adults are living in the home of the child victim?
- What part, if any, did they have to play in the abuse?
- If an adult in the home is recognised as an abuser, what did the partner know about this activity?
- What are the alleged abuser's social networks? May anyone from outside the family home also be involved?
- If, after investigation, none of the adults living in the home are suspected of abusing the child, how has the abuse occurred and who might be responsible?
- What contacts may the child have outside the family home which require investigation?
- Are there other children living in the home?
- Are they also victims of sexual abuse?
- Are there other children within the victim's social network who may also have been at risk?

The purpose of mentioning the above is to highlight the many issues involved and to contextualise the ramifications of such investigations where there is a new complex matrix of factors for consideration. The types of questions raised and requiring answers would have equal significance when investigating matters relating to people who are known to have downloaded abusive images and to be living in a household where there are children.

Investigative interview

Social workers and police officers tasked with interviewing child victims of abuse are now placed in a situation never experienced before. Previously, when interviewing children who had been sexually abused the interviewers would be armed with limited information regarding the offence against the child and the purpose of them carrying out such an interview would be to establish what had happened and who the perpetrator may be. When abusive images have been discovered this is not the situation. The interviewers have first hand evidence of what has occurred to the child. What they probably would not have, however, from the images is evidence regarding who the perpetrator may be. There are two avenues of investigation that the police may take to establishing the identity of the abuser. Firstly they can ask the child victim and secondly, through forensic examination of the images, which represent a crime scene, they may be able to pick up enough clues to trace the whereabouts of the perpetrator and to identify him.

Our practice experience when interviewing children who have been the subjects of abusive images tells us that they limit disclosure to the very minimum – if they disclose at all – and the majority will only proffer information when the interviewer gives hints or prompts them about the sequence of events. Thus the children will only tell the interviewer what the child thinks they know. In a sense we have a somewhat worrying form of 'game playing' where the police officer and social worker know what has occurred but ask the child to tell them for evidential purposes when they (the interviewers) already have that evidence. Because of the very nature of the grooming and silencing process on the part of the perpetrator and the shame and humiliation felt by the child victims, disclosure interviewing, in the initial stages, is likely to be a stilted process at best and a damaging one for the child at the worst.

Once images have been discovered of child victims the police would want to investigate the matter with the dual purpose of protecting the child and apprehending the perpetrators. There is no doubt that once child victims have been traced they need to be informed about the concerns that the police hold and they may, in most cases, need to be interviewed – the interview at this initial stage, however, needs to be far more generic in nature than would normally be the case. Issues regarding who the perpetrator may be, the possible involvement of other children who may remain at risk and the immediate protection needs of all children affected should take precedence. Immediate detailed questioning of the child victim's sexually abusive experiences will not necessarily need to be the priority and in these circumstances, in fact, if such an approach were taken it could be potentially highly damaging to the children's emotional and psychological well-being. Timing of such intimate enquiry is of the essence. The child victim may well be able to assist with the more generic issues at an early stage of the process of their realisation that their abuse is known about but details regarding what has happened to themselves takes on a different dimension.

Disclosure and revelations about what has happened to children are more likely to come out when they have recovered from the initial shock of knowing that 'others' have seen the images, when they feel reassured that the adults know that it was not their fault and when they feel safe to talk about the abuse – many children are abused by someone well known to them, before they can be expected to speak freely they need to feel protected from their abuser. Disclosure of trauma by victims of sexual assault whether they be adults or children does not occur in one interview. Victims need to stagger what they reveal and by so doing they are able to cope with the realisation of what has happened to them and to feel comfortable that the person they are telling can cope with the information. Thus disclosure by child victims of abuse images needs to take place over weeks and months rather than there is the expectation that they reveal all in a one off interview when they are recoiling from the shock of the discovery of the abusive activity.

In some cases both the child victim and the perpetrator have been traced. In such situations the initial contact with the child may not need to take the form of attempting to establish who the perpetrator may be. There have been cases where the perpetrator has been identified through forensic examination of the images and the police have been able to prove, without doubt, that the adult in the image and the adult they have traced is one and the same person. In such a situation, there is categorical proof that the adult depicted has committed sexual offences against the child victim. In the UK, such cases have resulted in 100 per cent conviction rates – not only can the judge and jury see with their own eyes what has occurred, so can the defence barrister whose advice to his client will invariably be to plead guilty.

Therefore, when we are considering practice guidance and procedures we need to address the following questions:

- Is it always necessary to interview the child for evidential purposes?

- In what circumstances might it not be necessary?

- Is it necessary to interview the child for other purposes?

- When would we do this and why?

- How do we need to change the way we help children whose abuse has been the subject of photography, disclose what has happened to them?

Finally, when carrying out investigative/disclosure interviews with children we need to be mindful of the manner in which the interviews are recorded. It is now general practice to video record children's evidence in chief and there is national guidance to this effect as laid out in Achieving Best Evidence in Criminal Proceedings: Guidance for Vulnerable or Intimidated Witnesses, including Children (Home Office, 2000). Practice on this specific point with regard to victims of abusive images has been disparate throughout the UK – some police forces have continued to video record, others have checked with the child victim about their wishes, whilst others have chosen not to video record in such circumstances. In any of our dealings with child victims, professionals have a duty of care which should ensure that harm is minimised.

If we use audio visual equipment to record the evidence given by child victims of abusive images, we are more than likely going to evoke feelings and responses in the child which echo those when their abuse took place. Such secondary traumatisation should be resisted at all costs and Q and A written evidence needs to be the norm. The rationale for carrying out interviews in this way needs to be conveyed to the judiciary who, in the UK, are now of a view that all children should give their evidence in chief via audio visual means. If practice ensues where children, in these particular circumstances, give their statement in written form, consideration needs to be given to the circumstances in which their cross examination occurs:

- Would they do this via the video-link in the court-room?

- Would this be equally traumatising for the child victim bearing in mind such technology was used in their abuse?

- Would the use of screens be suitable?

Each case will be different, but we need to ensure we are asking the right questions to enable the child to give 'best evidence' in a way that is least traumatic.

Assessment

The traumatic effects of sexual abuse on children are by now well understood (Barnardo's, 1998; Sgroi, 1982). They may include all, or a combination of some of the following:

- Guilt and a feeling of being responsible for the abuse.

- Fear of what may happen once the abuse has been recognised. This fear may refer to the child victims themselves or to their fear of what might happen to significant others on whom they are dependent.

- Depression which may take the form of a reactive episode but may well become indigenous in nature as the child matures.

- Low self-esteem which is often exhibited through what seems to be poor social skills.

- Repressed anger and hostility which may well surface unexpectedly and out of context.

- An inability to trust which may sometimes be displayed by the child appearing to be over trustful.
- Blurred role boundaries and role confusion. This may be demonstrated, for example, by the child acting in an age inappropriate manner.
- Psuedomaturity.
- Lack of mastery and control. The child may feel that whatever happens to them they will have no 'say' in the matter.
- Cognitive confusion. This is usually caused by the nature of the grooming process by the perpetrator.
- Damaged goods syndrome. Child victims may be fearful that they are physically damaged and/or that they are 'soiled' in such a way that others will not want to associate with them.

There are also known indicators which, when considered together, inform us of the potential degree of the impact of the sexual abuse on a child victim and their potential for recovery. These are:

- The nature of the abusive activity.
- The length of time the abuse has occurred.
- The perpetrator's relationship with the child.
- The nature of the grooming process.
- The nature of the child's previous life experiences.
- The natural resilience of the child.

When the sexual abuse is recorded via still or video photography the nature and the dynamic of the abuse takes on a different meaning for the child victim. Once the abuse is discovered, the child victim traced and the necessary investigatory interviews taken place, there are further impact issues to consider when assessing the child's therapeutic needs. In particular there is the impact of the impotence felt by the child regarding the disclosure process, the additional shame of 'being seen to let it happen', the subsequent added personal responsibility felt by the child and there is the serious issue of non-resolution of the abuse. Non-resolution carries with it the realisation by the child victim that the images of their sexual abuse have not only been seen by many people but will continue to be available, forever. Their images will remain on the World Wide Web and they can do nothing about it – they are impotent.

Therapuetic intervention

When working therapeutically with children who have been sexually abused there are key areas which need addressing:

- Their perception of safety.
- Allowing and assisting them to express and ventilate their feelings.
- Enabling them to become empowered.
- Sex education which is age appropriate and which clarifies the confusion they have regarding sex and relationships.
- Assertiveness and communication skills.

- Guilt, trust and ambivalence.
- Education about the way sexual abusers groom people – not only the victim but also, often, those close to the victim.
- Wishes and fears for the future.

When children have been the subjects of abusive images there are additional key areas which also need to be addressed. The impotence that such victims experience regarding the nature and timing of the disclosure of their abuse has a serious impact and makes them feel that they have little mastery over their lives. The shame and responsibility that they feel, often because of the way they are seen to be behaving in the images, is an extremely sensitive issue and its importance for the children and how they view themselves should not be undermined. Finally, the issue of this specific way of sexually abusing children with its pathology of non-resolution is a totally new phenomenon.

When working with children who have **not** been the subjects of abusive images but have been sexually abused, it is generally possible to help them to resolve what has happened to them and to enable them to go forward into adulthood without fear or concerns that people will know about what they have experienced. However, to grow up knowing that there are images of yourself being sexually abused which are available in perpetuity has complex implications for the child victim and poses new challenges for therapists. The age at which the images were made may have some relevance. If the child is of tender years when the images are made, there is the possibility that the impact of the fact that the images are available forever may be lesser than that for an adolescent whose fear of being identified through the images may be heightened and, in fact, a reality. To enable victims to cope with this knowledge and to go forward to a positive future life will require some serious attention on the part of therapists. These issues may not be insurmountable and it may be possible to transfer what we know 'works' for children who have been sexually abused, per se, to our work with those children whose sexual abuse has been photographed and distributed. One example of this is the process that can be followed to assist victims cope with flashbacks of their abuse – maybe this technique, or one similar, can be used to assist victims in coping with non resolution.

A systemic model for safeguarding and policing: some national and international issues

The above discussion raises many points which require serious and timely consideration. Within the UK over the past three years much attention has been paid to preventative matters but less has been paid to the need for a cohesive systemic approach to policing and safeguarding issues. The UK child protection framework and structures currently in place need re-defining to meet the new challenges that face professionals working in the field of child protection.

We have a comprehensive guide to interagency working to safeguard and promote the welfare of children which is entitled *Working Together to Safeguard Children* (DoH, 1999). However, this guidance does not address the child protection concerns raised through the new technology. There is an evident need for a more 'joined up' child protection response not only within the UK but between the UK and the rest of the world. The development of a way of working which addresses both national and international co-operation and co-ordination seems somewhat daunting. We are all too aware of the implications of the differences between countries – current laws and legal systems, ages for consensual sexual behaviour, levels of child protection and infra-structures in place, cultural beliefs and customs and the nature of policing activities are but a few aspects that need to be borne in mind. Putting such barriers to one side, how might we develop a more co-ordinated response? The Barnardo's report *Just One Click*! (Barnardo's, 2004) introduced, for the first time, the concept of a UK Centre to meet operational requirements. Such a centre would be tasked with the role of safeguarding children through a policing approach which would need to give equal priority to seeking out the victims and to apprehending the perpetrators. Its aims would be twofold:

- To ensure that communications between the different regions of the UK and between the UK and agencies abroad runs effectively.

- To ensure that good practice is disseminated to all professionals working in this particular field of abuse.

The proposed outcomes of a UK Centre would need to include the following:

- A central resource which acts as a conduit for intelligence and evidence gathering – serving police forces, social services departments and NGOs locally within the UK and police and child care personnel working in other countries.

- A central point of contact for UK based professionals and those working internationally – with particular reference to the policing and safeguarding activities relating to abusive images of children, children abused through prostitution and trafficking, online enticement and sex tourism.

- Development of appropriate investigative and intervention strategies both in respect of the child victims and the perpetrators.

- An advisory, information and support resource for professionals.

- A database for disseminating best practice both in relation to the UK and the international perspective.

In order to achieve these outcomes within the UK, we would need to build on our current practice of co-working that exists between police, social service and NGO personnel. The UK Centre could reflect a new, radical way of working where staff from different disciplines may be co-located to the Centre, may work a number of days a week at the Centre or may work remotely from the Centre but have an inbuilt system for communication. To guide the working of the Centre, the development of a Reference Group, the membership of which should be experienced professionals drawn from all organisations involved in safeguarding and policing activities, would ensure that 'best advice' is at hand and that the Centre carries out the functions for which it is intended.

There would need to be clear systems in place which link the activity which passes through the Centre to the local police forces and social service departments within the UK and these systems would need to be reflected in reviewed protocols and procedures for the way investigations and operations should be carried out. One of the problems currently facing the UK in relation to offences connected to the new technology is our policing structure. The current National Policing Plan has four policing priorities which do not include child protection. All Chief Constables have the duty of ensuring that the national policing priorities are met and, indeed, the performance of their respective police forces will be judged on how they have achieved the targets set by these priorities. Although each force may set further, local priorities, they do not have to do so and, quite understandably, would not do so at the expense of possible under-achievement on the four national ones. To enable a UK Centre to work effectively for and on behalf of the child victims, child protection needs to be placed on the national policing agenda as a fifth priority.

A logistical and geographical problem faces police forces – abuse via the internet and other forms of new technology knows no physical boundaries. Thus, concerns regarding a child's safety might be discovered by a police force in one part of the UK but the child be living in the jurisdiction of a police force in another part of country. This has particular implications when a police force might decide to take a pro-active policing approach and carry out an 'Operation' or 'sting' which traces a number of people who, for example, are viewing abusive images of children and these perpetrators are living in various parts of the UK. How police forces react to such initiatives and their differential prioritisation of such work will remain an issue whilst child protection is not a national policing priority. The issues multiply when the image of a child is discovered in the UK and the evidence depicted in the picture would suggest that the image was made in another country.

One of the principal outcomes when measuring policing effectiveness is the number of convictions achieved and appropriate sentences meted out. In one sense, therefore, it is not surprising that there has, to date, been only a few initiatives which have actively attempted to seek out the child victims as well as the perpetrator. If we are going to establish a dual approach to the policing of this matter, protection of a child should be a national and measurable standard and of equal standing when it comes to police practice as is the conviction of a perpetrator.

The lack of geographical boundaries peculiar to new technology abuse also, as mentioned earlier in this chapter, has implications for international collaboration and co-operation. A UK centre would be able to act as a conduit not only for policing and safeguarding issues within the UK but also between the UK and other countries. The need for international collaboration is recognised and the G8 countries are beginning to address the issues of the new technology. Interpol has a pivotal role to play in the schema of things. It offers an international policing service and is able to serve as the central 'collector' of abusive images as well as the source of assistance for all other issues related to abuse via the new technology which could include the selling of children online for sex, arrangements for trafficking children and so on. However, for Interpol to be effective it needs endorsement by the entire international community and not just by those countries which are members and it needs funding and resourcing in a way that is commensurate to the task. Thus an additional factor in the whole equation arises, namely what commitment is each country prepared to make to Interpol in terms of financial, personnel and other resources? The development of a UK Centre which over time, other countries might emulate ideally needs to take place in the context of its relationship to the International Centre – namely Interpol.

Conclusion

The introduction of the new technology as a conduit of abuse will impact on and radically change the way we operate at all levels within the child protection arena both within the UK and internationally. The main body of this chapter has considered the implications for policies, practice and procedures when assisting children who have been the subjects of but one form of abuse – that of abusive images. However, it has also related such implications to the wider national and international forum and suggested the basis of a model which may enable effective pro-active policing and safeguarding practices to ensue.

The task may, at times, seem impossible bearing in mind not only the national and international systemic re-organisation that will need to take place but also the way in which professionals working in the field will need to change their 'mindset' regarding territorial/geographical interests. Adapting to new challenges is not always easy, when they involve an international perspective additional obstacles arise. However, the bottom line remains – we have undeniable proof that children are currently being sexually abused via the new technology and we are doing very little to actively seek them out.

If we take a step at a time, the solutions may appear more obtainable. The UK can start to get its own 'house in order' by establishing a UK Centre and developing good models for practice which may then impinge on and influence the international landscape.

References

Barnardo's (1998) *Bridgeway Annual Report 1997–1998*. Essex: Middlesbrough.

Bentovim, A., Elton, A., Hildebrand, J., Tranter, M. and Vizard, E. (Eds.) (1988) *Child Sexual Abuse Within the Family: Assessment and Treatment*. London: Wright.

Briere, J. (1989) *Therapy for Adults Molested as Children*. New York: Springer.

Burgess, A.W. and Hartman, C. (1987) Child Abuse Aspects of Child Pornography. *Psychiatric Annals*. 248–53.

Crown Prosecution Service (2004) *Achieving Best Evidence in Criminal Proceedings: Guidance for Vulnerable or Intimidated Witnesses, Including Children*. London: Home Office.

DoH (1999) *Working Together to Safeguard Children: A Guide to Arrangements for Interagency Co-operation for the Protection of Children from Abuse*. London: HMSO.

Finkelhor, D. (Ed.) (1986) *A Sourcebook on Child Sexual Abuse*. London: Sage.

Jehu, D. (1988) *Beyond Sexual Abuse: Therapy with Women who were Childhood Victims*. Chichester: Wiley.

Jones, D.P.H. and Ramachandani, P. (1999) *Child Sexual Abuse: Informing Practice from Research*. Oxford: Radcliffe Medical Press.

Jones, T. (2004) *Barnardo's Just One Click! Conference* – conference presentation, February, 2004.

McCulloch, H. (2004) Interpol presentation at the COPINE conference, 24–26th May. Cork.

Palmer, T. (2001) Pre-trial Therapy for Children who have been Sexually Abused, in Richardson, S. and Bacon, H. (Eds.) *Creative Responses to Child Sexual Abuse*. London: Jessica Kingsley.

Palmer, T. with Stacey, L. (2004) *Just One Click! – Sexual Abuse of Children and Young People Through the Internet and Mobile Phone Technology*. Essex: Barnardo's.

Scott, S. (2001) *The Politics and Experience of Sexual Abuse: Beyond Disbelief*. Buckingham: Open University Press.

Sgroi, S. (1982) *Handbook of Clinical Intervention in Child Sexual Abuse*. Lexington, MA: Lexington Books.

Silbert, M.H. (1989) The Effects on Juveniles of Being Used for Pornography and Prostitution, in Zillman, D. and Bryant, C. (Eds.) *Pornography: Research Advances and Policy Considerations*, Hillside, NJ: Lawrence Erlbaum.

Svedin, C.G. and Back, K. (1996) *Children who Don't Speak Out*, Stockholm: Swedish Save the Children.

Taylor, M. (2004) Barnardo's Just One Click! Conference – conference presentation, February, 2004.

Taylor, M. and Quayle, E. (2003) *Child Pornography: An Internet Crime*. New York: Brunner Routledge.

Chapter 6

Identifying Victims of Child Abuse Images: An Analysis of Successful Identifications

Gemma Holland

Introduction

There is little known about investigations of child abuse images where identifications of the victims have occurred. The reason for this is that the law enforcement focus has been on disrupting the distribution of abusive images rather than on identifications (Taylor and Quayle, 2003). Additionally, there is relatively little documentation of such cases in the public domain. Therefore the lessons learnt in these cases, in successful identifications, are not informing practice. Consequently it is essential that such cases are studied so that we better understand how such investigations are conducted and what issues emerge.

This chapter will outline the scale of the problem of child abuse images, society's response to the images, and the strategies which exist for identifying the victims in the images. In addition, the process of identification will be described which has emerged from a number of interviews conducted with those involved in a number of identifications, which form part of an ongoing study. It includes research material from the Victim Identification Project (VIP), an EU funded project from 2000–2003, which looked at the problem of child abuse images on the Internet from the victims' perspective, and in addition data from the author's doctoral thesis (in progress) which involves the qualitative analysis of interviews with people involved in such cases; police, social workers, a parent of some of the victims and an adult victim. The objectives of the study are to elucidate the methods used in investigations and to identify emergent issues which could contribute to future research. It is orientated towards bringing about change in practice in policing, support services and policy.

What is the problem?

Child sexual abuse is shrouded in secrecy, as unsurprisingly is the recording of that abuse. Photographic images of children engaging in sexual activity have been available since the mid 1800s (Tyler and Stone, 1985). However the rapid development of imaging and computer technologies and the widespread use of the Internet since the 1990s have reduced the risks of production and distribution. The nature of the Internet has facilitated the distribution of, and increased the accessibility to, child abuse images. It has also highlighted the large numbers of children who are involved in child abuse images. The Internet has contributed further to the problem, making it more complex, because the problem now has both a global and a local aspect to it. The global aspect relates to the fact that the children in the images could be seen anywhere in the world, while the local aspect is that the abused children are living within our local communities.

No data currently exists on how many children are sexually abused and photographed. Without quantitative data on the numbers, some authors believe that the scale of the child abuse image problem has been overestimated. Anne Higonnet asserts that the 'disparity between the numbers of child pornographers being convicted and the numbers of real children is staggering . . . clearly child pornography is a small area of child sexual abuse, a tiny corner of all child abuse' (1998: 188). Higonnet has linked the low conviction rates of 'child pornographers' to the amount of children who are abused and photographed.

However, it would appear that the number of convicted 'child pornographers' is not representative of the actual number of children who are both abused and photographed. Higonnet fails to recognise the very essence of child sexual abuse which has secrecy at its heart. Perpetrators groom their victims, ensuring that they feel responsible, guilty and fearful. This effectively silences the children (Barnardo's, 2004) leading to under reporting which is a consistent feature of child sexual abuse (Itzin, 2000).

Until May 2004 the COPINE database held over 700,000 abusive images. This figure does not represent 700,000 children because while hundreds of images could exist of one child, only one or two images may exist of another. Therefore one could deduce that there could be anything from 7,000 to 70,000 children portrayed in these images. Furthermore COPINE retrieved these images from publicly available newsgroups: it would be naive to assume that these images represent all abusive images in existence. Many more could exist in private collections. The number of public images combined with private images would suggest that thousands of children are abused and simultaneously photographed.

As mentioned previously there are hundreds of thousands of images of child abuse available on the Internet alone. Surely then the question which needs to be addressed is – what are we doing to identify the children? Considering the scale of the problem, and the fact that it has been pushed into the public arena, meaning that it is harder to ignore it, what has been the response to child abuse images?

Response to the problem

Nearly twenty years ago Summit (Final Report of the Attorney General's Commission on Pornography, 1986) coined the phrase 'conceptual chaos' to describe the inadequate societal response largely ignorant of how to deal with victims of child abuse images. Today conceptual chaos still proliferates with little progress in our response.

Higonnet (1998: 189) highlights the most critical difficulty with the response to child abuse images. She criticises the American government for 'controlling pictures of children' and for not spending money 'on children themselves'. This has been the major failure in combating the problem worldwide (Holland, 2003, COPINE Colloquium). The police have devoted resources towards convictions for the possession of abusive images rather than attempting to identify and support the children in the images. This has been reflected in the large numbers of recent arrests for possession of the images used as evidence to convict the perpetrator for possession, while the identification of the victim is relegated to second place. Images are rarely examined in order to identify the children therein. The images should receive a child protection focus where the children are identified in order to protect them from future abuse and to offer them support.

The lack of concern towards victims is reflected in the low number of identifications. According to Interpol 297 victims of child abuse images on the Internet have been identified worldwide (Anders

Perrson, 2004). This is not a concrete figure for the number of identifications as Interpol does not receive notification of all identifications (a secondary problem in itself highlighting a need for countries to collate this information). Nonetheless, this figure highlights the chronically low number of identifications. What underpins this is an ad hoc approach to identification with a lack of local or global policies that focus on identifying victims. The predominant focus of controlling the problem by concentrating on tracking the distribution and possession of the images has resulted in a universal lack of child focus in investigations.

Another problem is the lack of policy relating to the identification of victims. There appear to be no national or international policies on the identification of children in child abuse images whereas most countries have laws that respond to the production, distribution and possession of these images. The children have been lost; society has failed to take responsibility in their identification.

Ownership: who will 'own' the problem?

There are so many images on the Internet that a major issue is deciding which ones will be investigated.

Ownership relates to location, and location will be the deciding factor in determining who has ownership. If an analysis can prove that an image was produced in a particular country then the onus is on the police in that area to investigate the case but, if there is no obvious location, who will investigate? At present the onus falls on a motivated few who actively attempt to identify victims. This is an unacceptable end result with obvious limitations: we need a global policy for a global problem, a policy where ownership through location identification is not an issue. The current response is hindered by geographical factors whereas the Internet has no geographical boundaries.

Victim identification strategies

At present identification is done in an ad-hoc manner. Strategies are primarily left to the various police agencies rather than strategic planning at national and international level. This has led to a situation where those who have made a concerted effort to focus on victim identification have basically produced their own terms of reference and made decisions on how they approach victim identification. This explains the disparity of responses which exists amongst countries worldwide. It appears that the level of response or rather the engagement in victim identification relies heavily on the interest taken by those working in the local and national units etc. Strategies developed at an international and national level are required. They must originate at, and filter down from, the highest level to ensure that the response is comprehensive, cohesive and inclusive at both national and international level.

The G8 holds a central position in the process of global governance. Its deliberations and declarations shape key decisions in the management of global political and economic affairs. Most of the world's major economic and security initiatives are discussed first by the G8 leaders and their ministers before the other multilateral organisations take action. This power affords the G8 immense influence on policies, programmes, and decisions.

The G8 has devised a strategy to protect children from sexual exploitation on the Internet in November 2002.

The actions outlined in relation to Victim Identification are:

- To explore the use of image databases, and other relevant sources of information and intelligence such as cyber tip-lines, for the identification and location of victims.
- To work in partnership with non-law enforcement bodies, including NGOs involved with missing and exploited children, to identify and locate victims.
- To build international procedures and relationships using the relevant bodies to identify victims.

The objective of this strategy is to identify children who have been sexually exploited, both past and present and to locate new victims as quickly as possible.

Examination of the guidelines laid out above shows that while well intentioned the guidelines are insufficient. Databases are useful tools in storing information on images but as Taylor and Quayle argue 'Recent investments in databases of child pornography photographs, although presented as aids to the identifications of victims, will contribute little if anything to the issue' (206). The co-operation advocated with NGOs is an essential element and would ensure that the responsibility would not fall solely on the police to deal with the problem. The G8 strategy recognises that the issue of child abuse images is a societal problem and not just a policing one. The last action of building international procedures and relationships is crucial in the formation of an appropriate response and needs serious attention and illustrates the G8's acceptance that no current standardised global approach to the issue of victim identification exists. However the strategy fails to address two critical factors: the need for a child centred approach and how to address the ownership problem.

While the points above outline the G8's suggested strategy for Victim Identification, the study introduced below details the actual steps taken in a number of 'successful' identifications.

Successful identifications

Fourteen investigations were examined with four in Germany, one in Sweden and nine in the UK. Ninety-five children were identified in these investigations. Twenty seven interviews were conducted with investigating officers, child protection officers, social workers, one parent and an adult survivor. In twelve of the cases in the UK, Germany and Sweden, the victims were abused and photographed with those images subsequently appearing on the Internet. In two of the cases, the images of 39 children have not been seen, as of yet, on the Internet. The cases comprising the study have been numbered from 1 to 14.

Identification is traditionally thought of as the moment where the victim's identity is revealed. Identification is not one distinct, specific moment when a child is identified. Each identification has a life cycle which can be described as the process beginning the instant the case is initiated continuing through to the identification itself and finally to the outcome of the identification; the support received by victim and family. The process falls into three phases:

- Pre-Identification Phase.
- Identification Phase.
- Post Identification Phase.

The pre-identification phase details how the case was initiated. The identification phase describes the investigative methods employed which resulted in the identification. Finally, the post identification phase comprises of what happens to the victims after identification.

Pre-identification phase

Initiation

In the cases studied there are three main categories of triggers which initiate an investigation: child disclosure, public tips and agency action. These categories will be outlined with illustrative detail from the cases.

1. Child disclosure

Only two of the investigations were prompted by a child's disclosure. This supports findings by Silbert, (1989) and Svedin and Back (1996) that exploited children keep their abuse secret. In Case 3, a girl disclosed that she was abused by her friend's step-father. She did not mention that she was photographed but abusive images of her and her friends were freely available on the Internet. A five-year-old girl disclosed in Case 6 that she was abused and photographed by a stranger in the tenement flat where she lived. The police carried out house-to-house investigations and made numerous enquiries which resulted in no further leads. Two months later a six-year-old girl disclosed to her parents that she was sexually abused and photographed by a man in the stairwell of the tenement block where she lived. This time the child gave the police vital information which ultimately led to the offender's arrest.

Interestingly, in the only two cases where the children disclosed, the children were not related to the offender.

2. Public tips

Two of the investigations began as the consequence of tips from the public. The police received information from a member of the public, in Case 8, that a man was downloading child abuse images from the Internet. An analysis of his computer revealed that he was producing abusive images of young boys. In Case 10, an Austrian journalist discovered a series of child abuse images in a newsgroup which facilitates the distribution of child abuse images. He believed elements in the images pointed to the series having been created in a German speaking country. The Federal Police in Germany, the BKA, assumed ownership and decided to investigate the case.

3. Agency action

The remainder of the investigations (ten), were initiated by agencies acting on information from the proactive monitoring of the Internet (seven), and information acquired in the course of other investigations (three).

A: Proactive monitoring of the Internet

An FBI agent came across a person in a chat room in Case 1 who was trading 22 abusive images of a 12-year-old girl. He surmised from the conversations that the suspect was abusing the girl in real time and taking instructions from other users on how to carry out the abuse. The suspect's IP address was available and the Internet Service Provider (ISP) he used to access the Internet was identified in the UK. In Case 2 COPINE, which constantly monitored newsgroups dedicated to child sexual abuse, downloaded a series of abusive image which, following an analysis, appeared to have been produced in the UK. COPINE contacted Greater Manchester Police (GMP) in the UK, who assumed ownership of the investigation.

In Case 12 the Internet Monitoring Squad, within the BKA, discovered a message posted in a newsgroup, written in German, asking if any one was willing to the exchange of photographs of their daughter. The Monitoring Squad observed the responses to the message and one of the respondents posted a message with three digital images of a girl approximately 10-years-old. The police deduced that the environs visible in the images pointed to Germany as the locus of production: thus they took ownership and investigated the case.

In total, half of all cases were initiated as the result of proactive monitoring of the Internet which meant that the agency took a degree of responsibility in either investigating the case themselves or passing it onto the relevant police force.

If the police hadn't been proactive in these cases they may have never been investigated. Case 14 is an excellent example of a case where the issue of ownership impeded the series being investigated. COPINE became aware of an abusive series in 1997. It consisted of thousands of images of at least 36 young girls. The series was released over a period of three years from 1997–2000 and was a major cause of concern because it was apparent the abuse was ongoing – the images were obviously taken over a period of a few years because the same girls physically matured in the images. COPINE made enquires with a number of law enforcement agencies about the series and the general response was that while they were aware of the series, it was available on the Internet for years, but no force was investigating it. The main obstacle in accepting responsibility was that there were no obvious identifiers in the images which suggested a country of origin therefore no national law enforcement agency was prepared to conduct an investigation without proof of jurisdiction. COPINE believed that there were enough clues in the images which could lead to the identification of the victims – their faces were clearly visible and there were clues in the environs which pointed to a possible geographic location.

Frustrated at the lack of investigation or interest in the series, COPINE undertook an analysis of the series in 2001 and came to a number of conclusions; the images were definitely produced in the later half of the 1990s, the locus of production appeared to be Northern Europe and the most severely abused and photographed victim was probably related or close to the offender because of the level of access the offender had to her (the offender turned out to be her father – this is an important point if a media search had been considered. If the police had publicly searched for the girl the offender would have been quickly identified). COPINE wrote a report on the findings of the analysis in April 2001 which was distributed to law enforcement agencies world wide. Subsequently COPINE was invited to present the report to a Meeting of the Interpol Specialist Group on Crimes against Minors in June 2001. COPINE presented the case and made a plea for a police force to begin an investigation in an effort to identify the children in the images. The National Criminal Investigation Service, Norway (Kripos), decided that they would take on a co-ordinating role in the investigation. The investigation was initiated in July 2001. It took four years before a police force took ownership of this case.

B: *information acquired in the course of other investigations (3)*

In Case 7, US Customs received information during an investigation, from informants, about the identity of an offender and his victim in a series of images which were widely available on the

Internet. It was alleged that the perpetrator was living in the UK and therefore the information was passed on to UK police.

Identification phase

Investigative techniques

A number of investigative techniques employed in the identification phase are common to the various cases in the study:

- image analysis
- forensic investigation
- information sharing and agency co-operation
- public searches

Image analysis

Image analysis involves an in-depth examination of the images where all features of the image are analysed such as the environs, the child, the offender (if present) and metadata of the image (technical information stored within the image such as camera model). These features, known as identifiers, can help in determining the origin of the images. While this may seem a very obvious feature of investigations it rarely happens. Seized collections are often examined with the aim of proving possession of illegal material, rather than of identifying the victims.

An important point is that while image analysis may seem to be an objective activity, in practice this is not the case. The senior investigating officer in Case 9 made an interesting point here about assumptions:

> . . . it is strange how when you see things in this sort of context you fill it with assumptions, you fill it with your experiences and you put things into the picture, interpretations that are not really there sometimes . . . we actually assumed, wrongly as it turned out, that it was one child in one particular house.

It turned out that the images depicted two individual children in two different houses. Because it is a subjective analytical tool, image analysis is error prone, and its success depends on the thoroughness, expertise and training of the investigating officers. Some might say that reliance on human analysis is the weak point in this approach and would suggest the use of technology such as databases etc. as a preferred method. However the technology does not currently exist to supersede the expertise provided by human agents as is the case with many technological solutions, their usefulness again depends on the skill of the operator and often on the quality of the input.

Forensic investigation

Forensic investigation entails what can be described as 'good old fashioned police work' where each piece of evidence in the case is followed up and investigated. Forensic investigation goes hand in hand with image analysis as each clue obtained through image analysis needs to be investigated. When abusive images are under investigation there are a number of clues that are available to the investigator. These clues may relate exclusively to the image or they present themselves as contextual or supplementary evidence e.g. IP addresses of distributors from message headers.

Together, image analysis and forensic investigation are essential elements in the identification process. One must bear in mind that while image analysis must be followed by forensic investigation, forensic investigation can proceed without image analysis. All of the cases examined employed both image analysis and forensic investigation.

Information sharing and agency co-operation

This is another important element which was found to be present in the majority of the cases studied. As the problem is a global one, with images available worldwide, it is essential that the various agencies involved share information with each other. Again as mentioned previously cases are ultimately local in that the children are usually abused by someone they know in their community. Therefore the different agencies (not just law enforcement) in the community can provide each other with a great deal of information relevant to the case. Quite often different agencies hold different pieces of the puzzle which when combined can lead to victim identification. For example, in Case 6 the police arrested an offender who was photographing children in an area of the UK. They seized a number of images produced by the perpetrator in various council flats. The police contacted the council, which maintained the council flats in the area, and showed them sanitised images where stairwells were visible in the background. Amazingly they were able to identify the tenement flats by the colour scheme used. Information sharing and agency co-operation also occurred in all of the cases in the study.

Case 9 is an excellent example of a case where image analysis, forensic investigation and information sharing all culminated in the identification of the victim and the offender. An investigating officer from GMP attended a Europol course in November 2001. At the time there were enquiries into a Bulletin Board and officers from various countries were discussing the material which was being posted. The officer saw 14 images which appeared on the Bulletin Board which looked very British. He decided to bring the images back to GMP where the unit concluded that a number of identifiers pointed to a possible UK origin and therefore they decided to investigate the case. Initially they analysed the content of the images which showed the interior of a house. They contacted an architectural expert who was able to tell them that the house was most likely built in the early 1900s (it turned out that there were two houses in the images which were built circa 1902). This information supported the police's reasoning that the images were produced in the UK. GMP also circulated images of a blue and white check dress which looked like a school uniform, on a private law enforcement Internet group. The general consensus was that it wasn't a familiar uniform in any other country so this further supported the notion that the images were of UK origin.

The best clues came from image analysis of the bedroom scene, in which there were three cardboard boxes. These boxes were from Epson and Time Computer products. The police made contact with Epson and discovered that the Epson labelled box was for a printer released in February 2000. This helped them to produce a possible time line for the abuse i.e. between February 2000 and November 2001. Labels on the Time computer box showed that it was delivered by a UK delivery company which delivered only in the UK. This confirmed the location as being in the UK. The Time Computer Company sold the three items together as a package. They had 4,000 customer names in a database who bought this package. The police obtained these names under the UK Data Protection Act.

COPINE had further additional images from the series which they gave to GMP. These additional images contained metadata which included the name of the camera model: a Fuji camera. Fuji had sold 28,000 of that model camera in the UK alone. GMP did not have the resources to go through 28,000 names and addresses but then learnt from discussions with Fuji that there was a shorter list of 4,000 names of those customers who had returned the camera for repair. GMP felt that there was a high probability that the offender returned his camera for repair if he was using it a lot so they decided to cross reference them against the 4,000 names of those who had bought the package from Time Computers. Two names matched. One was a man in his 60s and the other in his late 30s. It was evident from the images that the offender was in the age range 25–45: in addition, the younger man had a record of previous convictions, one for a minor assault against a child. Enquiries were also made with the child support agency. They had an order for him to pay child support for a girl of approximately the same age as the girl seen in the images. All of this information pointed overwhelmingly to the younger man being the offender GMP was looking for. The offender's identification led to the identification of two girls.

What is remarkable about the investigation in Case 9 is the level of analysis conducted by the police. They considered every single clue and the possible lines of enquiry they could follow in the identification process. They did not follow up on every clue initially because for efficiency's sake it was necessary to identify the most valuable clues first. So in essence they 'cherry picked' the clues they considered would be most productive. A crucial aspect in the success of this case was the persistence of GMP during this case. They did not know where in the UK the images were produced therefore it did not necessarily fall under their remit in Manchester. There was no onus on GMP to take on this investigation. They convinced their force that it was a case worth investigating. They were given six weeks to look into the case with no added resources to investigate. They solved the case in just over six weeks. Without such relentless persistence from GMP, the question remains as to whether, without this effort, these children would have been identified.

Public searches

A public search is where the public are asked whether they can supply any information to aid the identification of the victim or offender. This is done by putting sanitised images of the victim or offender in the media i.e. TV, newspapers and websites. This occurred in two cases in Germany and only after the above investigative techniques had been exhausted.

The public search involved sanitised images of the children and the environs being made publicly available on a German television crime watch programme. As a result of the public search, the children were identified within a few days. This method is controversial because it has been criticised for invasion of privacy for the victim which could lead to re-victimisation and also there is a 'killing argument'; some argue that public disclosure could put the victim in danger as the perpetrator may harm or kill them once the abuse becomes public.

The first case ever in which a public search was conducted occurred in Germany in 1999 – Case 10. The police were nearly certain that the images had been produced in Germany but after approximately two months of investigation, involving image analysis, forensic investigation and queries with other police forces, they were no nearer to narrowing down the possible location in Germany. At this juncture in the investigation, with no fixed location, the BKA decided that the final solution was to conduct a public search. An interesting point is that they had to prove to the prosecutor that they had exhausted all other means of identifying the child and to prove that going public was the only available solution. Images of the child and identifiers in the background were featured on a 'crime watch' type TV programme. The public was informed that it was a case involving sexual abuse because it was anticipated that this information would ensure that the public would be more willing to come forward with information. Interestingly 90 per cent of the responses related to the environs rather than the identity of the child. With a number of the tips pointing to a school in the southern part of Germany, the police visited the school and identified the girl. In interview she disclosed that the abuser was a close family friend.

A number of media searches have been conducted since the first case in 1999 in each of the following countries: Germany, the Netherlands, Austria, and Australia. All of the public searches resulted in the identification of the victims. Recently the US has conducted public searches where they have only publicly showed the offender's face – these also resulted in the identification of victims. This is not possible in many cases because the offender is rarely visible in the images. Although only a handful of public searches have been conducted worldwide, all of them have led to successful victim identification. This success rate would suggest that this method demands serious attention, despite its invasive nature for the victim.

In conclusion, the investigative techniques detailed above i.e. image analysis, forensic investigation, information sharing and agency co-operation and public searches can all contribute to successful investigations. These four techniques are not linear steps. They can occur at different stages of the investigation or they may not happen at all, although public searches can only happen after the other three steps have already occurred.

Post identification

Taylor and Quayle (2003) argue that there is little point in identifying victims if the support structures are not in place or adequately developed. Although in all of the cases studied the victims were identified, this does not mean that child focus was maintained throughout all of the cases. A number of issues were raised after the children were identified. These relate to the a) focus of the investigation and b) the support received by the victims.

a) Focus of the investigation

In Case 6 the police successfully identified the victims but the children were effectively used as tools for a conviction by the prosecution service. The offender was convicted for abusing 35 young girls and sentenced, on appeal, to 10 years in prison. This was a case of stranger abuse where the offender abused the children in the stairwells of tenement flats. The case went to court before all of the girls had been identified. Therefore the abuse against all of the victims, identified or not, was included in a composite charge. The police continued to identify the children following the conviction and managed to identify them all within a few months. However, it was not until March 2003, a year after the offender was sentenced, that 13 of the families were notified of their daughter's abuse. Naturally the parents were very angry that they were not informed about the abuse. Social services were dissatisfied with the position they now found themselves in, dealing with angry parents who felt they had been let down by the legal/justice system. The victims who were identified pre-trial (and their families) received significantly more support than those who were identified after the trial i.e. a consistent child focus was not maintained throughout the course of the case. This was not the fault of the police, who made every effort to identify the victims, but rather of the legal system whose focus was on convicting the offender.

b) *Support for victims*

As of yet there is little understanding around the short and long-term impact of photography on abuse victims. A child's awareness is obviously a critical factor: children photographed at different ages and developmental stages will have differing perspectives of the abuse. Another concern is the child's potential lack of closure. The images can never be destroyed or retrieved once they are distributed on the Internet. They become public property. The victim may find it difficult to gain a sense of closure on the abuse, which could be considered as ongoing because the images are available as a permanent record of the abuse.

In Case 3, a parent of three abused children was very satisfied with the support her family received from the police and social services. The children had been very much aware that the abuse was recorded and that the images were distributed on the Internet because the offender encouraged them to pick out their favourite photographs. As a result of knowing that other people saw images of their abuse the children expressed fear of being recognised by people in the street. The social workers were very mindful of the fact that children were photographed and this was an issue that they worked on with the children during therapy sessions. Interestingly the two social workers who worked on the case said that the case became a priority for social services due to its high profile in the media. The offender was a member of an online group called Wonderland, which received considerable publicity when discovered in 1998. The social workers believed that ordinarily other cases just as severe would not have received the same input from social services.

A social worker on a different case did not think that the existence of the photographs made any difference and suggested that the impact on the victims would be the same irrespective of whether the abuse had been recorded or not. She did admit however that she had not thought about the potential impact when she was working on the case or prior to the interview.

Parental consent also played a large part in the kind of support the child received. A few of the children did not receive any therapeutic support because their mothers felt it was unnecessary. In these cases their partners were the abusers. This is an obstacle faced by social services in child abuse cases in general.

Summary

If we analyse successful cases, i.e. cases where the child has benefited, the singular moment of identification, although pivotal, is not what is noteworthy in itself: it is all the steps that the case underwent or the entire 'process' that should be considered and analysed.

If the process is not broken down into phases then there is a tendency to neglect all the relevant issues at each point. If we are mindful of the child's best interests at each stage of the process then there is a higher probability that the entire process will be child centred.

The means of initiation is critical to each identification yet, as is evident from the low identification rates, it appears that we have not yet figured out what the focus of the response should be. Do we want to control the distribution of the images or do we want to identify the victims? This does not mean that the offenders who possess and trade images should not be targeted but the many victims in the images deserve more. The reasons why children are not being identified relate to issues such as ownership/responsibility and policy development and need to be seriously considered.

Emergent issues from cases

In this ongoing study a number of issues have emerged thus far which appear to be central to the victim identification process. They can be broadly categorised into three areas:

- victim issues
- law enforcement issues
- support services issues

1. Victim issues

Are there support structures in place to support the victims post-identification? Some of the victims in the cases examined were effectively abandoned once the offender was convicted i.e. conviction of the offender took priority. Svedin and Back (1996) found that in their study of children who were abused and photographed that the attention was focused on the offender. This study supports their findings that victims of abusive images can be lost in the legal process.

In some cases the support offered was not mindful of the fact that the abuse was recorded. Children whose abuse is photographed must live with the fact that there is a permanent record of the abuse. It can never be destroyed. There are problems in teasing out the different effects of victimisation. What are the effects of the abuse itself and what are the effects of being photographed? Are they different? Does the recording of the abuse exacerbate the problems for the child?

An important factor relates to the child's awareness of being photographed, the existence of the photographs and the child's knowledge of the very public nature of the Internet and its potential for photograph exchange. The child's age and awareness are important here. This may affect how they deal with the abuse. The short-term and long-term impact on the child needs to be considered in detail.

2. Law enforcement issues

In relation to the investigations, comprising the study, the issues which were raised highlighted the lack of standard procedures in the investigative process. Interestingly four of the investigations were undertaken by two units who have a proven track record in identifications – they are motivated in this area and have built up a level of experience and expertise which appears to be useful in such cases (as in any other kinds of investigations). This suggests the importance of experience and motivation within law enforcement units tasked with solving crimes where child abuse crimes have been photographed.

In the pre-identification phase described above, the initiation of 7 out of the 14 cases was the result of proactive monitoring of the Internet. If we cannot, as the evidence would seem to suggest, rely on children's disclosure then law enforcement needs to take a more proactive stance.

An impediment to the response as previously mentioned is the lack of a standard global victim identification policy and procedure. This has made it difficult for law enforcement to deal with the problem. While those who deal with the problem, as in these cases, basically assume responsibility themselves for the cases, this is ultimately not an approach that will tackle the global problem.

However, there have been developments in this area. There has been a noticeable difference in the last couple of years in the amount of interest in victims and their identification. This has been greatly influenced by the issue of reality which has been an explosive issue for the US. In Ashcroft vs. Free Speech Coalition, 535 US 234 (2002) the Supreme Court declared certain aspects of the Child Pornography Prevention Act unconstitutional. The contentious clause defined 'child pornography' as images that appear to depict or convey the impression that they depict minors. This ultimately meant that the burden was on law enforcement to prove that the children in the child abuse images were real children in order to prove abuse had taken place. The GAO report (2002) referred to this need to prove the images depict a real child as an 'affirmative burden' and that it became a challenge for the government to meet its 'burden of proof'. The impact of this change in the US law had reverberations in a way that was not anticipated at the time. What it meant was that police were obliged to actively identify the children in some of the images in a seizure of child abuse images, so that they could make charges of possession of 'child pornography'. The result was that this kick-started victim identification in the US which was not previously a priority and it also influenced victim identification worldwide because US LEAs were making constant queries across the globe regarding images found in seizures.

Surprisingly, however, this development did more to bring the issue of identification to the fore rather than dramatically increase the number of identifications: in many cases the court's attention was directed towards victims already identified in order to prove a child in the collection was 'real'. In essence the law encouraged a more systematic compilation of the list of previously identified children rather then actively trying to identify unidentified other children depicted in other images.

Another recent development relates to a recent increase in the number of positive identifications recorded by Interpol. As mentioned previously, the number of identifications in the Interpol database rests at about 297. In May 2004 that figure was at 261. Anders Persson, who works on the database at Interpol, believes that the recent increase in identifications is the result of an increase in the number of law enforcement officers who are actively trying to identify victims. They belong to Interpol's International Victim Identification Group which consists of over 20 investigators from Sweden, Norway, Denmark, The Netherlands, Belgium, Germany, UK, France, Switzerland, USA and Canada. They are in constant contact through a virtual network forum which was created in 2003. This real time forum appears to be much more effective than the previous approach which involved face-to-face meetings facilitated by Interpol. The constant access to other investigators and the fact that they receive newly produced images on a regular basis is undoubtedly useful. This is an informal group not overly constrained by 'red tape' helping them to be flexible, dynamic and to be able to react rapidly to information. These factors appear to have contributed to an increase in identifications. Nonetheless, this success can only be considered on a small scale. If the number of identifications is to increase dramatically then a formalised approach is required: one that incorporates the experience and lessons learnt (i.e. the importance of sharing information and inter-agency cooperation) from those with experience in the area.

3. Support services issues

Some of the social workers interviewed had never before worked with children who had been photographed. Some said that before they had worked on these cases they had never asked sexual abuse victims whether the abuse was photographed. While this may seem a very obvious point it is one worth noting. The question of whether the abuse was recorded should be considered by both law enforcement and social services in any sexual abuse cases primarily so that a more complete understanding of the role of photography in child sexual abuse could be gained. Furthermore this information could lead to the discovery of images which could provide evidence against the offender and possibly lead to the identification of other children. Support services need to recognise the added impact of child abuse images on the victims and this should be incorporated into long-term strategies of support.

Another issue for support services is that the investigating team may hold vital information on the abuse from either the images or the perpetrators which they may not be privy to. Therefore co-operation between police and the support services is essential in order to properly assess and deal with the victim's needs (e.g. in one of the cases the social worker had no idea what occurred in the images as she did not see them nor were they described to her. This appears to have led her to disregard their effect on the victim).

Recommendations

- Child protection focus for investigations rather than controlling the problem of possession and distribution.

- Prioritise service needs for victims and their families.

- Development of global and national policies on the identification of children.

- Discussion of the ownership problem.

- Increased co-operation between and within agencies who work in the area.

- Multi-disciplinary teams to investigate cases (multi-disciplinary teams with a diverse range of experience and perspective would ensure the most comprehensive and holistic approach. All members of any team should be educated in the importance of a consistent child centred approach).

References

Attorney General (1986) *Final Report of the Attorney General's Commission on Pornography* Nashville: Rutledge Hill Press.

Barnardo's (2004). *Just One Click: Sexual Abuse of Children and Young People through the Internet and Mobile Telephone Technology*. Essex: Barnardo's.

COE (2003) *G8 Strategy* to Protect Children from Sexual Exploitation on the Internet 2002. 30/07/03 at: http://www.coe.int/T/E/Legal_affairs/Legal_cooperation/Fight_against_terrorism/Texts_&_documents/Child%20Protection%20Strategy.pdf

Higonnet, A. (1998) *Pictures of Innocence: The History and Crisis of Ideal Childhood*. Thames and Hudson.

Holland, G. (2003) *Victim Identification: An Analysis of Successful Identifications*, paper presented at the COPINE Colloquium, Cork.

Itzin, C. (2000) (Ed.) *Home Truths about Child Sexual Abuse; Influencing Policy and Practice: A Reader*. London: Routledge.

Persson, A. (2004) Personal Communication re Interpol Database of abuse images. Figure of 297 victims accurate as at 8 November 2004.

Silbert, M.H. (1989) The Effects on Juveniles of Being Used for Pornography and Prostitution, in Zillman, D. and Bryant, C. (Eds.) *Pornography: Research Advances and Policy Considerations*, Hillside, NJ: Lawrence Erlbaum.

Svedin, C.G. and Back, K. (1996) *Children who don't Speak Out*. Stockholm: Swedish Save the Children.

Taylor, M. and Quayle, E. (2003) *Child Pornography: An Internet Crime*. Hove: Bruner Routledge.

Tyler, R.P. and Stone, L.E. (1985) Child Pornography: Perpetuating the Sexual Victimization of Children. *Child Abuse and Neglect: The International Journal*, 9: 313–8.

Chapter 7

Understanding Sexually Abusive Youth: New Research and Clinical Directions

John A. Hunter

New research directed at understanding the apparent heterogeneity of the juvenile sexual offender population is reviewed. This research examines developmental risk and protective factors associated with youth-perpetrated sexual aggression, and assesses the presence of three prototypic subtypes of adolescent male sexual offenders. The personality, sexual interests, and developmental characteristics of each subtype are discussed, along with hypothesized subtype-specific developmental trajectories. This research is related to new directions in the clinical and legal management of sexually abusive youth.

Introduction

The problem of juvenile sexual offending has received increased professional attention in the United States over the past decade. Youth under the age of 18 account for approximately one-fifth of all arrests each year for forcible rape, and one-fourth of arrests for other sexual offences (forcible rape and prostitution excluded) (Uniform Crime reports, 2002). The vast majority of arrested youth are adolescent males; adolescent females represent only about 2 per cent of juvenile arrests for rape, and 8 per cent of juvenile arrests for child sexual molestation.

While there is general professional consensus that treatment plays a potentially important role in the management and rehabilitation of juvenile sex offenders (National Task Force on Juvenile Sexual Offending, 1993) at issue in individual cases is the most appropriate level of care. For adjudicated youth, the courts must decide whether the youth can be safely and effectively managed in the community, or requires placement in a secure setting. Both statutory guidelines, and clinical assessment of risk and intervention needs, guide such disposition decisions.

Due to the enactment of an array of new legislation in the 1990s designed to 'get tough' on juvenile crime, a number of US states permit juvenile sex offenders to be prosecuted and sentenced in the adult courts, or placed on sex offender registries (Hunter and Lexier, 1998). These dispositions may have long-term consequences for the youth. Hence, in each individual case there is the need to balance public safety with what is believed to be in the best interest of the offending youth. These decisions can be difficult, as the stakes for both parties can be high.

Complicating clinical assessment and judicial decision-making, is the observed heterogeneity of the juvenile sex offender population. Some youth engage in less aggressive and invasive behaviours, and appear remorseful and motivated for treatment. Others commit violent offences, manifest deviant sexual interests, or display long-standing anti-social behaviour and attitudes. Absent in the field are empirically validated decision-support tools, and perhaps a less than complete theoretical understanding of the causes and courses of sexually abusive behaviour in youth.

The author's research on understanding developmental pathways into youth-perpetrated sexual aggression, and differential clinical manifestation and course, is reviewed. This research is directed at fostering a better understanding of major subtypes of juvenile sexual offenders and their unique characteristics and developmental trajectories. The clinical implications of this research, and new directions in the treatment of juvenile sexual offenders, are discussed.

On-going typology research: initial study

With the support of a grant from the US Office of Juvenile Justice and Delinquency Prevention (OJJDP), Hunter and colleagues (Hunter, Figueredo, Malamuth and Becker, 2003; Hunter et al., 2004; Hunter et al., in press) studied a sample of 182 adolescent males with documented histories of 'hands-on' sexual offending. This study focused on the hypothesised link between developmental risk factors, explanatory personality constructs, victim characteristics, and offence characteristics. Three developmental risk factors were examined: child maltreatment (physical and sexual), exposure to violence against females, and exposure to male-modelled anti-social behaviour.

Using structural equation modelling as the primary statistical tool, exposure to violence against females was found to be positively related to engagement in non-sexual delinquency, and to sexual aggression as mediated by psychosocial deficits. Exposure to violence against females predicted psychosocial deficits, which in turn predicted sexual offences against children.

Childhood exposure to male-modelled anti-social behaviour predicted greater adolescent involvement in non-sexual delinquency, and was positively associated with dominance traits and endorsement of aggression as a means of resolving conflicts and satisfying needs. Childhood sexual abuse, when non-coercive and perpetrated by a non-relative male, predicted sexual offending against a male child. Both childhood physical abuse by a father or step-father, and exposure to violence against females, were found to be associated with higher levels of co-morbid anxiety and depression.

In related analyses, exposure to violence against females was found to be associated with lower levels of emotional empathy in the studied sample. Conversely, higher levels of emotional empathy were found to be associated with self-reported attachment to father and positive fathering experiences. Offenders against pre-pubescent children were distinguished from youth who sexually assaulted peer or adult females on the basis of more pronounced psychosocial deficits. These youth were also less violent in the commission of their sexual crimes, less likely to use a weapon, and less likely to assault an acquaintance or stranger than their peer/adult-offending counterparts.

The conducted study both offered insight into developmental risk and protective factors associated with juvenile sexual offending, and differences between juvenile rapists and child molesters. In particular, it suggested that the latter group of youth were less generally criminal in their personality make-up and more driven by deficits in social self-esteem and social competency. These differences were further explored in subsequent typology research.

Subsequent study and research in progress

The same research team conducted a follow-up, cross-sectional study of 256 adolescent male sexual offenders with the support of a second grant from OJJDP. Preliminary analyses have been conducted on these data in support of identifying three prototypic subtypes of adolescent male sexual offenders:

1. life-course-persistent
2. adolescent-onset, non-paraphilic
3. early adolescent onset, paraphilic

A longitudinal study of the identified subtypes has been funded by the National Institute of Mental Health, and is currently underway. This research builds on the work of Terri Moffitt (Moffitt, 1993) who has developed a typology of anti-social and aggressive youth.

The first subtype is hypothesised to represent youth who begin to engage in delinquent and anti-social behaviour in childhood, and continue to offend into adolescence and beyond. The sexual offending of these youth is believed to be primarily directed at peer and adult-age females and reflect both psychopathic personality traits and hostility toward females. The latter is thought to represent a cluster of negative, stereotypic attitudes toward females and endorsement of rape myths. The developmental trajectory of these youth is believed to be negative, and downward spiralling.

The second subtype of youth is believed to engage in transient sexual offending during adolescence as a form of adolescent experimentation or in compensation for deficits in social competency. These youth are hypothesised to predominantly offend against pre-pubescent children, especially females. It is presumed that the majority will favourably respond to treatment if not ensnared by complications of engagement in anti-social behaviour (e.g. drugs and alcohol, negative peer influences, etc.). The sexual interests of these youth are thought to be essentially age-appropriate.

Deviant or paraphilic sexual interests in children characterise the third of the hypothesised subtypes of adolescent male sexual offenders. These youth are thought to be at risk for continued sexual offending into adulthood, and to have more male victims than the other two subtypes.

Cluster analysis was used to identify the discussed subtypes in the referenced cross-sectional sample of 256 youth. Youth were sequentially clustered on the following personality factors:

1. paedophilic interests
2. hostile masculinity, life-style delinquency (i.e. psychopathy and impulsivity) and egotistical-antagonistic masculinity (i.e. dominance traits and endorsement of instrumental aggression)
3. psychosocial deficits (i.e. social self-esteem and anxiety/depression).

This resulted in five clusters:

1. Youth who scored high on paedophilic sexual interests.
2. Youth who scored high on hostile masculinity, lifestyle delinquency, and egotistical-antagonistic masculinity and low on psychosocial deficits.
3. Youth who scored high on the named three factors and high on psychosocial deficits.
4. Youth who scored low on the named three factors and high on psychosocial deficits.
5. Youth who scored low on all five factors.

Clusters 2 and 3 were judged to represent Life-Course Persistent youth. Clusters 4 and 5 were thought to represent Adolescent-onset, Non-Paraphilic youth, and Cluster 1 Early Adolescent Onset-Paraphilic youth. Consistent with these assumptions, and hypothesised differences between the prototypic subtypes, Clusters 2 and 3 reported more violent delinquent behaviour in the prior twelve months, had the highest childhood exposure to anti-social males, the highest level of pre-adolescent substance and pornography use, and the highest percent of sexual assaults against pubescent/post-pubescent female victims. As predicted, Cluster 1 had the highest composite index of sexual offences against male children.

The referenced longitudinal study will sample 330 adolescent male sexual offenders placed in community-based and residential treatment programmes following adjudication. The study involves prospectively tracking these youth through treatment, and post-discharge into the community. Youth will be compared on three independently measured outcomes:

1. response to treatment
2. long-term psychosocial and psychosexual adjustment
3. sexual and non-sexual recidivism

Therapists and teachers, who are blind to subtype assignment and study hypotheses, will provide ratings of their adjustment. Ratings of response to treatment will include: the youth's acceptance of responsibility for his offences, his motivation for change, his understanding of risk factors and risk management strategies, his level of empathy, his remorse and guilt, the extent of cognitive distortions, and the quality of his peer relationships (note: these items are from the J-SOAP-II).

Clinical implications and new directions for treatment programming

The described research supports the observation that juvenile sexual offenders represent a heterogeneous population, and that within the population there are likely identifiable subtypes of youth with differential clinical characteristics and developmental trajectories. These youth may not only differ in their patterns of offending behaviour, but in their motives for offending, amenability to treatment, and risk for sexual and non-sexual recidivism. Furthermore, subsequent research may point to specific developmental pathways leading to particular patterns of sexual offending in youth.

As such, this research is of potential importance in understanding the intervention needs of youth who engage in sexually abusive behaviour. Most salient, the research supports the necessity of establishing a continuum of care to meet the varied needs of the population. In particular, both clinical observation and the reviewed research suggest that not all youth require placement in a secure setting, and that many can be managed in the community. The problem in the US in effecting the latter disposition is two-fold: firstly there is a dearth of community-based programming for juvenile sex offenders in many areas of the country and secondly existent clinical programming is typically limited in scope and ancillary services offered. In particular, few communities have adequate alternative placement resources for this population (i.e. group or foster homes). As a result, most community-based programmes can only accommodate the least maladjusted youth and those who do not require out-of-home placement.

As discussed by Hunter, Gilbertson, Vedros, and Morton (2004), States' reliance on residential programming for containment and treatment of juvenile sex offenders has both fiscal and clinical implications. The costs of residential care are typically quite high, and can easily exceed $100,000.00 annually per placed youth. Such costs can rapidly exhaust local and state resources, and make it difficult for communities to invest in developing the infrastructure for comprehensive community-based care. This phenomenon has the potential to result in an ever-growing dependence on residential care, and ultimately in the restriction of clinical services to the most seriously disturbed youth (or those committing the most serious offences).

Beyond the issue of spiralling costs of care, a reliance on residential care for management of heterogeneous groups of juvenile sex offenders may produce negative and complicating treatment effects. Research points to the potential for clinical aggregation of delinquent youth to result in harmful, iatrogenic treatment effects (Dishion, McCord and Poulin, 1999). In this regard, the developmental trajectories of younger and less anti-social youth may be permanently altered by their exposure to older and more anti-social peers (i.e. 'deviancy training'). Thus, the careful clinical assessment and judicious placement of youth who have engaged in sexual offending behaviour is indicated. The reviewed typology research suggests that clinicians must be particularly sensitive to disparate levels of character pathology and sexual deviancy amongst these youth. Indiscriminate grouping of these youth for treatment or living environment purposes may therefore only enhance their risk of re-engaging in sexual offending, and other forms of delinquent behaviour.

Hunter et al. (2004) discuss concepts and systems innovations that are critical to strengthening community-based programming for juvenile sex offenders, and expanding the base of youth that it can serve. These include training community-based providers, and stakeholder agencies, in better understanding the heterogeneity of the population and using newly developed risk and needs assessment instruments to support clinical decision-making. Also addressed is the establishment within states of a 'seamless' continuum of care, wherein community-based programmes are linked to residential or institutional programmes through common assessment and treatment methodologies, and collaborative case management.

These authors also discuss the importance of holistic treatment planning that addresses the frequently found psychiatric co-morbidity of juvenile sexual offenders, and shifting from strictly cognitive-behavioral to social-ecological intervention models. The latter models stress the importance of conceptualising and strategically addressing the multiple, and oftentimes interactive, dynamic systems that support delinquent behaviour (Henggeler, 1999). Interventions are delivered in and directed at all relevant systems and environments, including the home, school, and community.

While beyond the scope of the current paper to review in detail, social-ecological approaches (e.g. Multi-Systemic Therapy) have produced superior clinical and cost outcomes in the treatment of adolescent conduct, and psychiatrically related, disorders, and show promise in the treatment of juvenile sexual offenders (Borduin, 1999).

The discussed typology research may also ultimately inform risk assessment and treatment programming for juveniles who have engaged in sexually abusive behaviour. As discussed by Hunter and Longo (2004), treatment programmes for juvenile sex offenders historically have been heavily influenced by the adult sex offender treatment field. They observe that the field largely began as a 'trickle down' effect of studying adult sex offenders and discovering that a number of these individuals began to engage in deviant sexual behaviour as juveniles. Implicit in the early design of treatment programmes for juveniles was the assumption that youth sexually offend largely for the same reasons that adults do, and therefore have essentially the same treatment and legal management needs. It was furthermore assumed that sexual behaviour problems manifest in juveniles were likely to be chronic in nature, and only worsen over time in the absence of intensive clinical and legal intervention.

Noticeably absent in the juvenile sex offender field have been longitudinal studies of children and adolescents who manifest sexual behaviour problems. It is unknown as to how many juvenile sex offenders continue to exhibit sexual behaviour problems into adulthood, and what factors or characteristics predict long-term recidivism in this population. While not definitive, existent programme evaluation studies suggest that short-term ($\parallel = 5$ years) recidivism rates are relatively low in treated youth (5–15 per cent), and that the great majority of these youth may not be destined to life-long offending behaviour (Becker, 1998). Longitudinal typology research has the potential to more precisely define the characteristics of youth who are at heightened risk for continued sexual and non-sexual offending into adulthood, as well as identify critical protective factors and treatment issues.

Likewise, typology research may provide guidance for the refinement of treatment programme content and approach. Presently, juvenile sexual offenders are treated in a relatively generic manner. In this regard, whether community-based or residential, and regardless of presenting problem and underlying dynamics, all youth typically receive essentially the same treatment, delivered in the same format (i.e. group) over the same period of time.

Paralleling the adult sex offender field, most juvenile sex offenders receive therapy directed at establishing accountability for their offences, correcting cognitive distortions or thinking errors, improving social and communication skills, attenuating or controlling deviant sexual urges, enhancing victim empathy, and teaching relapse prevention (Hunter et al., 2004). This popular treatment approach has never been subjected to rigorous experimental evaluation. Typology research may provide guidance in the development of subtype-specific approaches based on an advanced understanding of the unique developmental, clinical, and legal characteristics of specific subtypes. Thus, the delivered treatment may be more precisely focused on subtype-specific endogenous and external, systemic determinants of the sexual misbehaviour and reflect an understanding of dose requirements. Finally, it is suggested that the delineation through longitudinal research of developmental pathways and processes leading to specific types of sexual behaviour problems in youth may provide insight into the development of effective early intervention and prevention programming for at-risk youth.

References

Becker, J.V. (1998) What we Know About the Characteristics and Treatment of Adolescents Who Have Committed Sexual Offences. *Child Maltreatment: Journal of the American Professional Society on the Abuse of Children*. 3: 4, 317–29.

Borduin, C.M. (1999) Multisystemic Treatment of Criminality and Violence in Adolescents. *Journal of the American Academy of Child and Adolescent Psychiatry*. 38: 3, 242–9.

Dishion, T.J., McCord, J. and Poulin, F. (1999) When Interventions Harm: Peer Groups and Problem Behavior. *American Psychologist*. 54: 9, 755–64.

FBI (2002) *Uniform Crime Reports*. Federal Bureau of Investigation, www.fbi.gov.

Henggeler, S.W. (1999) Multisystemic Therapy: An Overview of Clinical Procedures, Outcomes, and Policy Implications. *Child Psychology and Psychiatry Review*. 4: 1, 2–10.

Hunter, J.A., Gilbertson, S.A., Vedros, D. and Morton, M. (2004) Strengthening Community-based Programming for Juvenile Sexual Offenders: Key Concepts and Paradigm Shifts. *Child Maltreatment*. 9: 2, 177–89.

Hunter, J.A. and Longo, R.E. (2004) Relapse Prevention with Juvenile Sexual Abusers: A Holistic/Integrated Approach, in O'Reilly, G. and Marshall, W. *Handbook of Clinical Intervention with Young People who Sexually Abuse*. Brunner Routledge.

Hunter, J.A., Figueredo, A.J., Malamuth, N. and Becker, J.V. (in press) Emotional Empathy as a Mediator and Moderator of Non-sexual Delinquency in Juvenile Sexual Offenders. *Journal of Family Violence*.

Hunter, J.A., Figueredo, A.J., Malamuth, N.M. and Becker, J.V. (2003) Juvenile Sex Offenders: Toward the Development of a Typology. *Sexual Abuse: Journal of Research and Treatment*. 15: 1, 27–48.

Hunter, J.A., Jr. and Lexier, L.J. (1998) Ethical and Legal Issues in the Assessment and Treatment of Juvenile Sex Offenders. *Child Maltreatment: Journal of the American Professional Society on the Abuse of Children*. 3: 4, 339–48.

Moffitt, T.E. (1993) Adolescence-limited and Life-course-persistent Antisocial Behavior: A Developmental Taxonomy. *Psychological Review*. 100: 4, 674–701.

National Task Force on Juvenile Sexual Offending (1993) *Final report*. A Function of National Adolescent Perpetration Network, C.H. Kempe National Center, University of Colorado Health Sciences.

Chapter 8

What Sort of Person could do that? Psychological Profiles of Internet Pornography Users

David Middleton, Anthony Beech and Rebecca Mandeville-Norden

Introduction

This chapter seeks to explore the applicability of the Ward and Siegert 'Pathways Model of Sexual Offending' to a sample of offenders convicted of making, possessing and distributing indecent images of children using the Internet. The Model is presented as a useful example of 'theory knitting' in seeking to combine elements of other offending models to build on their strengths and overcome some of their weaknesses.

The sample of 42 cases drawn from the National Probation Service Caseload appears to demonstrate the relevance of the theoretical model. In particular two clusters of offenders are identified as sharing the psychological characteristics of those who have 'Intimacy Deficits' and the other with 'Emotional Dysregulation'. The paper suggests how these two groups may present and the possible function of their offence behaviour in meeting their needs. The implications for sex offender treatment programmes are also discussed. Finally the data supports the view that offenders who exhibit this type of offence behaviour may form a continuum from low deviance to high deviance and that individual assessment will be required to determine treatment needs.

How do Internet offenders who derive gratification from viewing child abuse images fit into a theoretical framework for understanding child sexual abusers?

Previous studies have relied on adapting existing models e.g. Finkelhor (Middleton, 2004) or in developing a stand-alone model (Taylor and Quayle, 2003). Other models which could contribute to understanding the aetiology of sex offending such as the Marshall and Barbaree (1990) Integrated Theory appear relevant to some offenders but inevitably some offenders seem to fall outside the model. Critiques of models of sexual offending (Ward and Hudson, 2001; Ward and Siegert, 2002; Ward and Stewart, 2003; Beech and Ward, 2003) question how these models may explain some aspects of sexual offending behaviour, but often leave significant gaps which become exceptions to the model.

This question is also relevant to considering the application of such general theories to the Internet offending phenomenon. Put simply it appears that just as the 'sexual offender' population is a heterogenic population which is difficult to categorise so too is the 'Internet Offender'.

The term 'sex offender' is used to cover diverse behaviours from inappropriate sexual activity between juveniles to the rape of an 80-year-old woman. The paradox is that 'Internet Offenders' are another manifestation within the general spectrum of sexual offending behaviour and yet the generic term 'Internet Offender' also serves as an umbrella covering a wide variety of sexual behaviours associated with online activities. These range, for example, from use of the Internet to access abuse images, distribution of abuse images, a means of contact between individuals engaged in similar behaviours, to more instrumental uses as part of an offence chain. This could include behaviour such as grooming victims online, real-time sexualised inter-action and depictions of sexual abuse. For example Wolak et al., (2003) found that in a study of 2,577 cases processed by law enforcement agencies in the USA during a 12-month period 998 cases involved identified victims being solicited, groomed and subsequently involved in face-to-face meetings through use of the Internet. A further 644 cases were arrested by law enforcement officers posing as minors in chat rooms who were 'solicited' by the offenders to engage in both online and offline sexual behaviour. Finally 935 cases involved cases of possession, trading and distribution of indecent images.

Can one model seek to encompass such diverse behaviour? Ward and Siegert (2002) in attempting a resolution specifically in respect of models of general sexual offending, have applied the approach of 'theory knitting'. This draws on the salient features of existing models of sexual offending and seeks to encompass them into a 'Pathway Model of Child Sexual Abuse'. Therefore they draw on the Finkelhor Precondition Model (1984), Hall and Hirschman's Quadripartite Theory (1992) and Marshall and Barbaree's Integrated Theory (1990) taking the virtues of each model to construct a more comprehensive explanation of child sexual abuse. Briefly, the pathways model suggests that there are multiple pathways leading to the sexual abuse of a child and that each pathway involves a core set of dysfunctional psychological mechanisms that cause specific outcomes. The model postulates that the four distinct psychological mechanisms are intimacy and social skill deficits; distorted sexual scripts; emotional dysregulation and cognitive distortions. However the mechanisms interact to cause a sexual crime. A brief representation of this model is described in Table One below.

Since every sexual offence involves emotional, intimacy, cognitive and arousal components the pathways are not to be viewed as separate.

> *Although each pathway is hypothesised to be associated with a unique set of primary mechanisms and cluster of symptoms or problems, the mechanisms always interact to cause a sexual crime. That is, every sexual offence involves emotional, intimacy, cognitive and arousal components; however, each distinct pathway will have at its centre a set of primary dysfunctional mechanisms that impact on the others.* (Ward and Sorbello, 2003)

In considering the implication for individuals who engage in sexualised behaviour associated with problematic Internet use, it would appear possible to test out whether this model has utility for assessment and determining treatment needs. It is likely that such individuals will have differing distal factors that have impacted on their emotional, cognitive, arousal and intimacy behaviours. Because of the variety of 'Internet Offence' behaviours detailed above it is proposed to examine the application of the model to one form of behaviour – that of making, distributing and possession of indecent images.

What is the evidence for a link between viewing such images and other forms of sexual abuse?

Check and Gullion (1989) found that 'men who are predisposed to aggression are particularly vulnerable to negative influences from pornography'. Marshall (2000) states that it is possible to 'infer from the available literature that pornography exposure may influence . . . the development of sexual offending in some men'. Such individuals would be those who have experienced childhood development of vulnerability that in turn leads to a variety of problems including 'a greater focus on

Table 8.1 Schematic representation of the pathways model of child sexual abuse

Pathway	Distal factors	Sexual preference	Associated deficits	Behaviour
Intimacy deficits (intimacy)	Insecure attachment Inability to sustain adult intimacy	Normal sexual script operates until rejection, blockage Arousal to child although not preference	Emotional loneliness Social skills Cognitive distortions Entitlement beliefs	Target vulnerable child Create pseudo adult-adult 'loving relationship'
Distorted sexual scripts (arousal)	Early or inappropriate sexual experiences Victimisation Fear of rejection	Relationships seen as purely sexual Intimacy is equated with sex Children more trustworthy and accepting	Low self-esteem Craving for love and approval Misreading sexual cues	Unsatisfying adult sexual encounters, frustration Seek sex in inappropriate situations (e.g. when angry), inappropriate partners (children), inappropriate activities (e.g. sadistic)
Emotional dys-regulation (emotions)	Compulsive masturbation in early adolescence Lack of alternatives to increase self-esteem or alleviate negative mood	Preference for age related partners but opportunistically use children at times of stress Sex used as coping strategy	Problem in emotional recognition Dealing with negative emotion Problem in utilising social supports	Inability to manage mood may result in loss of control, which in conjunction with sexual desire leads to disinhibited behaviour

Table 8.1 *Continued*

Pathway	Distal factors	Sexual preference	Associated deficits	Behaviour
Anti-social cognitions (cognitive)	Specific belief systems such as the world is a dangerous place and you have to fight to have your needs satisfied General and extensive record of criminal and anti-social behaviour in youth and adolescence, possible conduct disorder	A right to have sexual needs met irrespective of needs and rights of others Sexual abuse justified and acceptable if alternatives not available	Entrenched cognitive distortions which make offenders vulnerable to sexual offending and to justify it	Positive emotional state when abusing a child because of the pleasure experienced and meeting needs for self-gratification in personally acceptable manner
Multiple dysfunctional mechanisms	Early sexualisation Impaired relationship and attachment style Multiple maladaptive development responses	Deviant sexual fantasy Approach goal of sexual gratification linked with others e.g. sense of control	High self-esteem since interests are legitimate and healthy Children seen as legitimate sexual partners Intimacy deficits	Inappropriate emotional regulation Multitude of offence related behaviours The 'pure paedophile'

sex, and the need to control events during sex'. However, Marshall cautions against ascribing a direct causal link between viewing pornography and other forms of sexual offending, rather that viewing pornography may accelerate a process already underway or may further justify an established set of antisocial beliefs.

Itzin (1992) has argued that the research consistently produces correlations between pornography and harm such as negative effects on attitudes, beliefs and behaviour and should therefore be re-conceptualised as evidence of causal – although not solely causal – relationships.

In summary pornography can be used to stimulate, develop and fuel sexual fantasy. Frequent use may be linked to sexual pre-occupation and attitudes that normalise deviant behaviour with potential victims. Many sex offenders appear to use pornography to increase arousal pre-offence. However, many men who use pornography do not sexually assault others and assessment needs to focus on the context and meaning of pornography for each individual along with an assessment of other dynamic factors associated with sexual offence behaviours.

Method

The National Probation Service collects data on convicted sexual offenders who have completed the standardised psychometric battery for the accredited sex offender treatment programmes (Beech, Fisher and Beckett, 1999). A sample of offenders who had been convicted of offences relating to making, distributing and possessing indecent images by the use of the Internet was drawn from this data set. Cluster analysis was undertaken of the psychometric profiles of this group in relation to the 'Pathways Model' described above.

Description of sample

The sample comprised 43 subjects, with an average age when sentenced of 42.06 years (SD = 14.43). Sixty per cent were married/cohabiting; 32 per cent single; 8 per cent widowed. Ethnicity (where known) was recorded as white. Risk of reconviction was assessed using the Risk Matrix 2000 (Thornton et al., 2002) however risk data was only available on 19 offenders of which 68 per cent were classified as Low risk, 16 per cent as Medium and 16 per cent as High risk.

At the time of arrest 15 per cent of the men were in daily contact with children; 3 per cent reported contact of more than three times a week; 13 per cent were in weekly contact with children and 32 per cent had contact less than once a month. None of these offenders was working with children.

Information on the gender of victims (i.e. portrayed in the indecent images) recorded that 70 per cent were images of female children; 5 per cent were male children and 25 per cent were depictions of both male and female children. The number of images downloaded ranged between 6 and 3000. Given the time period in which this data was recorded it is likely that the majority of offenders were prosecuted as a result of Operation Ore.

Psychological profiles

It is noteworthy that a number of the sample have scores that are above average or very much above average on the Impression Management sub-scale of the Social Desirability scale.

In relation to the 'Pathways Model' 26 men (60 per cent of the total sample) men could be relatively easily classified to four of the five pathways. The relative ease of doing this classification says something about treatment needs. The clusters were as follows:

Intimacy deficits (N = 10) (38 per cent of the coded sample) (Cluster 1)

- All report high level of emotional loneliness.
- None report high levels of problems in dealing with negative emotions.
- None report cognitive distortions with children.
- Self-esteem generally high.
- 60 per cent (6) report high levels of emotional congruence towards children.

Distorted sexual scripts (N = 4) (16 per cent of the coded sample) (Cluster 2)

- All report low levels of self-esteem.
- All report high levels of emotional congruence/ emotional identification with children.
- None report high levels of problems in dealing with negative emotions.
- None report cognitive distortions with children.
- None report high levels of emotional loneliness problems.

Emotional dysregulation (N = 9) (35 per cent of the coded sample) (Cluster 3)

- All report high levels of problems in dealing with negative emotions.
- None report emotional loneliness problems.
- None report significant levels of cognitive distortions.
- Only 22 per cent (2) have low self-esteem.
- 78 per cent (7) report high levels of emotional congruence towards children.
- High levels of reported victim empathy distortions (average 27 per cent) on Internet questionnaire.

Anti-social cognitions (N = 1) (4 per cent of the coded sample) (Cluster 4)

- This type of offender rare in this sample.
- High levels of cognitive distortions.
- High levels of self-esteem.
- High levels of impulsivity.
- Would be predicted that this man would have an extensive criminal record.

Multiple dysfunctional mechanisms (N = 2) (8 per cent of the coded sample) (Cluster 5)

- Low levels of self-esteem.
- High levels of emotional loneliness.
- High levels of personal distress.
- Tendency for high levels of cognitive distortions.
- Tendency for high levels of emotional congruence.
- Index offence in both cases is making/possessing indecent photos of children.

Discussion

This group of offenders does not appear to possess the range of deviant attitudes that distinguishes high deviance sex offenders. Similarly whilst they contain some who are of high risk of reconviction, in general they are assessed as low risk of reconviction. In relation to the Pathways Model clearly the majority of this sample fell into either the Intimacy deficits (38 per cent of the coded sample) or Emotional Dysregulation (35 per cent) clusters. There did not appear to be high levels of general anti-social attitudes or cognitive distortions which are generally supportive of seeing children as sexual, manipulative or seeking sex. However there are differences between the two major clusters in that one (Emotional cluster) report high levels of problems in dealing with negative emotions such as anger, rejection and stress, but not emotional loneliness. This group would appear to be able to make and sustain intimate relationships, but are not able to gain support within the relationship for dealing with emotional stressors. The other group (Intimacy) may have more difficulty in entering age appropriate, intimate relationships although do not report general problems in dealing with emotional stressors. This group may be more socially isolated or, given the 60 per cent who were in marital relationships at time of arrest, may be in relationships which are emotionally unsatisfying. However, given that both groups have high emotional identification with children, it may be that they use sex as a coping strategy and that they seek to use the Internet, and sites depicting children, either to relieve stress or to seek pseudo-intimacy.

Implications for treatment

The findings suggest a positive potential for successful treatment. However these data suggest that individual assessment is required in order to ascertain the important treatment targets for each offender. For the majority of these offenders the treatment programme may be shorter in line with the National Probation Service programmes for low deviance sex offenders (Middleton, 2002, NPD, 2003). Typically these programmes are group programmes of around 100 hours. It may be that an individually tailored programme would be of shorter duration. The programme will need to work with the offender in a functional analysis of the on-line behaviour. Work would be targeted at overcoming intimacy deficits or acquisition of skills to deal with negative affect as appropriate to the needs of the individual. There is some indication that work would also be required in building on empathic responses to child victims and in some cases this would need to begin with work on identifying with the offender that children depicted in the indecent images are real victims of child abuse.

Conclusion

The research supports the suggestion that men who use the Internet to obtain indecent images of children are not a homogeneous group. With the addition of more cases for analysis it may be that these offenders can be placed along a continuum. These would range from low risk, low deviance offenders who are unlikely to pursue their sexual interests into 'contact' offences at one extreme, to those who are high risk and high deviance who display many of the pre-disposing attitudes and behaviour supportive of serial sexual abuse. For this latter group the abuse of children through accessing indecent images may be only one of many expressions of their offence behaviour.

References

Beech, A.R., Fisher, D. and Beckett, R. (1999) *STEP 3: An Evaluation of the Prison Sex Offender Treatment Programme*. London: Home Office.

Beech, A.R. and Ward, T. (2003) The Integration of Aetiology and Risk in Sexual Offenders: A Theoretical Framework. *Aggression and Violent Behavior* (In press).

Check, J.V.P. and Gullion, T.H. (1989) Reported Proclivity for Coercive Sex following Repeated Exposure to Sexually Violent Pornography, Non-violent Pornography and Erotica, in Zillmann, D. and Bryant, J. (Eds.) *Pornography: Research Advances and Policy Considerations*. Hillsdale, NJ: Erlbaum.

Hall, G.C.N. and Hirschman, R. (1992) Sexual Aggression Against Children: A Conceptual Perspective of Aetiology. *Criminal Justice and Behavior*. 19, 8–23.

Itzin, C. (1992) Pornography and Civil Liberties: Freedom, Harm and Human Rights, in Itzin, C. *Pornography: Women, Violence and Civil Liberties*. OUP: Oxford.

Finkelhor, D. (1984) *Child Sexual Abuse: New Theory and Research*. New York: Free Press.

Marshall, W.L. and Barbaree, H.E. (1990) An Integrated Theory of the Aetiology of Sexual Offending, in Marshall, W.L., Laws, D.R. and Barbaree, H.E. (Eds.) *Handbook of Sexual Assault: Issues, Theories and Treatment of the Offender*. New York: Plenum.

Marshall, W.L. (2000) Revisiting the Use of Pornography by Sexual Offenders: Implications for Theory and Practice. *The Journal of Sexual Aggression*. 6: 1, 2.

Middleton, D. (2002) Accredited Programmes for Sex Offenders in the Community: An Overview from the National Probation Service. *Nota News*. July.

Middleton, D. (2004) Current Treatment Approaches, in Calder, M.C. *Child Sexual Abuse and the Internet: Tackling the New Frontier*. Lyme Regis: Russell House Publishing.

National Probation Directorate (2004) *The Treatment and Risk Management of Sexual Offenders in Custody and in the Community*. NPD/037/2002 London: Home Office.

Taylor, M. and Quayle, E. (2003) *Child Pornography: An Internet Crime*. Hove: Brunner Routledge.

Thornton, D. and Beech, A. (2002) Integrating Statistical and Psychological Factors Through the Structured Risk Assessment Model. ATSA Conference. October, Montreal, Canada.

Ward, T. and Hudson, S.M. (2001) A Critique of Finkelhor's Precondition Model of Child Sexual Abuse. *Psychology, Crime and Law*. 7, 333–50.

Ward, T. and Siegert, R.J. (2002) Toward a Comprehensive Theory of Child Sexual Abuse: A Theory Knitting Perspective. *Psychology, Crime and Law*. 8, 319–51.

Ward, T.S. and Sorbello, L. (2003) Explaining Child Sexual Abuse: Integration and Elaboration, in Ward, T., Laws, D.R. and Hudson, S.M. (Eds.) *Sexual Deviance: Issues and Controversies in Sexual Deviance*. London: Sage.

Ward, T. and Stewart, C. (2003) The Good Lives Model of Offender Rehabilitation of Sexual Offenders, in Ward, T. Laws, D.R. and Hudson, S.M. (Eds.) *Sexual Deviance: Issues and Controversies in Sexual Deviance*. London: Sage.

Wolak, J. Mitchell, K. and Finkelhor, D. (2003) *National Juvenile Online Victimization Study*. Presentation to the Association for the Treatment of Sexual Abuse (ATSA) 22nd Annual Conference, '*Gateway to Knowledge: Steps to Effective Treatment*' Oct 8–11, St Louis, USA.

Chapter 9

A Relational Frame Approach to the Psychological Assessment of Sex Offenders

Bryan Roche, Maria R. Ruiz, Martina O'Riordan and Karen-Anne Hand

Relational Frame Theory (RFT) (Hayes, Barnes-Holmes, and Roche, 2001) is a recent technical and conceptual account of human language and cognition. As such it provides a range of conceptual and empirical tools for the investigation of a wide range of behaviours germane to thought and language. More specifically, RFT is concerned with a core language skill, known variously as stimulus equivalence (Sidman, 1971: 1986) or relational framing (Hayes et al., 2001). The stimulus equivalence phenomenon can be summarised briefly as follows. A research participant is seated before a computer on which a series of stimulus-matching tasks are presented. A sample stimulus (e.g., an abstract shape) is presented in the centre of the screen, and two choice stimuli (referred to as comparisons) are presented at the bottom of the screen (e.g., nonsense syllables). The sample stimulus is often referred to as A1 and the comparison stimuli as B1 and B2, respectively. The participant's task is to choose between B1 and B2 conditional upon the sample stimulus. That is, when A1 is the sample the subject should choose B1, but given A2 as a sample they should choose the B2 comparison (this performance is known as a conditional discrimination). The computer presents feedback on performance after each trial. On two further tasks either B1 or B2 is presented as a sample, but two further stimuli, C1 and C2, are presented as comparisons. On these trials the subject must choose C1 when B1 is the sample, and choose C2 when B2 is the sample (see Figure 1).

When the foregoing tasks are presented repeatedly new relations typically emerge between the stimuli without further feedback to the participant. More specifically, participants will spontaneously match A1 to B1, B1 to C1, A2 to B2, and B2 to C2 (i.e., reverse the taught relations, or demonstrate symmetry between the stimuli). Furthermore, they will match A1 to C1, C1 to A1, A2 to C2, and C2 to A2 (i.e., combine the taught relations, or demonstrate transitivity between the stimuli). When this occurs the stimuli are said to participate collectively in a stimulus equivalence relation. (see Sidman, 1986; Barnes, 1994; Fields, Adams, Verhave, and Newman, 1990)

Derived stimulus relations, such as stimulus equivalence, are of interest to behaviour analytic researchers because their emergence is not predicted by traditional behavioural accounts based on direct contingent reinforcement for classes of topographically similar behaviours, and because the phenomena appear to parallel many natural language phenomena. For example, if a child is taught to identify an object when presented with a written word, the child may point to the word when presented with the object, without any feedback or encouragement. More specifically, given training in the spoken word 'cookie' and actual cookies, and between the written word cookie and the spoken word 'cookie,' a child will spontaneously identify the written word cookie as equivalent to

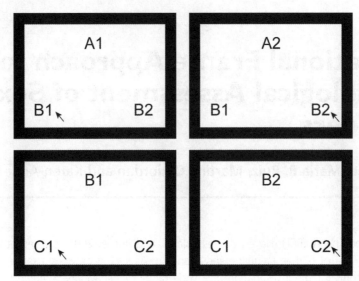

Figure 9.1 A standard set of matching-to-sample (MTS) tasks for training two three-member equivalence classes. The top two matching tasks together constitute the first conditional discrimination. The bottom two tasks together constitute the second conditional discrimination. The cursor indicates the correct choice.

'cookie', even though the performance has never been directly taught. In effect, the emergence of symmetry and transitivity between written words, spoken words, pictures and objects is commonplace in the acquisition of basic language skills (Hayes, Gifford, and Ruckstuhl, 1996). Insofar as this is the case, an analysis of derived stimulus relations may constitute an analysis of the very building blocks of language itself. (see Hayes and Blackledge, 2001)

As a technology and theory of language, RFT takes the position that deriving relations among stimuli, such as words and objects, represents the very essence of language activity itself (see Barnes-Holmes and Barnes-Holmes, 2000; Barnes-Holmes, Barnes-Holmes, Roche, Healy, Lyddy, Cullinan and Hayes, 2001; Lipkens, Hayes, and Hayes, 1993). Put simply, the complexity of spoken language and the creativity and generativity seen during the acquisition of language by young children can be understood in terms of the myriad derived relations that obtain between numerous words and events in the vernacular. RFT researchers refer to these collective trained and derived relations as a relational network.

Relational Frame Theory constitutes more than a functional account of language and relevant processes. Rather, it attempts to apply its technical nomenclature to the analysis of a wide range of complex behaviours, including complex attitudes and emotions. In one study relevant to the current chapter, for example, it was found that unusual patterns of sexual arousal could be understood in terms of the derivation of relations between stimuli (Roche and Barnes, 1997). In that study, seven subjects were trained on a series of conditional discrimination tasks (i.e., see A1 pick B1, see B1 pick C1, see A2 pick B2, see B2 pick C2, see A3 pick B3, see B3 pick C3, where all stimuli were nonsense syllables). Training on these tasks led to the emergence of the following equivalence relations during testing; A1–B1–C1, A2–B2–C2, and A3–B3–C3. Sexual and nonsexual functions were then established for the C1 and C3 stimuli, respectively, using a respondent conditioning procedure. That is, brief presentations of the C1 and C3 stimuli on a monitor were followed contingently and contiguously with presentations of sexual and nonsexual film clips, respectively. The acquisition of sexual arousal functions by the C1 stimulus was monitored physiologically. Following conditioning, subjects showed differential arousal responses to the stimuli (i.e., C1 produced significantly greater arousal than C3, because C1 predicted the presentation of a sexual film clip and C3 did not). More importantly, these respondently conditioned sexual arousal functions spontaneously transformed the functions of the A1 and A3 stimuli, in the absence of any further respondent conditioning or reinforcement. Specifically, five of seven subjects showing significantly greater arousal to C1 over C3 also showed a significant arousal response differential to A1 over A3. This effect can only be explained in terms of the derived relations between the C and A stimuli, as neither stimulus had any direct association with the sexual film clips (i.e., A1 is equivalent to C1 which predicts a sexual film clip). Based on these findings, the authors suggested that derived relations among events (e.g., clothing, aromas, tactile sensations) might be used to account for the arousal many paraphiliacs show in response to inanimate objects for which there appears to be no direct conditioning or learning history (see also Roche and Barnes, 1998).

Derived relations researchers have also noted the relevance of derived relations to the analysis of sexual attitudes. In one study Grey and Barnes (1996) proposed that an attitude can be conceived as a network of derived and explicitly reinforced stimulus relations according to which the functions of events are transformed (e.g., a negative attitude towards normal heterosexual interactions can be seen as responding in accordance with an equivalence relation between normal opposite-sex adults and descriptive terms such as 'disgusting' see also Moxon, Keenan, and Hine, 1993; Schauss, Chase and Hawkins, 1997; Watt, Keenan, Barnes and Cairns, 1991). In the Grey and Barnes study, participants were provided with the necessary conditional discrimination training to form the following derived equivalence relations; A1–B1–C1, A2–B2–C2, and A3–B3–C3, using nonsense syllables as stimuli. One member from each of two of these relations (i.e., A1 and A2) was then used to clearly label one of two VHS videocassettes. The cassettes contained films of either a sexual/romantic or religious theme. Participants viewed the films and were subsequently required to categorise four further novel cassettes as 'good' or 'bad'. Participants were given no information about these novel cassettes and were not allowed to watch their contents, but each was labelled with one of the nonsense syllables; B1, C1, B2 or C2. Participants categorised the novel cassettes according to the derived equivalence classes, even though they could not have known what the videocassettes contained. More specifically, subjects classified the B1 and C1 cassettes in the same way as the A1 cassette, and the B2 and C2 cassette in the same way as the A2 cassette. In effect, the study demonstrated the transformation of an attitudinal or evaluative response from A1 to other stimuli only indirectly related to it.

While the foregoing procedure may be useful in a laboratory analysis of attitude formation and the assessment of current attitude, it suffers from the limitation that participants become immediately aware of the nature of the task during the critical probe stage. That is, participants can clearly see that what is required of them is to provide the experimenter with the correct associations between sexual/religious stimuli and other stimuli (e.g., nonsense syllables) with which they are associated. Thus, the participant is free to produce responses that do not conform to their true attitude or affective state. However, one group of researchers have developed a categorisation paradigm based on derived stimulus relations that would appear to assess attitudes without necessarily alerting the participant as to the nature of the task, and thereby circumventing problems of experimental demand.

Assessing implicit attitudes using a derived relations paradigm

Watt et al., (1991) used a simple stimulus equivalence paradigm to take advantage of the fact that people in Northern Ireland often respond to each other's names as indicative of religious background. During the study, Northern Irish and English subjects were trained to relate three Catholic names to three nonsense syllables, and subsequently to relate the three nonsense syllables to three traditionally Protestant symbols (i.e., the words, 'Union Jack', 'Orange Order' and 'Lambeg Drum'). During the test for derived relations, subjects were presented with Protestant symbols as samples and Catholic names as comparisons, along with a novel Protestant name as a further comparison choice. All of the English subjects correctly chose the Catholic name (related through equivalence to the Protestant symbols), but 12 of the 19 Northern Irish subjects chose the novel Protestant name in the presence of the Protestant symbols, thereby failing to form equivalence relations. These findings strongly suggest that the social contingencies operating in Northern Ireland were responsible for the non-equivalence responding of the 12 Northern Irish subjects. In other words, only the Northern Irish subjects had been socially trained to respond to Protestant symbols and Catholic names as belonging to socially exclusive categories. The important point here, however, is that the derived relations (i.e., equivalence) paradigm was used successfully to assess the social knowledge or attitudes of the research participants without alerting them as to the nature of the task.

The foregoing research paradigm suggests the basis for a behavioural screening procedure that might be used for the assessment of a wide variety of attitudes and knowledge without the awareness of participants. This development is particularly exciting for those applying behavioural assessment methodologies in the forensic field as it may allow for the identification of knowledge or attitudes held by an individual that might be concealed in overt paper and pencil tests. For example, a paedophile population may wish to hide their unchanged sexual attitude towards children following a therapeutic intervention for fear of legal sanctions. Alternatively, they may wish to fake more acceptable attitudes as part of an assessment procedure that may increase chances of parole or other privileges.

One previous study has attempted to utilise a derived relations paradigm in the development of a screening procedure to identify sexually abused children without their awareness. In that study, McGlinchey, Keenan and Dillenburger (2000) examined the extent to which normal equivalence responding can be disrupted by socially loaded stimuli. A group of children first participated in a standard equivalence training and testing procedure, using nonsense syllables and a range of pictures. The trained relations were as follows; A1→a picture of goggles, B1→a triangle; C1→picture of a girl, arrow pointing to leg; A2→picture of a hat, B2→a triangle; C2→picture of a girl, arrow pointing to neck; X1→picture of braces; and X2→picture of shirt. Subjects were then tested for derived relations among the stimuli (e.g., B1 goes with B2 in a derived equivalence relation because both are related to a triangle). Each child subsequently took part in a dressing-up role-play in which the photographed hat, goggles, braces and shirt were employed. In order to socially load the clothing items and related stimuli, some of the clothes were purposely placed on inappropriate body parts. This was intended to indirectly recombine the relations between the stimuli in the naturalistic manner in which a child might acquire confusing or inappropriate information during an abusive episode. Each child was then re-exposed to the equivalence test. It was expected that equivalence responding (e.g., matching B1 to B2) would be disrupted following the role-play. While results were not easy to interpret,

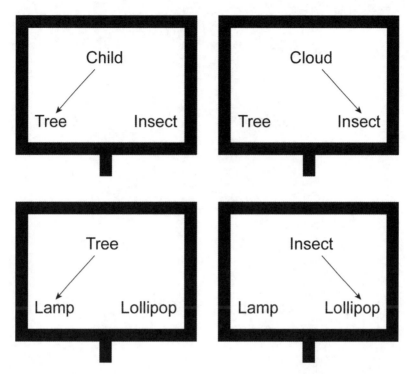

Figure 9.2 Four matching-to-sample tasks used to train two three-member equivalence relations. Solid arrows represent the trained relations.

McGlinchey et al., (2000) did find support for the use of a derived relations-based screening procedure in their data. In effect, the final equivalence test did reveal patterns of responding that were sensitive to the inappropriate information that the children had knowingly or unknowingly acquired during the dress-up role-play.

In on-going research, the current authors have recently applied a derived relations paradigm to the analysis of sexual attitudes of convicted sex offenders towards children. More specifically, our research attempts to identify whether or not a range of convicted sex offenders categorise children as sexual or nonsexual. In one study, we have employed a small number of sex offenders against the adult, contact sex offenders against the child, several offenders convicted of child pornography offences, as well as several male and female control participants from the general population. All participants are presented with a series of conditional discriminations on a computer screen. More specifically, subjects are exposed to the following equivalence training relations; Child→Tree, Tree→Lamp, Cloud→Insect, Insect→Lollipop (see Figure 2). Each task is presented 8 times each in a quasi-random order in blocks of 32 trials. Subjects match the comparison stimuli (e.g., Insect or Tree) to the sample (e.g., Child) by clicking on their choice using the computer mouse and cursor. All choices are followed by corrective feedback delivered by the computer. Subjects are exposed to training until they produce consistent and correct responding across a block of 32 training trials. Under normal testing situations this training can be expected to give rise to the derived equivalence relations; Child→Lamp and Cloud→Lollipop. However, the tasks are loaded with a term relevant to paedophiles and child pornographers. More specifically, the word 'Lollipop' is often used to describe sexually available children and is an appellation widely applied to child pornography picture sets.

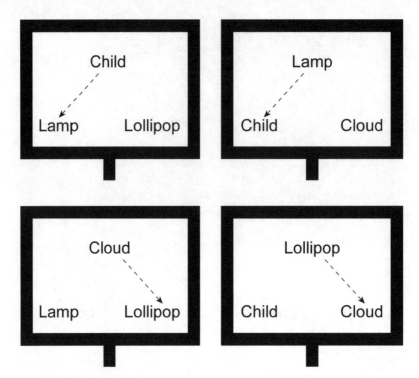

Figure 9.3   Four matching-to-sample tasks used to test for derived equivalence relations. Hashed arrows indicate the expected derived relations.

Thus, individuals with this knowledge should be more likely to mistake the derived equivalence task for a simple choice task involving matching the word Child and Lollipop (even though this not a derived equivalence relation; see Figure 3). In simple terms, we might consider the equivalence test tasks involving the word 'Lollipop' as distracter tasks which will distract specific subject populations from the derivation of the Child→Lamp equivalence relation.

Participants are exposed to a block of 32 testing tasks, in which the four tasks are administered in a quasi-random order 8 times each. The testing proceeds without a break in blocks of 32 trials until the subject consistently produces the correct equivalence-based matching response (i.e., Child→Lamp, Cloud→Lollipop) or until 12 blocks have been administered, whichever comes first. Feedback is not presented on any trial. Preliminary results suggest that those participants who have been convicted of sexual offences against children (both contact offences and pornography offences) require more blocks of testing in order to derive the equivalence-based relations than convicted sex-offenders against the adult. In fact, not a single one of the first four contact offenders against the child has managed to derive the equivalence relations at all within the 12-block limit. Similarly, three of four subjects with child pornography offences have also failed to derive the equivalence relations within 12 blocks of testing. The remaining subject required 10 blocks of testing in order to produce consistently correct equivalence responding across a block of 32 trials. In contrast, of the first four sex offenders against the adult, only one failed to derive the equivalence relations within 12 blocks of testing, whereas the other three all produced perfectly correct and consistent equivalence responding (i.e., Child→Lamp, Cloud→Lollipop) on the very first block of testing. Similarly, of the first four male control subjects from the general population, only one failed to produce the derived equivalence relations within 12 blocks; the remaining three subjects produced the correct relations within 1, 11, and 1 block, respectively.

The foregoing findings are very promising for the derived relations approach to the development of subtle, easily administered screening tests for sex offenders. Of course, these data are preliminary and allow only for a descriptive group analysis at this stage. They can scarcely identify an individual sex offender against the child with any confidence. Nevertheless, the power of the group effect obtained using this methodology suggests that the use of a derived relations paradigm represents a potentially powerful method for the identification of the covert sexual predilections of individuals while simultaneously allowing the researcher to circumvent problems of experimental demand. Moreover, as the procedure is computer-based it does not allow for the possibility of experimenter bias and can be delivered dynamically on-line.

The implicit association test

The research reviewed thus far could be said to be moving towards the development of a diagnostic tool for the analysis of individuals' social history and the identification of current social contingencies controlling behaviour. Interestingly, this parallels recent developments in attitude measurement in mainstream social psychology. Specifically, the Implicit Association Test (IAT; Greenwald, McGhee and Schwartz, 1998) was designed to study implicit attitudes that may be beneath awareness. The IAT is said to measure hidden prejudices regarding race, age and gender, etc., by recording the speed with which subjects associate words and images in a format not unlike a matching-to sample preparation described thus far. Specifically, a subject responds to a series of items that can be classified into four categories; usually two representing a concept, such as flowers and insects, and two representing an attribute, such as pleasant and unpleasant. Subjects are asked to respond rapidly with a right-hand key press to items representing one concept and one attribute (e.g., insects and pleasant), and with a left-hand key press to items from the remaining two categories (e.g., flowers and unpleasant). Subjects then perform a second task in which the requirements are switched (e.g., such that flowers and pleasant share a response and insects and unpleasant share a response). The IAT records the latencies and accuracies of responses to these two tasks. These measures are interpreted in terms of association strengths by assuming that subjects respond more rapidly when the concept and attribute sharing the same response are pre-experimentally strongly associated (e.g., flowers and pleasant) than when they are weakly associated (e.g., insects and pleasant).

Greenwald et al. (1998) suggested the following thought experiment to illustrate the IAT procedure. Imagine an experiment in which a series of male and female faces are shown, and to which the subject must respond as rapidly as possible by saying 'hello' if the face is male and 'goodbye' if it is female. Now imagine a second task in which the subject is shown a series of male and female names, to which they must respond rapidly with 'hello' for male names and 'goodbye' for female names. The faces and names are unambiguously male or female and so the tasks are relatively easy. However, now imagine that the subject is asked to perform both of these discriminations alternately. That is, a series of alternating faces and names would be shown, and the subject must respond 'hello' if the face or name is male and 'goodbye' if the face or name is female. This task is somewhat more difficult, but not as difficult as one remaining task type. Specifically, a small variation of the foregoing task is then administered in which the first component is the same as before (e.g., 'hello' to male faces, 'goodbye' to female faces) but the second component is reversed. That is, subjects are now required to respond 'goodbye' for male names, 'hello' for female names. While these two latter task types are on their own relatively easy, when all four tasks are combined (i.e., 'hello' to male face or female name and 'goodbye' to female face or male name), the resultant task is extremely difficult. Subjects make more errors on these latter task types and in an attempt to reduce errors subjects respond considerably more slowly. Greenwald and colleagues assert that the expected difficulty of the experiment with the reversed second discrimination follows from the likely existence of strong pre-experimental associations of male names with male faces and female names with female faces. The attempt to map the same two responses ('hello' and 'goodbye') in opposite ways onto the two gender opposites is resisted by well-established associations that link the face and name domains.

Greenwald et al. (1998) have used the IAT to detect evaluative differences (e.g., flower versus insect) expected individual differences in evaluative associations (Japanese and pleasant versus Korean and pleasant for Japanese versus Korean subjects) and consciously 'repressed' evaluative differences (Black and pleasant versus White and pleasant for self-described unprejudiced White subjects).

One significant problem with the IAT, however, is its conceptual foundation on the idea of implicit attitudes or association strength. Greenwald has yet to provide an operational definition of these terms. More specifically, it is important to distinguish between attitudes or associations that are implicit in the individual's psyche and those that are implicit in the verbal practices of a community. Several researchers have responded to this and other problems with the conceptualisation of the test (e.g., De Houwer, 2001; De Jong, van der Hout, Rietbroek and Huiijding, 2003; Fazio and Olson, 2003; Karpinski and Hilton, 2001; Mierke and Klauer, 2003; Olson and Fazio, 2003; Sherman, Rose, Koch, Presson and Chassin, 2003). Given these considerations and our own behavioural orientation toward attitude measurement, we will now outline an explicitly behavioural approach that provides a new conceptual framework for the analysis of the IAT effect and the measurement of implicit attitudes.

A behavioural model

Stimulus equivalence research may reveal some clues as to the core processes involved in IAT performances. For instance, researchers have shown that when a response function is explicitly established for one stimulus that participates in an equivalence relation, that function often spontaneously transfers to the remaining class members (e.g., Roche and Barnes, 1997). Consider for instance, an individual who salivates when they hear the word 'chocolate'. Now let's suppose that we tell this individual that the Irish word for chocolate is 'Seacláid' (i.e., the two words are equivalent). We can expect that the individual will now spontaneously salivate whenever they hear the word 'Seacláid', even though it has never been associated directly with actual chocolate. This well-established derived transformation of functions effect has exciting implications for a behaviour-analytic understanding of some of the most important properties of human language, in particular novelty and generativity. Indeed, equivalence classes parallel verbal classes in many ways. For example, consider the words 'White', 'Pure' and 'Clean', that participate in an equivalence relation with one another (i.e., they often mean the same thing). When a child has been taught the meaning of 'White' (i.e., spotless, pure, clean, etc.), the child is likely to respond in the same way to the words 'Pure' and 'Clean' without further training and to use them appropriately in the place of 'White' without reinforcement. Indeed, it would likely be impossible to explicitly teach a child every possible meaning or context usage of every single word in the vernacular. Thus, stimulus equivalence and the derived transformation of functions constitute a core process in the formation and development of verbal classes and have been used to explain rapid language acquisition in children and what is widely known as the language explosion (Barnes-Holmes, Barnes-Holmes, Roche, Healy, Lyddy, Cullinan and Hayes, 2001).

Given the foregoing, the authors have begun to construct a functional-analytic model of the IAT in which its effects are construed in terms of subjects' fluency with the relevant verbal categories and their degree of experience at juxtaposing members of those verbal categories. For instance, an experienced zoologist may have sufficient knowledge of both plants and insects that they are aware of many pleasant and unpleasant examples of both. Such an individual will posses a level of verbal skill in these domains that will allow him or her to juxtapose the unpleasant/pleasant and insect/flower classes with equal speed and accuracy (e.g., the term 'cockroach' can comfortably be associated with either the word 'filth' or 'amazing'). However, an individual displaying a phobic fear of insects will likely find it very difficult to classify insects in any other way than a negative one (e.g., the word cockroach is easily associated with 'filth' but not with 'amazing'). A test such as the IAT, that assesses categorisations of this kind may be sensitive to subjects' fluency and skill at various verbal categorisations, and may therefore be used as an indicator of behavioural dispositions (e.g., phobia).

Interestingly, recent research conducted in the field of social cognition has begun to suggest an environmental association interpretation of the IAT in which scores reflect the word associations a person has been exposed to in his or her social environment, rather than the extent to which the person endorses those evaluative associations (Karpinski and Hilton, 2001). In addition, other researchers have begun to realise that subjects' experience with the use of words employed in an IAT test can reduce the IAT effect itself (see McFarland and Crouch, 2002; Ottaway, Hayden and Oakes, 2001; but see also Dasgupta, Greenwald and Banaji, 2003; Gawronski, 2002). Thus, the Relational Frame approach construes the IAT as a measure of an individual's verbal practices that may or may not reflect personal attitudes or affective states and dispositions, per se. From this perspective, the IAT measures verbal practices and verbal categorisations in vivo, rather than affective evaluations per se. By moving the core IAT processes from the unconscious of the individual to their history of verbal and social interaction, the Relational Frame conceptualisation renders the implicit explicit and opens the way for a functional-analytic empirical investigation of the IAT effect as a potential screening device.

From the behavioural perspective outlined here, the IAT can be said to measure subjects' inability to juxtapose the members of specific verbal equivalence classes that are mutually exclusive, and to easily respond in the same way to common members of established verbal classes. The Relational Frame model can be described technically in terms of a series of equivalence relations, the functions of a limited number of participating stimuli, and a categorisation test that requires subjects to produce the same operant response when presented with members of mutually exclusive classes. The model is depicted in Figure 4.

This model was first examined empirically by Roche, Ruiz and Hand (2003). Those authors trained subjects to form four separate three-member equivalence relations using 12 nonsense syllables as stimuli. In the interest of clarity, these nonsense syllables will be referred to using alphanumerics. The four trained and tested classes were; A1–B1–C1, D1–E1–F1, A2–B2–C2 and D2–E2–F2. Subjects were then exposed to a matching-to-sample procedure whereby the classes were linked together to form two superordinate 6-member equivalence relations (i.e., A1–B1–C1–D1–E1–F1 and A2–B2–C2–D2–E2–F2). Specifically, subjects were trained to match C1 with D1 and C2 with D2 in a conditional discrimination format. Colour functions were then established for one member from each of the four

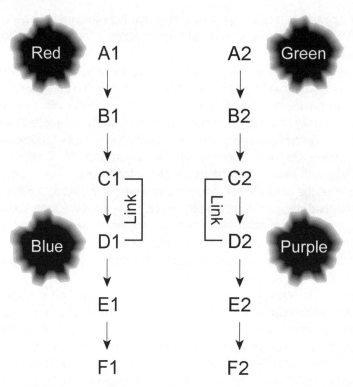

Figure 9.4 A behavioural model of the Implicit Association Test in terms of derived equivalence relations and the transformation of functions effect.

equivalence classes. More specifically, using a respondent conditioning procedure, a picture of a red blob was paired with presentations of A1 on a computer screen. Similarly, D1, A2 and D2 were associated with blue, green and purple blobs, respectively. The transformation of functions effect ensured that subjects spontaneously associated the colours with all other members of the relevant three-member equivalence class established at the outset. For instance, during a test phase, subjects spontaneously matched C1 with a red blob and F2 with a purple blob, without instruction, feedback or reinforcement. In effect, there were two colours associated with each six-member superordinate class; red and blue for A1–B1–C1–D1–E1–F1 and green and purple for A2–B2–C2–D2–E2–F2 (see Figure 4). Thus, the experimenters had succeeded in establishing two functional stimulus classes, based on colour. Finally, subjects were exposed to an IAT-type test during which they were required to respond rapidly with a left or right-hand key press to each of a series of nonsense syllables from the established equivalence relations. For example, on one trial C1 might appear on the screen, along with the instructions; 'Press left for red or blue' and 'Press right for green or purple' (see Figure 5). Left presses were made by pressing the Z key on a computer keyboard, whereas right presses were made by pressing the M key. Tasks of this kind are described as within-class tasks, as they require subjects to respond to the same key for stimuli from the same superordinate equivalence relation (e.g., red and blue). These tasks are relatively easy because the subject need only remember the members of two superordinate classes and respond to the left for all instances of one, and to the right for all instances of the other. The block of within-class tasks consisted of four trial-types. Specifically, given the foregoing response instructions, subjects were presented with one of the four

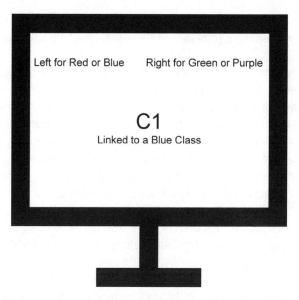

Figure 9.5 A sample 'within-class' task used to test a behavioural model of the IAT.

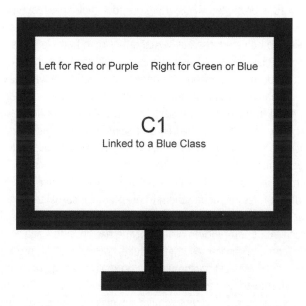

Figure 9.6 A sample 'across-class' task used to test a behavioural model of the IAT.

stimuli; C1, F1, C2 or F2 on any given trial. Each trial was presented to the subject 20 times in a quasi-random order until the subject had been exposed to 80 within-class trial-types.

On another block of testing, subjects were exposed to 80 across-class tasks (see Figure 6). These tasks required subjects to produce the same operant response (e.g., left key press) to members of mutually exclusive superordinate equivalence classes. Specifically, on all trials subjects were presented with the instructions; 'Press left for red or purple' and 'Press right for green or blue', and presented with one of the stimuli C1, F1, C2 or F2. Subjects were required to respond by pressing either the Z (left) or M (right) key. This and ongoing current research (Ruiz, Roche and Florio, 2004) is showing that subjects tend to respond more accurately on the within-class tasks compared to the across-class tasks.

These findings suggest that the Relational Frame model of the IAT does explain the core processes involved in the IAT effect and may help us go some way toward building a functional-analytic method for the analysis of implicit attitudes and dispositions without the need for recourse to mentalistic or other ill-defined terms (e.g., attitudinal bias). Using this model as part of a behavioural conceptual framework, the current authors have embarked on a preliminary investigation of the utility of an IAT-type test in distinguishing between sex-offender and control populations. If successful, the development of such methods may be of enormous potential benefit to those requiring easy-to use, reliable and powerful methods for the assessment of sex offenders both before and after therapeutic intervention.

In our ongoing research we administer an IAT-type test, as described in the previous section, to individuals from a range of populations. The test is designed to assess subjects' fluency in associating terms related to sexuality with images of children as compared to images of adults. More specifically, on one block of tasks subjects are presented with rules that instruct them to press left for sexual terms and images of children and right for horrible words and images of adults (see Figure 7). On any given trial a cartoon image of a child, a cartoon of an adult, a sexually explicit word, or a nonsexual disgusting word is presented. Thus, there are four trial-types, each presented 20 times in a quasi-random order. For sex offenders against children these tasks are class-consistent. That is, children are already likely to be categorised as sexual rather than horrible. Thus, for this group these tasks are defined as within-class tasks and should pose little difficulty for many or most sex offenders against children. For a random sample from the general population, however, producing the same operant response for sexual terms and images of children is likely to represent a categorisation conflict. That is, such a task requires the non-deviant individual to respond in the same way to two normally mutually exclusive classes (i.e., children and sex). Thus, we should expect these 'normal' individuals to find this task more difficult and to make more errors across a block of trials than will a child sex offender population.

As is traditional with the IAT format, the rules are changed for a further block of trials. Specifically, subjects are presented with rules instructing them to press left for sexual terms and images of adults, and to press right for horrible words and images of children. The same stimulus types are again presented 20 times each in a quasi-random order. For the sex offenders against children these tasks pose a categorisation conflict, insofar as they require the subject to produce distinct operant responses (i.e., left and right presses) to stimuli that normally go together (i.e., sex and children). Thus, these tasks are referred to as across-class tasks. However, for the general population, these tasks should be relatively easy, insofar as they require subjects to produce distinct operant responses to stimuli that are normally categorised as mutually exclusive (i.e., sex and children).

Preliminary data gathered from the current authors' research within the Irish penal system do suggest that the IAT may have the potential to distinguish sex-offender groups from the general population. Table 1 illustrates the number of correct responses that our initial subjects have made on the within-class and across-class task blocks. Three groups of subjects are considered here; contact sex offenders against children, Internet offenders (convicted of child pornography possession or distribution), and a random sample of males and females from the general population. Table 1 shows that both child sex offender groups, on average, make more correct responses on within-class tasks (i.e., child images and sexual terms require the same operant response). More specifically, of the first

Figure 9.7   Sample IAT tasks used in a potential screening test for sex-offenders against children. This group should find the top task-type more difficult than the bottom task-type. This difference should be reflected in reaction times and total number correct across a block of each.

four contact offenders against children examined, only one produced more correct responses on the across-class tasks. Similarly, of the first four Internet offenders examined, three of the four produced more correct responses on within-class tasks compared to across-class tasks. In contrast, however, of the first two males and two females assessed from the general population, all four produced more correct responses to the across-class tasks than to the within-class tasks, indicating less fluency at associating children with sex than the child sex-offender population.

Of course, a greater number of subjects are required to more fully assess the utility of the IAT and its variants as a screening tool for sex offenders against children. However, such work is slow,

Table 9.1 Total correct responses out of 80 within-class and 80 across-class tasks for contact offenders against the child ((OC), internet offenders (IO) and control subjects (Male and Female)

Subject code	Within-class (out of 80)	Across-class (out of 80)
Contact offenders against children		
OC 1	55	56
OC 2	60	50
OC 3	62	53
OC 4	43	40
Mean	55	49.75
Internet offenders		
IO 1	40	33
IO 2	49	64
IO 3	43	37
IO 4	64	48
Mean	49	45.5
Control Subjects		
Male 1	75	78
Male 2	56	57
Female 1	48	66
Female 2	75	78
Mean	63.5	69.75

laborious and politically and ethically sensitive. A great deal of co-operation is required from the state, from prisons, from probation services and from the participants themselves in order for this work to be completed. In addition, the number of Internet offenders available for research of this kind is extremely limited. Nevertheless, preliminary results are promising insofar as they suggest that sex offenders against children may indeed categorise children in a unique way and that these categorisation histories can be detected using an IAT-type test. Given the subtlety of the test format (i.e., the subject is not aware what is being tested), and the fact that test outcomes cannot be controlled or 'faked' by subjects (see Kim, 2003), it should have great potential benefit to those interested in assessing the sexual tendencies of offenders both before and after rehabilitation.

Conclusion

It is important to remember that any IAT or derived relations test is only as effective as the stimulus words chosen by the researchers. For instance, for the IAT, word sets must be chosen with great care so that responses are not ambiguous on any one trial. Moreover, the word sets must represent an array of words categorised in distinctly different ways by different social groups. Only systematic research across a range of offenders, using different arrays of stimulus words, will reveal the optimal word set for IAT research aimed at developing screening procedures for sex offenders.

Another important consideration is that the performances of subjects from different populations cannot be readily compared. More specifically, intellectual differences between offenders of different types and the general population may greatly influence subjects' performances on an IAT (see McFarland and Crouch, 2002). Nevertheless, subjects' own performances on within-class and across-class tasks can be compared to reveal a fluency or lack of fluency in associating various terms, images and concepts. With these considerations in mind researchers are already beginning to use the IAT in the clinical setting for psychological assessment (Palfai and Ostafin, 2003; see also De Houwer, 2002).

Even within groups of sex offenders there is enormous variation in sources of motivation and perhaps even in the typology of the offending behaviour. As most clinicians are aware, the Diagnostic and Statistical Manual (DSM-IV; American Psychiatric Association, 1994) provides diagnostic criteria for sex offenders, but these serve only as guides for clinical judgments. Definitions of paraphilia in the DSM-IV also pose the problem that they do not clearly specify whether sexual interest in children is clinically relevant when it involves sexual fantasies, sexual urges, or overt sexual contact. To add further confusion, recent qualitative findings suggest that some users of child pornography are not specifically interested in children, but may have interest in children only as part of some other overarching sexual proclivity (see Quayle and Taylor, 2002). For these reasons, we should not expect to find perfect consistency in the IAT performances of offenders of any one type. It may be, for instance, that users of child pornography can be meaningfully differentiated as a sex offender population in their own right, with their own unique behavioural etiologies, trajectories of clinical behaviour and necessary treatments. Or perhaps it will turn out that sex offenders in general are also more likely to categorise children as sexual than are members of the general population, leading to even more homogenous definitions of paraphilia. By examining the behavioural categorisations of various populations of sex offenders with regard to ranges of sexual stimuli and concepts, using the types of subtle screening procedures suggested here, it is hoped that we will at least move closer to providing answers to these questions.

References

Barnes, D. (1994) Stimulus Equivalence and Relational Frame Theory. *The Psychological Record*. 44, 91–124.

Barnes-Holmes, D. and Barnes-Holmes, Y. (2000) Explaining Complex Behavior: Two Perspectives on the Concept of Generalized Operant Classes. *The Psychological Record*. 50, 251–66.

Barnes-Holmes, Y. et al. (2001) Psychological Development, in Hayes, S.C., Barnes-Holmes, D. and Roche, B. (Eds.) *Relational Frame Theory: A Post-Skinnerian Account of Human Language and Cognition*. New York: Plenum Press.

Dasgupta, N., Greenwald, A.G. and Banaji, M.R. (2003) The First Ontological Challenge to the IAT: Attitude or Mere Familiarity? *Psychological Inquiry*. 14, 238–43.

De Houwer, J. (2001) A Structural and Process Analysis of the Implicit Association Test. *Journal of Experimental Social Psychology*. 37, 443–51.

De Houwer, J. (2002) The Implicit Association Test as a Tool for Studying Dysfunctional Associations in Psychopathology: Strengths and Limitations. *Journal of Behavior Therapy and Experimental Psychiatry*. 33, 115–223.

De Jong, P., van den Hout, M.A., Rietbroek, H. and Huijding, J. (2003) Dissociations between Implicit and Explicit Attitudes Toward Phobic Stimuli. *Cognition and Emotion*. 17, 521–45.

Fazio, R.H. and Olson, M.A. (2003) Implicit Measures in Social Cognition Research: Their Meaning and Uses. *Annual Review of Psychology*. 54, 297–327.

Fields, L., Adams, B.J., Verhave, T. and Newman, S. (1990) The Effects of Modality on the Formation of Equivalence Classes. *Journal of the Experimental Analysis of Behavior*. 53, 345–58.

Gawronski, B. (2002) What does the Implicit Association Test Measure? A Test of the Convergent and Discriminant Validity of Prejudice-related IATs. *Experimental Psychology*. 49, 171–80.

Greenwald, A.G., McGhee, D.E. and Schwartz, J.L. (1998) Measuring Individual Differences in Implicit Cognition: The Implicit Association Test. *Journal of Personality and Social Psychology*. 74, 1464–80.

Grey, I., and Barnes, D. (1996) Stimulus Equivalence and Attitudes. *The Psychological Record*. 46, 243–70.

Hayes, S.C. and Blackledge, J.T. (2001) Language and Cognition: Constructing an Alternative Account within the Behavioral Tradition, in Hayes, S.C., Barnes-Holmes, D. and Roche, B. (Eds.) *Relational Frame Theory: A Post-Skinnerian Account of Human Language and Cognition*. New York: Plenum Press.

Hayes, S.C., Gifford, E.V. and Ruckstuhl, Jr., L.E. (1996) Relational Frame Theory and Executive Function, in Lyon, G.R. and Krasnegor, N.A. (Eds.) *Attention, Memory and Executive Function*. Baltimore: Brookes.

Hayes, S.C., Barnes-Holmes, D. and Roche, B. (Eds.) (2001). *Relational Frame Theory: A Post-Skinnerian Analysis of Human Language and Cognition*. New York: Plenum Press.

Karpsinki, A. and Hilton, J.L. (2004) Attitudes and the Implicit Association Test. *Journal of Personality and Social Psychology*. 81, 774–88.

Kim, D. (2003) Voluntary Controllability of the Implicit Association Test (IAT). *Social Psychology Quarterly*. 66, 83–96.

Lipkens, G., Hayes, S.C. and Hayes, L.J. (1993) Longitudinal Study of Derived Stimulus Relations in an Infant. *Journal of Experimental Child Psychology*. 56, 201–39.

McFarland, S.G. and Crouch, Z. (2002) A Cognitive Skill Confound on the Implicit Association Test. *Social Cognition*. 20, 483–510.

McGlinchey, A., Keenan, M. and Dillenburger, K. (2000) Outline for the Development of a Screening Procedure for Children who Have Been Sexually Abused. *Research on Social Work Practice*. 10, 721–47.

Mierke, J. and Klauer, K.C. (2003) Method-specific Variance in the Implicit Association Test. *Journal of Personality and Social Psychology*. 85, 1180–92.

Moxon, P.D., Keenan, M. and Hine, L. (1993). Gender-role Stereotyping and Stimulus Equivalence. *The Psychological Record*. 43, 381–94.

Olson, M.A. and Fazio, R.H. (2003) Relations between Implicit Measures of Prejudice: What are we Measuring? *Psychological Science*. 14, 636–39.

Ottaway, S.A., Hayden, D.C. and Oakes, M.A. (2001) Implicit Attitudes and Racism: Effects of Word Familiarity and Frequency on the Implicit Association Test. *Social Cognition*. 19, 97–144.

Palfai, T.P. and Ostafin, B.D. (2003) Alcohol-related Motivational Tendencies in Hazardous Drinkers: Assessing Implicit Response Tendencies using the Modified IAT. *Behavior Research and Therapy*. 41, 1149–62.

Quayle, E. and Taylor, M. (2002) Child Pornography and the Internet: Perpetrating a Cycle of Abuse. *Deviant Behavior*. 23, 331–62.

Roche, B. and Barnes, D. (1997) A Transformation of Respondently Conditioned Function in Accordance with Arbitrarily Applicable Relations. *Journal of the Experimental Analysis of Behavior*. 67, 275–301.

Roche, B. and Barnes, D. (1998) The Experimental Analysis of Human Sexual Arousal: Some Recent Developments. *The Behavior Analyst*. 21, 37–52.

Roche, B., Ruiz, M. and Hand, K. (2003) *An Experimental Analysis of Social Discrimination using Relational Frame Theory*. Paper presented at the Annual Conference of the Association for Behavior Analysis, San Francisco, May 23–27.

Ruiz, M.R., Roche, B. and Florio, A. (2004) *Implicit Associations: Empirical Analysis of Explicit Learning Histories*. Paper presented at the Annual Conference of the Association for Behavior Analysis, Boston, May 25–30.

Schauss, S.L., Chase, P.N. and Hawkins, R.P. (1997) Environment-behavior Relations, Behavior Therapy and the Process of Persuasion and Attitude Change. *Journal of Behavior Therapy and Experimental Psychiatry*. 28, 31–40.

Sherman, S.J., Rose, J.S., Koch, K., Presson, C.C. and Chassin, L. (2003) Implicit and Explicit Attitudes towards Cigarette Smoking: The Effects of Context and Motivation. *Journal of Social and Clinical Psychology*. 22, 13–39.

Sidman, M. (1971) Reading and Auditory-visual Equivalences. *Journal of Speech and Hearing Research*. 14, 5–13.

Sidman, M. (1986) Functional Analysis of Emergent Verbal Classes, in Thompson, T. and Zeiler, M.E. (Eds.) *Analysis and Integration of Behavioral Units*. Hillsdale, NJ: Laurence Erlbaum Associates.

Watt, A., Keenan, M., Barnes, D. and Cairns, E. (1991) Social Categorization and Stimulus Equivalence. *The Psychological Record*. 41, 33–50.

Chapter 10

The Internet as a Therapeutic Medium?

Ethel Quayle

Clearly, treatment will never eliminate crime, but if effective work with offenders can reduce the human and financial costs of victimization then the effort is surely worthwhile. (Hollin, 1999)

The Internet and sexuality

From the beginning, the Internet has been associated with sexuality and sexual behaviour in all its manifestations. More than any other medium it has provided a window through which we can see, writ large, sexual fantasies and relationships through text and images. Some 20 per cent of Internet users engage in some form of online sexual activity (OSA), as estimated by Cooper and Griffin-Shelley (2002: 3), that involves sexuality 'for purposes of recreation, entertainment, exploration, support, education, commerce, efforts to attain and secure sexual or romantic partners and so on'. Cybersex is seen as one category of OSA whereby the individual uses the medium of the Internet to engage in sexually gratifying activities such as looking at or exchanging sexual images, participating in sexual chat with others and engaging in online sexual activity through fantasy sharing and masturbation. Goodrum and Spink (2001) estimated that 25 of the most frequently occurring terms submitted to the Excite commercial Web search engine were clearly sexually related. Such sexually related web searching seemed to take longer than other types of information seeking on the Web and was described as using a very limited vocabulary (Spink et al., 2004). These authors qualitatively analysed the logs of 1,025,910 Alta Vista and All the Web user queries from 2001 and found that there was a higher percentage of queries for sexual material from European users than others, but that many queries which started with a search for sexual information eventually converted into non-sexual searches. In a survey of 7,037 respondents, Cooper et al., (2002a) indicated that the typical adult who engages in OSA is married, male, professional and in their early 30s. They also appeared to be more experienced Internet users and gave 'distraction' as the most common reason for their engagement. Within their sample, three-quarters of OSA users reported that they had masturbated when viewing online sexually explicit materials or activities, and men were more likely to masturbate at that time than later.

Such Internet use for sexual purposes may become problematic for some people when it impacts negatively on offline relationships with family and friends, financially on the individual, or where the activity becomes illegal because of the content of the material accessed within a given jurisdiction. Problems may also relate to the degree of the activity, which for some may take on a compulsive quality that may indicate a loss of personal control. The context of the behaviour may also be problematic. Most people access the Internet either at home or in the workplace. Young and Case (2004) have described how Internet activity, which included within their sample accessing pornography (42 per cent), online chatting (13 per cent), and gaming (12 per cent), were the leading causes of disciplinary action or termination of employment. A challenge to such disciplinary action has come in the form of allegations of Internet addiction as a disability (Young and Case, 2004), the symptoms of which are described as:

- Preoccupation with the Internet.
- Increased anxiety when offline.
- Hiding or lying about the extent of online use.
- Impairment to real-life functioning.

Such problematic online behaviour (variously described as addictive or pathological) includes dependence, obsessive thoughts, tolerance, diminished impulse control, inability to cease and withdrawal. This clearly overlaps with the domain of normal media consumption where the dominant paradigms relate to uses and gratifications (Song et al., 2004). Rotunda et al., (2003: 488) have hypothesised that feelings of boredom may push people towards maladaptive behaviours and that the Internet may lead to impairment in some people because, similar to other potentially addictive behaviours, it provides 'an easily accessible and individually tailored escape from boredom'. These authors used an Internet user survey to examine Internet use and misuse and found that people with a greater tendency to become bored experience more negative consequences related to Internet use and higher levels of absorption and over involvement. In a study of OSA in students, seeking sexual information and masturbating online were the two activities most strongly associated with dissatisfaction in people's offline lives. (Boies et al., 2004)

Cooper et al., (2002b) have expressed concern that for some people OSA can escalate, even for those who had not previously experienced any difficulties. These authors felt that for people with a prior history of mental health or sexual problems, the Internet is likely to reinforce and further increase these problems. It is also inevitable that concern is already being expressed that mobile and wireless computing will make detecting incidents of occupational abuse even more difficult. Research from Japan has suggested that over 40 per cent of Japanese have access to the Internet via mobile phones and that this has grown more rapidly than PC Internet access (Ishi, 2003).

That people are fascinated by sexual material is not new, nor is it confined to the Internet. Other authors have traced the history of pornography and its use, noting a rise in availability with the advent of photography (Edwards, 1994). However, the Internet has brought with it both a quantity and variety of materials such as has never been seen before (Taylor and Quayle, 2003). For those willing to search, any sexual predilections can be catered for. Much of this material may be offensive to some, but it is not necessarily illegal. Along with availability have come ease of access and an assumed level of anonymity, which Cooper and Griffin-Shelley (2002) have referred to as the Triple A Engine. It is almost as though because much online sexual activity takes place in peoples' homes an assumption is made (largely false) that it is totally private and untraceable. As Cooper et al., (2002b) have indicated, this is the first time in history that sexually explicit material is easily accessible via the Internet to any one with a computer modem 24 hours a day and 365 days a year. In an earlier study King (1999) reviewed the number of messages posted to various Usenet pornography newsgroups and this demonstrated that the more popular ones were those that were devoted to types of pornography not available in adult bookstores in the United States. 'Teen pornography, child pornography, hard core bondage, and bizarre fetishes are amongst the largest groups. This reflects the fact that part of the attraction to internet pornography is the ability to view pictures that are not available from traditional print sources' (p. 189).

That there is an increase in the availability of such images and text is not in question. What is of concern, however, is the effect of such availability on both online and offline sexual behaviour. In the past, research has tended to focus on the relationship between viewing pornographic images and the commission of sexually violent or coercive acts (e.g. Seto et al., 2001). While it has been impossible to establish any causal relationship between the two, it has been implied that for some, viewing such images increases the likelihood of the commission of a contact offence. However, the Internet does not function simply as a provider of sexual materials, in the same way that a sex shop might. It is also a forum for potential interaction with a limitless number of like minded others. Such interaction may take place at a number of levels from passive consumer to active participant (Taylor and Quayle, in press), but in some way each individual is part of an online community.

In the context of OSA, people may access material and individuals on the Internet for a number of reasons. They may be curious, they may feel isolated within the confines of their existing relationships, they may be distressed and seeking solace or they may see the Internet as a way of fulfilling sexual needs that in the offline world are illegal if expressed. 'There are a wide variety of sexually explicit possibilities available via the Internet. Consequently, an individual struggling with paraphilic behaviours may be easily caught up in the Web. In some instances, persons with paraphilias who are involved in illegal sexual activities over the Internet have a prior criminal history. On the other hand, clinicians may encounter a number of cases where the presence of the Internet itself seems to have been the primary impetus for such contact' (Galbreath et al., 2002). This forces us to contend with the possibility that exposure to available 'paraphilic' material on the Internet may in fact result in the emergence of fantasies, feelings and behaviours that would otherwise have remained dormant (Quayle et al., 2000). Galbreath et al., (2002) have questioned the homogeneity of people who engage in OSA which is illegal and suggested that many of the individuals that they have encountered are conflicted and struggling people whose sexual behaviours are driven more by intense yearnings, than by a lack of conscience or decency. Barak and Fisher (2002) have similarly contended that the increasing accessibility and affordability of the Internet will likely enlarge the number of people who will be classified as sex offenders and the range and reach of sexual offences. They concluded that this might result in cyberspace becoming 'a relatively congenial environment for wrong-doing'. It may also be the case that the Internet, and the availability of illegal materials, has acted for some as a catalyst to wrongdoing and a destructive element in their lives.

Several authors have suggested that OSA, cybersex and the use of illegal sexual materials serve many functions for the individual (Quayle and Taylor, 2002), which may include components of 'escape and self-medication' (Delmonico et al., 2002: 149). Cooper et al., (1999) had earlier suggested that two functions may be:

1. Stress reactive – where Internet sex is used as a way to relieve high levels of stress.
2. Depressive subtypes – where Internet sex functions as an escape from depression.

Cooper et al., (2001) has added a third subtype to this:

3. Fantasy – an escape from the daily routine of life into a world of fiction and fantasy that fulfils one's sexual desires.

More recent research by Cooper et al., (2004) examined the responses of 384 men who were identified through a survey on the MSNBC web site as having online sexual problems. Two broad behaviour patterns were manifested by men identified as having problems and these were: men who used the Internet to further their real-time sex lives and those who used the Internet as a substitute for their real-time sex lives. The former may not be so problematic as they may have adaptive reasons for doing so, such as education or to purchase sex materials.

In the context of the use of illegal images of children, Quayle et al., (in press) have examined the role of emotional avoidance and suggested the likelihood not only that individuals are using the Internet to change or avoid negative mood states, but that the material accessed is highly reinforcing, particularly as access often culminates in masturbation (Quayle and Taylor, 2002). One explanation for this may be seen in the work of Marshall and Marshall (2000) who have looked at affective states and coping behaviour. These authors proposed that when in a state of negative affect, sex offenders are more likely to use sexual behaviours as a means of coping than are non-offenders. Sex becomes a way of resolving non-sexual problems, which Howells et al., (2004) have suggested is reinforced and learned precisely because it is effective in reducing a state of negative affect.

In the context of illegal images of children (usually called child pornography and increasingly child abuse images (Quayle, 2004)), there are four broad classes of activities that people engage in that in most jurisdictions are illegal. These include:

- downloading
- trading
- producing
- seduction

At the heart of all such offending are child abuse images (see Taylor and Quayle, 2003, and Quayle, 2004 for more detailed accounts). However, it would be simplistic to argue that all people who access abuse images on the Internet are motivated by exactly the same factors. Internet abuse images also function: as an aid to fantasy and masturbation; as a means of avoiding negative emotional states; as a way of socialising with others and as a form of collecting behaviour (Quayle and Taylor, 2002). This is important in relation to treatment planning as increasingly authors such as Beech et al., (2003) have emphasised the need for functional analysis in the context of offender assessment to determine the underlying motives and functions of the offending behaviour. Functional analysis typically involves obtaining detailed information about the antecedents, the behaviours and the consequences of offending for the individual, which includes such private events as thoughts and feelings (Sturmey, 1996). This may provide the offender with an understanding of the process that lead to the commission of an offence and the choices that the person made at each stage in the process. Functional analysis emphasises the purpose that the behaviour serves for the person and places importance on the part that the environment plays in causing, controlling and maintaining behaviour. Such a functionalist approach de-emphasises the form that the problem takes and shifts attention to the purposes that the behaviour might serve for the individual. This means that behaviours may be topographically similar, but serve different functions. For example, research related to the function of images had suggested that while images served initially as an aid to arousal and masturbation, this function could change over time so that the purpose of the activity became social rather than sexual. This is important as it may guide both assessment and intervention.

Treatment issues

Hollin (1999) has reviewed the components of effective treatment programmes across all offender groups and concluded that:

- The focus should be on criminogenic targets.
- They should be structured.
- There is a strong evidence base for cognitive behavioural therapy (CBT).
- There is a need for a high level of offender responsivity.
- Treatment in the community is more effective.
- There is a need for high integrity, which includes trained staff.

Intervention or treatment approaches to sexual offences are typically within a cognitive behavioural framework. In their review of behavioural and cognitive behavioural approaches to treatment, Marshall and Laws (2003: 110) concluded by saying that, '. . . cognitive behavioural procedures have developed into a comprehensive approach that is widely shared and appears to be effective. The breadth of treatment targets has progressively increased and research has been implemented to evaluate the basis for these expanded targets'. Cognitive-behavioural treatment has emerged as the principal type of treatment used to modify deviant sexual arousal, increase appropriate sexual desires, modify cognitive distortions and improve interpersonal coping skills (Terry and Tallon, 2004). Nicholaichuk and Yates (2002) have described how this treatment approach is based on the premise that 'cognitive and affective processes and behaviour are linked, and that cognitions, affect, and behaviour are mutually influential'. According to Marshall and Barbaree (1990) treatment typically includes targeting the following:

- Deviant sexual behaviour and interests.
- A wide range of social skills and relational deficits.
- Cognitive distortions, which permit the offender to justify, rationalise or minimise the offending behaviour.

As well as attempting to reduce deviant sexual behaviour and interests through techniques such as counter-conditioning, cognitive-behavioural treatment seeks to enhance the offender's interpersonal functioning, through targeting relationship skills, appropriate social interaction and empathy (Marshall et al., 1999). Social problem solving, conversational skills, managing social anxiety, assertiveness, conflict resolution, empathy and intimacy, anger management, self-confidence and the use of mood altering substances are also targeted (Laws and Marshall, 2003). Such intervention is based on the belief that the attitudes of sexual offenders toward their victims will change if they understand how the victim feels, and will inhibit future sexual abuse.

Cognitive restructuring is an integral part of cognitive-behavioural treatment, regardless of the focus of change. As we have already noted, child sex offenders are said to construct internal rationalisations, excuses and cognitive distortions in order to maintain their sexually deviant behaviour. Marshall and Barbaree (1990) have argued that it is important that an offender's cognitive distortions are challenged so that he can comprehend his faulty thinking and recognise its distorted, self-serving nature. The practitioner facilitates this through challenging beliefs and helping to present more socially appropriate and adaptive views. Within this framework, the benefits of accepting such views are identified. Implicit is the assumption that cognitive distortions are a product of an automatic way of processing information about the world and which are amenable to change. It is argued that changing such cognitions will also result in a change in behaviour. Central to this is an assumption that the offender can learn how these cognitive distortions are problematic in achieving a 'good life' (Ward, 2002) and lead the offender to engage in behaviours that make the achievements of such a good life impossible. One of the difficulties of most sex offender treatment programmes is that the practitioner makes the assumption that the offender really shares similar values and these become implicit, but not explicitly stated in any treatment programme. Ward and Brown (2004) have increasingly argued the need to make such values explicit.

Studies on treatment efficacy not only have to consider the changes that take place in the offenders behaviour both during and immediately at the end of treatment, but how treatment has impacted on behaviour over time. This is difficult to assess, as recidivism is invariably going to be based on statistics derived from future convictions. Most studies conducted on treatment efficacy focus on the rate of recidivism among offenders, usually comparing those who have been through treatment with those who have not. In itself, it could be argued that this is problematic as there may be differences amongst those who are offered treatment and those who are not. For example, many treatment programmes will only offer therapy to those who 'admit' their offence. In the UK, the current sentencing structure means that many offenders on short prison sentences are unlikely to be offered access to a sex offender treatment programme. However, given these reservations, in a follow-up study conducted on 89 sex offenders in Ontario, Looman et al., (2000) found that those offenders who participated in treatment had a sexual recidivism rate of 23.6 per cent, whereas those offenders who did not participate in treatment had a sexual recidivism rate of 51.7 per cent. Similarly, when 296 treated and 283 untreated offenders were followed for a six-year period, Nicholaichuk and Yates, (2002) found that convictions for new sexual offences among treated sex offenders were 14.5 per cent versus 33.2 per cent for untreated offenders. Further, during the follow-up period, 48 per cent of treated offenders remained out of prison as compared to 28.3 per cent of untreated offenders.

Time series comparisons of treated offenders and comparison samples also showed that treated offenders re-offended at significantly lower rates after ten years. In reviewing studies pertaining to the efficacy of a particular type of treatment, there is significant evidence that cognitive-behavioural treatment has emerged as the principle type of sex offender treatment targeting deviant arousal, increasing appropriate sexual desires, modifying distorted thinking and improving interpersonal coping skills (Marshall and Barbaree, 1990; Marshall and Eccles, 1996; Marshall and Pithers, 1994; Becker, 1994; Hall, 1995; Abracen and Looman, 2001; Burdon and Gallaher, 2002; Nicholaichuk and Yates, 2002; Craig et al., 2003). Further, Marshall and Anderson (2000) found that cognitive-behavioural treatment programmes that have an internal self-management relapse prevention component appear to be the most successful in reducing recidivism rates. Studies of the effects of treatment completion on recidivism have also supported the effectiveness of treatment (Hall, 1995; Hanson and Bussière, 1998; Hanson et al., 2002). For example, a retrospective study, conducted by McGrath et al., (2003), found that the reduction in the sexual recidivism rate among those offenders who participated in treatment was statistically, as well as clinically, significant. Treatment completers were almost six times less likely to be charged with a new sexual offence than were offenders who refused, dropped out or were terminated from treatment.

In the context of the United Kingdom, the accredited treatment model is adapted from the work of Fisher and Beech (1999) and addresses four key components – denial, offence specific behaviours, social adequacy and relapse prevention skills. Middleton et al., (2004) had suggested that in spite of an absence of research concerning the specific characteristics of offenders who use the Internet in the commission of their offences, early analysis of psychometric testing in a small cohort has suggested evidence that these offenders have similar characteristics to those who commit other forms of sexual offending and present along a similar spectrum of high treatment need through to relative low treatment need. Middleton et al., (2004) also concluded that there may be additional treatment targets which will be determined through individual assessment and these may include the degree to which the offender has exhibited compulsive or obsessive behaviour in pursuing the on-line activity, the importance of community in the offending behaviour, and obsessive collecting activity. Again, Middleton (2004) has emphasised the importance of a specific assessment of the individual and the context in which the behaviour was developed and sustained. He concludes, 'Most human behaviour can be understood as meeting needs for the individual and, in order to be effective, treatment will help the individual to meet these needs in a more appropriate manner.' (p. 110)

Generic CBT programmes effect a measure of control over content and delivery. In the context of people who have used the Internet in the commission of their offence, Middleton (2004) has suggested that central to any therapeutic approach to such offenders should be:

- The recognition of a pattern of behaviour.
- The recognition of negative consequences of the behaviour: on inter-personal relationships, life-balance, work etc.
- The recognition of risk of escalation.
- The recognition that images are scenes of abuse to real victims.

Quayle and Taylor (in press) have suggested that additional offence specific targets may include:

- Fantasy escalation
- Socialisation
- Collecting
- Emotional avoidance

These targets arose out of a qualitative analysis of offender accounts (Quayle and Taylor, 2002) and led to the development of a model of offending behaviour (Quayle and Taylor, 2003).

Working with offenders: The role of self-help

There has been considerable investment of resources in intervention programmes with sex offenders, both in context of prison and community, but as yet there appears to be a mismatch between the availability of resources and those who are seeking help. In addition, outside of the unknown numbers privately seeking psychotherapy, intervention can only target those known to the services through prison and probation and welfare. A recent publication by Stop It Now indicated that 45 per cent of all calls to their telephone help line over a sampled period were made by people concerned about their behaviour and their perceived loss of control (Kemshall et al., 2004). While we may strive to ensure equality in service provision, the reality is that for many individuals the option of seeking help is limited and carries with it the potential penalty of a conviction. Suggestions by people such as Donald Findlater from the Lucy Faithful Foundation (Wheeler, 2003) of an 'amnesty' for Internet offenders, so that they might seek help without the threat of punishment was met by criticism, and yet we know that such a threat effectively debars many people from gaining help.

One alternative approach to intervention might be the provision of self-help materials. This has been described by Cuijpers (1997) as 'the patient receives a standardised treatment method with which he can help himself without major help from the therapist . . . it is necessary that treatment is described in sufficient detail, so that the patient can work it through independently.' Castelnuovo et al., (2003) also emphasised that self-help is characterised by a treatment programme (or part of it) that may be self-administered by patients with or without the therapist's guidance. Four substantial meta-analysis studies (Scogin and McElreath, 1990; Gould and Clum, 1993; Marrs, 1995; and Cuijpers, 1997) indicated that self-help approaches can be effective and that they are most effective for skills deficit training, and the treatment of anxiety, depression and sexual dysfunction. Such studies would suggest that additional therapist input appeared to have no effect on patient outcome above what is obtained by the self-help treatment alone.

What are the potential benefits of self-help approaches? Williams (2001) has suggested that the most obvious would seem to be that:

- Access is facilitated.
- They are cost effective.
- They avoid the stigma of treatment provision (either through a special programme or through mental health services).
- They foster responsibility for self-management, and enhance the sense of control that the person has over their problems.
- They offer the chance to reinforce or consolidate learning, as access to such material can be 'on demand' rather than controlled by the service provider.
- They can help the person to identify early warning signs of relapse and prepare a plan of action to deal with them.

There are equally potential disadvantages:

- Some people may not see this as a valid treatment option.
- The material needs a format and content that is accessible to and understandable by the specific user.
- Such an approach may exclude users from different ethnic and minority groups.
- The materials may be inappropriate for agitated or distressed people.
- It may be perceived that the approach offers a guarantee of cure.
- Drop out rates can be high.

Most studies evaluating self-help approaches have used a CBT format, and we can think of this as an explicitly educational form of psychotherapy, that has a clear underlying structure and theoretical model and focuses clearly on current problems. CBT approaches also adopt a collaborative stance and materials associated with this approach are amongst the group of self-help materials with the strongest evidence for effectiveness (Whitfield and Williams, 2003). Laszlo et al., (1999) have drawn our attention to the fact that cognitive behavioural interventions would be very compatible with a text based medium such as the Internet, as such a therapeutic approach relies heavily on conscious processes and thinking. There are many formats for the delivery of self-help programmes and these can include audiotape; videotape; written materials; interactive computer materials; virtual-reality presentations; interactive touch-tone or voice activated telephone access and Web media.

Internet based help

Over the last few years we have seen a massive increase in the availability of Internet based interventions, seen by many as a modern alternative to self-help manuals (e.g. Andersson and

Carlbring, 2003). The literature on the feasibility and utility of Internet interventions is limited, and as yet there are few outcome study findings. Nonetheless, it seems likely that while Internet interventions will not replace face-to-face care, there is little doubt that they will grow in importance as a powerful component of psychological treatment. (Ritterband et al., 2003)

The Internet combines attributes of mass communication (e.g. broad reach) with attributes of interpersonal communication (e.g. interactivity and rapid individual feedback), (Copeland and Martin, 2004). Internet based interventions also bring with them a high level of convenience and flexibility of use. They are not confined to a specific physical location and are available 24 hours a day. Time constraints are therefore removed in a way that would have been impossible with more traditional forms of therapy delivery. For example, Winzelberg (1997) found that members of an electronic support group for people with eating disorders posted more than half of the messages between 18.00 and 07.00 – a time frame when most consulting rooms would have been closed. There is also a consistency in the application of the therapeutic model as it does not require any input from a 'live' therapist and therefore avoids any bias from different therapeutic inputs. The nature of the medium also means that intervention can be updated centrally, in the light of new knowledge or data, and therefore can be reflexive in meeting the needs of that population. Several studies would support a heightened level of disclosure on the part of clients during assessment, and in this time of cost effectiveness it is a relatively inexpensive way of providing a therapeutic service to large numbers of people.

Such interventions are commonly called 'telehealth' – a tool for health promotion, described by Castelnuovo et al., (2003) as the use of telecommunication and information technology to promote access to health assessment, diagnosis, intervention, consultation, supervision, education and information across distance. Common to all definitions is the geographical distance between the person that provides the service and the user, and the use of telecommunication technologies to facilitate the interaction (Alcañiz et al., 2003). While Cooper and Griffin-Shelley (2002: 7) have cautioned against the unscrupulous use of new technologies, they have also asserted that 'As a communication tool, the Internet offers a means of promoting physical and mental health, especially sexual health, through innovative methods'. Tepper and Owens (2002) have also suggested that the use of the Internet for telehealth approaches provides a unique way of distributing basic sexual health information, education and specific advice for what they saw as a growing population. It is also the case that unique advantages exist in online work such as access for the home-based, geographically isolated, or stigmatised clients who will not, or cannot, access treatment locally (Fenichel et al., 2002).

Internet based psychological interventions can be divided into four categories:

1. self-administered therapy which is purely self-help;
2. predominantly self-help, but where the therapist assesses, provides an initial rationale and teaches how to use the self-help tool;
3. minimal contact therapy; and
4. predominantly therapist administered therapy , but in conjunction with self-help material. (Carlbring and Andersson, 2004).

There are a number of studies examining the effectiveness of CBT administered through the medium of the Internet. For example, Carlbring et al., (2003) have described an Internet self-help programme for the treatment of panic disorder, with minimum therapist contact through email. The subjects in this study showed significant improvement in diary measurements of the frequency of panic attacks, the total intensity of each attack, the total duration of each attack and levels of daily anxiety compared to wait list controls. However, when they compared their results with a group who had been administered applied relaxation, they found that the CBT programme was less effective, leading to the recommendation that more therapist help may be needed. Telehealth programmes have also evolved in the context of management of heart failure (Enneking et al., 2004). This study used a telehealth device to monitor and educate patients with heart failure. Those in the programme demonstrated improvement in self-management, reduced readmission into hospital and length of stay in hospital. In a similar programme, Schofield et al., (2004) examined the use of a telehealth programme with patients with refractory heart failure and demonstrated a reduction in hospitalisations, an increase in loop diuretic dose, a fall in weight and an improvement in patient dyspnoea.

Recent research by Farrell et al., (2004) has examined the role of Web technology for people with serious mental illness. In this study they utilised portal technology whereby the users of a homepage can utilise both the look and the placement of links to specialise content. At the same time, service providers can customise the content to be 'pushed' to the consumer. These authors suggested that with this 'push-pull' system, homepage portals can be designed to meet the individualised needs of the user. It was considered that: 'A computer portal designed to offer a doorway into a world of information about mental health services and community resources offers promise for improving the lives of persons with serious mental illness living in the community' (p. 122). The long term goals of these portals was to improve adherence to treatment plans, medication regimens and increased consumer satisfaction. However, while at the time of publication of the study the portal had been developed, it was not yet available through the Internet because issues related to security, confidentiality and privacy had yet to be addressed.

It is apparent that telehealth approaches are not without their problems, especially for the providers of the service. Some of the difficulties clearly relate to anonymity, both of the service providers and users. Anyone accessing the service has no way of ensuring that the information given is accurate or that any claims about the effectiveness or usefulness of the site can be substantiated. Toll et al., (2003) discussed this issue in relation to Internet based alcohol treatment programmes. These authors felt that brief interventions and self-help materials could easily be adapted to the medium of the Internet, but when they evaluated existing online treatments or interventions they discovered that while many were offered, very few had any basis in clinical or empirical research. In addition, for many users it was difficult to even know the source or provenance of the information. The authors felt that this was a cause for concern, particularly as many people with alcohol related problems, as with sexual difficulties, might be reluctant to seek more conventional help because of the stigma attached to both the problem and the intervention. There are equally ethical difficulties for the service provider. 'Consider a client acknowledging paedophile tendencies or someone who confirms being sexually abusive towards a child or a partner. How can the telehealth professional take the necessary steps to protect potential or actual victims if the physical location of those individuals cannot be revealed without involving major, ethically debatable efforts of tracing'. (Tepper et al., 2002: 82) The difficulties that come with potential disclosure are considerable and are not readily reconciled with what the service purports to offer.

CROGA

In 2002 the COPINE Project at University College Cork received funding from the EU Daphne Initiative to design and pilot a web based CBT programme, developed from prior research with Internet offenders. The programme, named CROGA because it had no actual meaning in English, Spanish and

Italian (the site languages), targeted people engaging in problematic Internet use through downloading, trading and producing images. The goals of the website were to provide a proactive education and intervention programme and to generate data that would help provide novel information about this population. Its structure reflected three important and related areas: education, self-exploration and self-help. CROGA did not purport to replace face-to-face intervention, but was rather seen as a first step towards acknowledging the presence of a problem and taking some action to change. This was emphasised through the use of an initial disclaimer, which the user had to acknowledge before entering the site. Other research in this area had stressed the role of education materials in raising awareness about the nature and consequences of sexual activity for the individual. In the context of cybersex, Delmonico et al., (2002) suggested that 'often, inappropriate recreational users are unaware of the impact of their behaviour on others. Education that raises awareness of such impact, informs them of social etiquette of sexual harassment policies in the workplace and addresses other topics will often resolve issues associated with this group. However, raising awareness is a critical task for the problematic user as well'. (p. 154) In the context of the present study, educational resources were provided that listed the various laws in European countries and suggested links to further education sources both online and offline.

The section in the website relating to 'self-exploration' reflected the ongoing ethical difficulties that such resources bring with them. While it was important for service users to be able to explore the nature of their difficulties, it was equally important that this should not be confused with an assessment that would lead to diagnosis, or that would provide a defence within the legal system should a person be caught engaging in illegal activities and be brought to court. An additional problem related to the fact that the process of cybersex assessment remains in its formative stages, and as yet there are no comprehensive, reliable and valid instruments available to clinicians (Delmonico et al., 2002). In addition, there are no current instruments that relate directly to the therapeutic goals of CROGA, nor that reflect the fact that users of online sexual activity are not a homogeneous group. The measures used in relation to CROGA were:

- Daily record of Internet use and illegal activity.
- Internet Dependency Checklist (Young, 1998).
- The Online Cognition Scale (Davis et al., 2002).
- Internet and Values (Luciano and Ortega, 2004).
- Illegal activities on the Internet matrix.

At the time of developing CROGA we were aware of potential difficulties in gaining information through these questionnaires, in particular the Internet matrix which described specific offending behaviours. Prior research by Riva et al., (2003: 78) which compared online and offline questionnaires of attitude change in Italian students had suggested that, '. . . web-based data collection neither statistically enhance nor diminish the consistency of responses, nor compromise the integrity of the test, and are a suitable alternative to more traditional methods'.

However, participants in Internet research remain unmonitored, are self-selected (usually skewed towards the high end of the socio-economic and educational spectrum) and any assessment tool requires the development of different web pages and administration of the data base in which the answers are stored. There is also anecdotal evidence to suggest that a large number of people who commence responding to sexually-related Internet-based questionnaires drop out before completion (Ross et al., 2003), and this may suggest one reason why Internet-based questionnaires are typically less than 15 minutes long. The study by Ross et al., (2003) attempted to examine drop out rates and the demographic characteristics of those who drop out of completing questionnaires as opposed to those who do not. The research design allowed them to track response rate throughout the consecutive items of the sexuality questionnaire. In this study the first question (which asked the age of the participant) was answered by 3,614 persons, whereas 1,851 answered the last question. Half of the males had dropped out by item 23, compared to half of the females who dropped out by item 49. There was a relatively rapid rate of dropout that flattened over time. This research clearly indicated that drop out rates for questionnaires about sexual behaviour were high and that critical data questions should be placed as early as possible in the questionnaire. Men, but not women, with slower Internet connections were significantly more likely to drop out, suggesting that time and impatience are more important to male than female respondents.

In traditional CBT interventions 'what works' is largely assessed by the administration of pre and post measures that relate to the target problems. With the Internet we not only have an increased likelihood that people will drop out before completing the questionnaires, but we also have an anonymised data set that then cannot distinguish (unless users are willing to identify themselves with a unique identifying alphanumeric) who has completed each set of questionnaires. How people use the site is therefore additional information that can be assessed through the collection of access and usage data (Sterne, 2002). In the context of CROGA it was decided that such webmetric data was possibly as important as the actual test data as it would tell us about people's interaction with the site. We therefore decided to focus on:

- Number of hits (daily score)?
- Referrer log – which site did they come from?
- Visitor url (annonymiser/nationality).
- Entry site page – which was first page they accessed?
- Exit page from site – what page did they leave site from?
- Length of time viewing each individual page.
- Overall length of time that was spent on the site by individuals.
- Number of downloads and of what?
- Paths used through the site (individual sequences which can be graphical representations).
- Test data – organised by the individual.
- Comments (sent by email, invited at the end of each section and organised by individual text).
- If individuals used a unique identifier, related pre and post test data.

However, what is apparent is that this would not let us identify multiple accesses by the same individual, which may affect data relating to such things as navigation through the site. It was possible to ask 'Is this your first visit to the site?' which would mean that some of the items could then be sorted between 'new user' and 'old user' without compromising anonymity. The test data was also reliant on self-report, with all the problems that this brings in relation to the accuracy of the responses. However we should note that paradoxically, there appears to be evidence that people are more 'honest' in their responses to Internet questionnaires and more willing to disclose personal information. For example Proudfoot et al., (2003) demonstrated that patients were more likely to disclose suicide plans to a computer than to a human being.

The CROGA site developed out of collaborative academic and practitioner research, which was subject to peer review and comment before it was launched. It attempted to target a population about which little was known and where there had been minimal empirical work. At the time of writing this chapter, the site has been in existence for three months, and had been launched with minimal publicity. An early concern related to the dissemination of the site to those who might benefit from it, and while this is still an ongoing concern the numbers accessing CROGA has surprised us. As anticipated from prior research, our early results suggest that while initial access levels are high, the majority of those who go to the site do not get past the disclaimer notice. Of those who do agree to the disclaimer, site usage falls off again in terms of how people work through both the explorations and the self-help material. What is encouraging is that we already have sufficient data from the questionnaires that will enable statistical analysis and comparison with other studies. Previous research by Davis et al., (2002) had led to the development of the Online Cognition Scale as a measure of problematic or addictive Internet use, and was one of the questionnaires used in the CROGA site. It will be of interest to see how our questionnaire data compares with that of Davis et al., (2002) and Young (1998).

As a parallel activity we are currently piloting the material with known sex offenders who have used the Internet. However, this cannot address the problems of being able to examine change in the short term over long-term change, which is a problem common to most treatment programmes. In line with recent research by Ward and Brown (2004), we have argued that we decrease the likelihood of future offending by helping people address their needs in more productive and valued ways. One aspect of the self-help materials on CROGA has been to help those accessing the site to look at how their emotional, sexual and social needs were being met through engagement with illegal images and how these needs may be met in other non-offending ways. We have, through the use of a values-based questionnaire (Luciano and Ortega, 2004) made it possible for people to make explicit what they value in life and how far their illegal use of the Internet has blocked them in their bid to meet these values. Central to the self-help materials is a non-judgemental and supportive stance, and this is reflected in the language used throughout the site. Aggressive, confrontational styles have been seen as problematic in sex offender intervention and we believed that this needed to be addressed through text as much as would be the case in any therapeutic alliance.

CROGA was created out of a belief that there are many people struggling with difficulties posed by the availability of illegal images of children on the Internet. In a world that views such activities as criminal, the likelihood of many people seeking help must, at best, be reduced. This also needs to be considered in the context of the availability of therapeutic services. The numbers who may avail themselves of help are unknown. It is apparent from the volume of illegal material available on the Internet that there is clearly a marketplace for illegal images of children and that this must be supported by a considerable number of people who access it. One focus of the self-help materials in CROGA is a bid to increase awareness that behind each of the images is a child who is being sexually exploited or abused, and it is important that we acknowledge that the goal of intervention is not only to reduce the problematic behaviour of those accessing such images but also to reduce the ongoing abuse and victimisation of the children in the images by reducing the market place. Clearly the data from CROGA will help us to learn more about this population and about those seeking help. While the data from the site is not without its problems, it should allow us to examine the effectiveness of both the site and its contents. However, while there is emerging evidence to suggest that the Internet can provide an accessible and cost-effective way of helping people, it is important that professional standards and not commercial considerations influence the development and use of self-help materials (Rosen, 1987). As we analyse the data from CROGA, this will inform us as both academics and practitioners about the changes that we need to make to increase the usability and effectiveness of the site.

References

Abracen, J. and Looman, J. (2001) Issues in the Treatment of Sexual Offenders: Recent Developments and Directions for Future Research. *Aggression and Violent Behavior*. 1, 1–19.

Alcañiz, M., Botella, C., Banos, R., Perpina, C., Rey, B., Lozano, J.A., Guillen, V., Barrera, F. and Gil, J.A. (2003) Internet-based Telehealth System for the Treatment of Agoraphobia. *CyberPsychology and Behavior*. 6: 4, 355–58.

Andersson, G. and Carlbring, P. (2003) Editorial – special issue: Internet and Cognitive Behaviour Therapy: New Opportunities for Treatment and Assessment. *Cognitive Behaviour Therapy*. 32, 97–9.

Barak, A., and Fisher, W.A. (2002) The Future of Internet Sexuality, in Cooper, A. (Ed.) *Sex and the Internet: A Guidebook for Clinicians*. New York: Brunner Routledge.

Becker, J.R. (1994). Offenders: Characteristics and Treatment. *The Future of Children: Sexual Abuse of Children*. 4, 176–97.

Beech, A., Fisher, D. and Thornton, D. (2003) Risk Assessment of Sex Offenders. *Professional Psychology: Research and Practice*, 34: 4, 339–52.

Boies, S., Cooper, A. and Osborne, C.S. (2004) Variations in Internet-related Problems and Psychosocial Functioning in Online Sexual Activities: Implications for Social and Sexual Development of Young Adults. *CyberPsychology and Behavior*, 7: 2, 207–30.

Burdon, W.M. and Gallagher, C.A. (2002) Coercion and Sex Offenders: Controlling Sex-offending Behavior Through Incapacitation and Treatment. *Criminal Justice and Behavior*. 29, 87–109.

Castelnuovo, G., Gagglioli, A., Mantovani, F. and Riva, G. (2003) From Psychotherapy to e-therapy: The Integration of Traditional Techniques and New Communication Tools in Clinical Settings. *CyberPsychology and Behavior*. 6: 4, 375–82.

Carlbring, P. and Andersson, G. (2004) Internet and Psychological Treatment. How Well can They be Combined? *Computers in Human Behavior*. (in press).

Carlbring, P., Ekselius, L. and Andersson, G. (2003) Treatment of Panic Disorder via the Internet: a Randomized Trial of CBT versus Applied Relaxation. *Journal of Behavior Therapy and Experimental Psychiatry*. 24, 129–40.

Cooper, A. (2004) Online Sexual Activity in the New Millennium. *Contemporary Sexuality*, 38, i–vii.

Cooper, A. and Griffin-Shelley, E. (2002) In Cooper, A. (Ed.) *Sex and the Internet. A Guidebook for Clinicians*. New York: Brunner Routledge.

Cooper, A., Morahan-Martin, J., Mathy, R.M. and Mahen, M. (2002a) Toward an Increasing Understanding of User Demographics in Online Sexual Activites. *Journal of Sex and Marital Therapy*. 28, 105–29.

Cooper, A., Golden, G.H. and Kent-Ferraro, J. (2002b) Online Sexual Behaviors in the Workplace: How can Human Resource Departments and Employee Assistance Programs Respond Effectively? *Sexual Addiction and Compulsivity*. 9, 149–65.

Cooper, A., Griffin-Shelley, E., Delmonico, D.L. and Mathy, R.M. (2001) Online Sexual Problems: Assessment and Predictive Variables. *Sexual Addiction and Compulsivity: The Journal of Treatment and Prevention*. 8: 3–4, 267–86.

Cooper, A., Scherer, C.R., Boies, S.C. and Gordon, B.L. (1999) Sexuality on the Internet: From Sexual Exploration to Pathological Expression. *Professional Psychology: Research and Practice.* 30: 2, 154–64.

Copeland, J. and Martin, G. (2004) Web-based Interventions for Substance Use Disorders: A Qualitative Review. *Journal of Substance Abuse Treatment.* 26: 2, 109–16.

Craig, L.A., Browne, K.D. and Stringer, I. (2003) Treatment and Sexual Offense Recidivism. *Trauma, Violence, and Abuse.* 4, 70–89.

Cuijpers, P. (1997) Bibliotherapy in Unipolar Depression: A Meta-analysis. *Journal of Behavioral Therapy and Experimental Psychiatry.* 28, 139–47.

Davis, R.A., Flett, G.L. and Besser, A. (2002) Validation of a New Scale for Measuring Problematic Internet Use: Implications for Pre-employment Screening. *CyberPsychology and Behavior.* 5: 4, 331–45.

Delmonico, D.L, Griffin, E. and Carnes, P.J. (2002) Treating Online Compulsive Sexual Behavior: When Cybersex is the Drug of Choice, in Cooper, A. (Ed.) *Sex and the Internet. A Guidebook for Clinicians.* New York: Brunner Routledge.

Edwards, S. (1994) Pretty Babies: Art, Erotica or Kiddie Porn? *History of Photography.* 18: 1, 34–6.

Enneking, J.M., Blake, P.A., McCleery, M.B., Gurgiolo, T., Cowe, R., Anderson, J., Sheriden, L. and Clonch, B. (2004) A Telehealth Program for Heart Failure: An Adjunct to Patient Management. *Journal of Cardiac Failure.* 10: 4, Suppl. 382.

Farrell, S.P., Mahone, I.H. and Guilbaud, P. (2004) Web Technology for Persons with Serious Mental Illness. *Archives of Psychiatric Nursing.* XVIII: 4, 121–25.

Fenichel, M., Suler, J., Barak, A., Zeluin, E., Jones, G., Munro, K., Meunier, V. and Walker-Schmucker, W. (2002) Myths and Realities of Online Clinical Work. *CyberPsychology and Behavior.* 5: 5, 481–97.

Fisher, D. and Beech, A.R. (1999) Current Practice in Britain with Sexual Offenders. *Journal of Interpersonal Violence.* 14, 240–56.

Galbraeth, N.W., Berlin, F.S. and Sawyer, D. (2002) Paraphilias and the Internet, in Cooper, A. (Ed.) *Sex and the Internet: A Guidebook for Clinicians.* New York: Brunner Routledge.

Goodrum, A. and Spink, A. (2001) Image Searching on the Excite Web Search Engine. *Information Processing and Management: An International Journal.* 37: 2, 295–311.

Gould, R.A. and Clum, A.A. (1993) Meta-analysis of Self-help Treatment Approaches. *Clinical Psychology Review.* 13, 169–86.

Hall, G.C.N. (1995) Sexual Offender Recidivism Revisited: A Meta-analysis of Recent Treatment Studies. *Journal of Consulting and Clinical Psychology.* 63, 802–9.

Hanson, R.K. et al. (2002) First Report of the Collaborative Outcome Data Project on the Effectiveness of Psychological Treatment for Sex Offenders. *Sexual Abuse: A Journal of Research and Treatment.* 14, 169–94.

Hanson, R.K. and Bussière, M.T. (1998). Predicting Relapse: A Meta-analysis of Sexual Offender Recidivism Studies. *Journal of Consulting and Clinical Psychology.* 66, 348–62.

Hollin, C. (1999) Treatment Programs for Offenders. Meta-analysis, What Works and Beyond. *International Journal of Law and Psychiatry.* 22: 3–4, 361–72.

Howells, K., Day, A. and Wright, S. (2004) Affect, Emotions and Sex Offending. *Psychology, Crime and Law,* 10: 2, 179–95.

Ishi, K. (2003) Internet Use via Mobile Phone in Japan. *Telecommunications Policy.*

Kemshall, H., Mackenzie, G. and Wood, J. (2004) *Stop It Now! UK and Ireland. An Evaluation.* Leicester: Community and Criminal Justice Division, De Montfort University.

King, S.A. (1999) Internet Gambling and Pornography: Illustrative Examples of the Psychological Consequences of Communication Anarchy. *CyberPsychology and Behavior*, 2: 3, 175–93.

Laszlo, J.V., Esterman, G. and Zabko, S. (1999) Therapy over the Internet? Theory, Research and Finances. *CyberPsychology and Behavior*, 2: 4, 293–307.

Laws, D.R. and Marshall, W.L. (2003) A Brief History of Behavioral and Cognitive Behavioral Approaches to Sex Offenders: Part 1. Early Developments. *Sexual Abuse: A Journal of Research and Treatment*. 15, 75–92.

Looman, J., Abracen, J. and Nicholaichuk, T.P. (2000) Recidivism Among Treated Sexual Offenders and Matched Controls: Data from the Regional Treatment Centre (Ontario). *Journal of Interpersonal Violence*, 15, 279–90.

Luciano, C. and Ortega, J. (2004) Internet and Values. Personal Communication.

Marrs, R. (1995) A Meta-analysis of Bibliotherapy Studies. *American Journal of Community Psychology*, 23, 843–70.

Marshall, W.L. and Laws, D.R. (2003) A Brief History of Behavioral and Cognitive Behavioral Approaches to Sex Offender Treatment: Part Two, The Modern Era. *Sexual Abuse: A Journal of Research and Treatment*. 15: 2, 93–120.

Marshall, W.L. and Anderson, D. (2000) Do Relapse Prevention Components Enhance Treatment Effectiveness? in Laws, D.R. (Ed.) *Remaking Relapse Prevention with Sex Offenders*. California: Sage Publications.

Marshall, W.L. and Marshall, L.E. (2000) The Origins of Sexual Offending. *Trauma, Violence and Abuse*. 1, 250–63.

Marshall, W.L., Anderson, D. and Fernandez, Y. (1999) *Cognitive Behavioral Treatment of Sexual Offenders*. England: John Wiley & Sons, Ltd.

Marshall, W.L. and Barbaree, H.E. (1990) Outcome of Comprehensive Cognitive-behavioral Treatment Programs, in Marshall, W.L. (Eds.) *Handbook of Sexual Assault: Issues, Theories, and Treatment of the Offender*. New York: Plenum Press.

Marshall, W.L. and Eccles, A. (1996) Cognitive-behavioral Treatment of Sex Offenders, in Van Hasselt, V.B. and Hersen, M. (Eds.) *Sourcebook of Psychological Treatment Manuals for Adult Disorders*. New York: Plenum Press.

Marshall, W.L. and Pithers, W.D. (1994) A Reconsideration of Treatment Outcome with Sex Offenders. *Criminal Justice and Behavior*. 21, 10–27.

McGrath, R.J., Cumming, G., Livingston, J.A. and Hoke, S.E. (2003) Outcome of a Treatment Program for Adult Sex Offenders: From Prison to Community. *Journal of Interpersonal Violence*. 18, 3–17.

Middleton, D., Beech, A. and Mandeville-Norden, R. (2004) *What Sort of a Person could do That? – Psychological Profiles of Internet Pornography Users*. Paper presented at 5th COPINE Conference, Cork, May.

Middleton, D. (2004) Current Treatment Approaches, in Calder, M. (Ed.) *Child Sexual Abuse and the Internet: Tackling the New Frontier*. Lyme Regis: Russell House Publishing.

Nicholaichuk, T. and Yates, P. (2002) Treatment Efficacy: Outcomes of the Clearwater Sex Offender Program, in Schwartz, B. (Ed.) *The Sex Offender: Current Treatment Modalities and Systems Issues*. Vol. 4. New Jersey: Civic Research Institute, Inc.

Proudfoot, J. et al. (2003) Computerised, Interactive, Multimedia Cognitive Behavioural Program for Anxiety in General Practice. *Psychological Medicine*, 33, 217–27.

Quayle, E., Vaughan, M. and Taylor, M. (in press) Sex Offenders, Internet Child Abuse Images and Emotional Avoidance: The Importance of Values. *Aggression and Violent Behaviour*.

Quayle, E. (2004) The Impact of Viewing on Offending Behaviour, in Calder, M.C. (Ed.) *Sexual Abuse and the Internet: Tackling the New Frontier*. Lyme Regis: Russell House Publishing.

Quayle, E. and Taylor, M. (2003) Model of Problematic Internet use in People with a Sexual Interest in Children. *CyberPsychology and Behavior*. 6: 1, 93–106.

Quayle, E. and Taylor, M. (2002) Child Pornography and the Internet: Perpetuating a Cycle of Abuse. *Deviant Behavior*. 23: 4, 331–62.

Quayle, E., Holland, G., Linehan, C. and Taylor, M. (2000) The Internet and Offending Behaviour: A Case Study. *Journal of Sexual Aggression*. 6: 1–2, 78–96.

Ritterband, L.M., Gonder-Frederick, L.A., Cox, D.J., Clifton, A.D., West, R.W. and Borowitz, S.M. (2003) Internet Interventions: In Review, in Use, and into the Future. *Professional Psychology: Research and Practice*. 34: 5, 527–34.

Riva, G., Teruzzi, T. and Anilli, L. (2003) The Use of the Internet in Psychological Research: Comparison of Online and Offline Questionnaires. *CyberPsychology and Behavior*. 6, 73–80.

Rosen, G. (1987) Self-help Treatment Books and the Commercialization of Psychotherapy. *American Psychologist*. 42, 46–51.

Ross, M.W., Daneback, K., Mansson, S-A., Tikkahen, R. and Cooper, A. (2003) Characteristics of Men and Women who Complete or Exit from an on-line Internet Sexuality Questionnaire: A Study of Instrument Drop-out Biases. *Journal of Sex Research*. 40: 4, 396–402.

Rotunda, R.J., Kass, S.J., Sutton, M.A. and Leon, D.T. (2003) Internet Use and Misuse. Preliminary Findings from a New Assessment Instrument. *Behavior Modification*. 77: 4, 484–504.

Schofield, R.S. et al. (2004) Telehealth Management of Chronic Heart Failure Optimizes the use of Diuretic Therapy. *Journal of Cardiac Failure*. 10: 4, Suppl. 387.

Scogin, F. and McElreath, L. (1994) Efficacy of Psychosocial Treatments for Geriatric Depression: A Quantitative Review. *Journal of Consulting and Clinical Psychology*. 62, 69–74.

Seto, M.C., Maric, A. and Barbaree, H.E. (2001) The Role of Pornography in the Etiology of Sexual Aggression. *Aggression and Violent Behaviour*. 6, 35–53.

Song, I., Larose, R., Eastin, M. and Lin, C.A. (2004) Internet Gratifications and Internet Addiction: On the Uses and Abuses of New Media. *CyberPsychology and Behavior*. 7: 4, 384–94.

Spink, A., Koricich, A., Jansen, B.J. and Cole, C. (2004) Sexual Information Seeking on Web Search Engines. *CyberPsychology and Behavior*. 7: 1, 65–72.

Sterne, J. (2002) *Web Metrics: Proven Methods for Measuring Web Site Success*. New York: Wiley.

Sturmey, P. (1996) *Functional Analysis in Clinical Psychology*. Chichester: Wiley.

Taylor, M. and Quayle, E. (2003) *Child Pornography: An Internet Crime*. Brighton: Routledge.

Taylor, M. and Quayle, E. (in press) Abusive Images of Children, in Cooper, S., Giardino, A., Vieth, V. and Kellogg, N. (Eds.) *Medical and Legal Aspects of Child Sexual Exploitation*. Saint Louis: GW Medical Publishing.

Tepper, M.S. and Owens, A.F. (2002) Access to Pleasure, in Cooper, A. (Ed.) *Sex and the Internet. A Guidebook for Clinicians*. New York: Brunner Routledge.

Terry, K.J. and Tallon, J. (2004) *Child Sexual Abuse: A Review of the Literature*. The Jon Jay College Research Team. Available online at http://www.usccb.org/nrb/johnjaystudy/litreview.pdf.

Toll, B.A., Sobell, L.C., D'Arienzo, J., Sobell, M.B., Eickleberry-Goldsmith, L. and Toll, H.J. (2003) What do Internet-based Alcohol Treatment Websites Offer? *CyberPsychology and Behavior*. 6: 6, 581–6.

Ward, T. and Brown, M. (2004) The Good Lives Model and Conceptual Issues in Offender Rehabilitation. *Psychology, Crime and Law*. 10: 3, 243–57.

Ward, T. (2002) Good Lives and the Rehabilitation of Offenders. Promises and Problems. *Aggression and Violent Behavior*. 7, 513–28.

Wheeler, B. (2003) An Amnesty for Internet Paedophiles. *BBC Online Magazine*, 9 December. Available at http://news.bbc.co.uk/2/hi/uk_news/magazine/3254382.stm.

Whitfield, G. and Williams, C. (2003) The Evidence Base for Cognitive-behavioural Therapy in Depression: Delivery in Busy Clinical Settings. *Advances in Psychiatric Treatment*. 9, 21–30.

Williams, C. (2001) Use of Written Cognitive-behavioural Therapy Self-help Materials to Treat Depression. *Advances in Psychiatric Treatment*. 7, 233–40.

Winzelberg, A. (1997) The Analysis of an Electronic Support Group for Individuals with Eating Disorders. *Computers in Human Behavior*. 13, 393–407.

Young, K.S. and Case, C.J. (2004) Internet Abuse in the Workplace: New Trends in Risk Management. *CyberPsychology and Behavior*. 7: 1, 105–111.

Young, K.S. (1998) Internet Addiction: The Emergence of a New Clinical Disorder. *CyberPsychology and Behavior*.1: 3, 237–44.

Chapter 11

Interpol and Crimes against Children

Hamish McCulloch

Interpol, the international criminal police organisation, was established in 1923, as a direct response to the recognition by police organisations in Europe that international co-operation was required to combat the growing threat of trans-national crime.

The organisation now has 181 member states and is truly global in every sense of the word. It is in fact the only global policing organisation operating a state of the art communication system that allows all member states to communicate with each other and pass vital police information through a totally secure and encrypted network. This is called I 24–7: Interpol – 24 hours a day, 7 days a week.

Despite Interpol being in existence for more that 80 years, it is only since 1989 that the organisation began involving itself in combating crimes against children. This coincided with the first World Congress on the Commercial Exploitation of Children which was held in Stockholm, Sweden the same year as the opening of the new Interpol General Secretariat in Lyon and the most ratified and popular convention ever – The UN Convention on the Rights of the Child.

During the early days resources were limited and the unit developed slowly until 1993 when the first Interpol Specialist Group on Crimes Against Children met in Lyon, France, to develop a strategy and decide the best way forward. The same group has now met on more than 21 occasions.

The group is made up of law enforcement officers working nationally to protect children and as crimes trends have changed, so has the group which now focuses on four specific theme groups:

- child prostitution and sex tourism
- missing and trafficking in children
- sex offenders
- child pornography

Since the group first met in 1993, child pornography has totally changed its focus following the development of the Internet.

In response Interpol has developed a greater proactive approach to assisting national law enforcement investigate crime, none more so than in the area of investigating crimes against children, especially crimes involving the sexual abuse of children whose images are distributed via the Internet. The main focus of the assistance provided involves the co-ordination of international investigations, analysis of information and intelligence recovered from police operations and more importantly, the operation of a child abuse image database with powerful software capable of matching images from the same series of abuse and images taken in the same location with different victims.

The role which is played by Interpol is developing on a daily basis and more countries than ever are tasking the Trafficking in Human Beings sub directorate in their efforts to combat crimes against children due to the vast amounts of data being recovered from computers all over the world which are seized during investigations into those persons who seek to produce, distribute and collect images of children being sexually abused.

Regarding the co-ordination of investigations, the first that Interpol were asked to assist with was Operation Cathedral, globally known as Wonderland. Much as been written and spoken about this network, and the investigation, which involved simultaneous arrests of networking paedophiles in many countries. That was in 1998, much has been learnt since and the amount of data being recovered has demanded that we move on.

As an example let me talk about Operation Landslide, Operation Ore in the United Kingdom, Operation Amethyst in Ireland and Avalanche in the United States. This investigation commenced in the United States and was undertaken by the US Postal Inspection Service, not by the FBI as has been claimed in many newspapers.

The US Postal Inspection Service identified a web site calling itself Landslide, which offered to provide access to a number of sites providing child pornography for a fee of $29.95. Payment was by credit card and those wishing to have access had to select the site they wanted and then enter their personal details and their credit card number, exactly as if you were booking a hotel or buying a product over the Internet.

In five months this site attracted hundreds of thousands of people, who paid a total of 5.5 million $US. When the operation was closed down and the arrests made the amount of data recovered was overwhelming. The US Postal Inspection Service were, as mandated, interested in persons in the US who had paid to access images, and the numbers involved precluded them from working on anyone outside North America. Consequently, Interpol offered to take responsibility for the analysis and processing of any information involving persons from the rest of the world to ensure that this valuable information on individuals with a sexual interest in children was not lost.

Subsequently, Interpol received a copy of the data recovered in the US that contained no less than 394,000 entries, which had to be analysed and sorted into individuals by country. More importantly, we had to be sure that the intelligence we passed out was accurate and referred to persons who had paid to access images of child abuse.

This was a challenge that we faced up to and within a short period we produced more than 60 different databases, one per country, and forwarded them to our Interpol bureaux who are our national points of contact in those countries. This may sound a simple task, but the UK alone had over 15,500 entries which represented more than 7,200 different individuals who, of course, had not entered the data in a standard format.

As a result operations have taken place in many countries, many thousands of searches and arrests have taken place, citizens from all walks of life have been identified as having a sexual interest in children, with police officers, judges, celebrities, clergy, schoolteachers and voluntary workers dealing with children to name a few. This was a remarkable list, individuals who had openly declared that they had a sexual interest in children. The very nature of material they wished to buy was evidence in itself and law enforcement agencies in different countries were shocked by the numbers of people involved.

New policing units were set up, countries reacted differently depending on their legislation, others were unable to act due to insufficient legislation, risk assessments were made on individuals, resources became stretched in some countries and others had to totally change their approach to child protection.

Other operations have since taken place, or are ongoing, and it is important that law enforcement globally uses the information which is constantly being passed to them by and through Interpol, to ensure that every effort is made to protect children from sexual abuse by swiftly undertaking positive action.

Interpol have also taken up the challenge handed down to them by member states and others, including the G8, to develop a state of the art image comparison database of images of child abuse. The necessity for a database was identified when the number of images in circulation rapidly exceeded those that the human brain could remember and analyse.

Investigators needed to know whether a victim was identified and was required to prevent law enforcement investigating already detected cases. If an image was new did the victim already appear in other images of abuse, if so which? Has the image been circulated? Important for the victim and the prosecutor? How old is the image, and where were the images taken?

The database which Interpol developed is based in the General Secretariat, and officers work with images received from member states, and others including COPINE, to fulfil the following objectives:

- The prevention of the sexual abuse of children through the identification of victims and abusers.
- Ensuring the best use of investigative resources by providing a global focal point for information on identified victims and ongoing investigations.

One of the major problems with this particular type of crime is identifying a country where the abuse took place as national law enforcement are responsible for investigating offences in their country. Consequently, very few agencies are prepared to invest their resources into trying to identify crime committed elsewhere than within their own borders.

When investigating the sexual abuse of children that is evidenced through images available on the Internet, the usual response is to prosecute for possession or distribution type offences. Very few investigators consider the possibility of trying to identify the victim but I believe that each and every investigator should be asking these three questions:

- Is this image known?
- Is the victim identified?
- Has the image been distributed?

Of course these are difficult questions to answer, but the identification of victims is possible and with the assistance of the officers working in Interpol investigators can ensure that no information is lost, that duplication of investigations are not taking place and most importantly, when a new image is identified it may just hold the final clue as to who or where the victim is.

So what problems prevent law enforcement from ensuring that all images of children being sexual abused are forwarded to Interpol for comparison?

Firstly, there are numerous, different law enforcement structures, both nationally and internationally. The United States has over 18,000 different law enforcement agencies; the United Kingdom has more than 50 different police forces alone. In France the towns and cities are the responsibility of the Police National whereas the more rural areas are policed by the Gendarmerie. In Italy we have three major police agencies; the Polizia Di Stato, the Carabinieri and the Guardia Di Finanzia, and in Germany the country is divided into regions which are policed by the Landeskriminalamt but Federal responsibility is under the jurisdiction of the Bundeskriminalamt.

Each country has a national point of contact through which Interpol information is passed. These points of contact are essential and have proved successful for many years. However, when dealing with images of children being circulated on the Internet, national points of contact need to identify the specialised units that many countries have set up, and allow them to interact directly with the officers operating the global database to ensure that all the evidence available, recovered in whichever country, is brought together to allow a complete analysis. Only then are we providing the best service to children who are the victims of Internet abuse, and inflexibility to change to allow access by investigators outside of the traditional national points of contact is unjustifiable.

Secondly, a major problem for any international investigation is language. Interpol operates in four languages; Arabic, English, French and Spanish. There are of course many other languages spoken in the organisation's member states and many investigators do not speak any of the official languages, others communicate other than in their mother tongue, but despite the difficulties of those working together in this crime area, the successful investigations which have led to the identification of victims and the prevention of continued abuse speak for themselves.

Thirdly, obstacles include national legal restrictions preventing prosecution for possession of images; other countries are yet to implement legislation dealing with this type of Internet crime. Different systems of investigation and prosecution occasionally hinder the cross border flow of information. For example, in the United Kingdom the police investigate and refer the evidence to the Crown Prosecution Service whereas in France, Belgium and many other countries, a Magistrate directs the investigation. Other legal restrictions are even more obstructive to investigations of Internet abuse, especially when national legislation exists preventing the police transmitting images of abuse to other law enforcement officers or to the Interpol database for comparison.

Fourthly, a system needs to be put in place to ensure that investigators dealing with images of child abuse are made aware of the global services that are available. However, logistically this is extremely difficult when different countries and agencies have varying priorities and objectives and new legislation may be required.

The investigation of sexual crimes against children has always been difficult. Corroboration has always been sought to back up an allegation made by a child. Historically this has been difficult, relying on medical evidence obtained through a traumatic examination, interview with police and social workers and, despite many countries improving their judicial practices to reduce the negative impact on children, ultimately having to attend court to provide evidence. The identification of a child from digital images recovered from the Internet or an offender now provides investigators with the corroboration they require. More importantly, in many cases they do not need the evidence from the victims, many of whom when interviewed actually deny any abuse took place.

Through use of the Internet the child sex offender is for the first time publicly announcing his sexual interest in children and it is the duty of law enforcement, in all countries, to ensure that any image which could have been instrumental in leading to the identification of a victim and the prevention of further abuse is forwarded to the Interpol database. It is equally important that images of identified victims are forwarded to avoid the duplication of investigations in the future. We must remember that those images circulating in cyberspace now will still be there in many years to come and we have a duty to future victims to ensure that the precious resources available are utilised to identify new victims and not those who are already identified.

Investigators must also ensure that any proactive initiatives they develop take into account other global activity. If a country is investing resources in the identification of persons possessing or exchanging images, or grooming children to sexually abuse, they need to be aware of what other countries are engaged in. Similarly, if a country has taken responsibility to investigate a particular series of images then Interpol must be aware to ensure any new images recovered from that series are made available to the investigators.

To conclude, the use of the Internet by persons to distribute images of children being sexually abused will continue to increase in line with accessibility. Interpol are at the heart of global policing efforts to combat the sexual abuse of children through the use of the Internet. Co-ordination and co-operation are vital to our success and to achieve our goal all available information must be made available through one centralised nexus at the Interpol General Secretariat.

Chapter 12

Global Issues and Regional Co-operation Fighting Child Exploitation

Lars Lööf

In Vilnius, the capital of Lithuania, two American men in their 30s met with two young teenage girls. The girls were persuaded by the Americans to follow them to an apartment where they were filmed in sexually explicit situations. The girls reported this to their parents who subsequently reported to the police. The Lithuanian police and the American police apprehended the two men who were sentenced for the production of child pornography.

Many countries in central and Eastern Europe, where some of the member states of the Council of the Baltic Sea States (CBSS) are situated, are struggling to fight poverty and people are striving to find a foothold in a world that has changed dramatically in the last ten years. The changing economies and the political changes have put a strain on individual families. Persons with a sexual interest in children have been known to use the situation in order to gain access to children and to abuse them sexually. Child abusive images that are produced in the eastern part of Europe find their way to the commercial sites, films showing minors in sexually explicit situations filmed in Ukraine or Russia are for sale on these sites. These disturbing facts are some of the reasons why the countries of the region have decided to prioritise the fight against abuse, violence and exploitation of children through establishing a special unit at the international secretariat of the CBSS; The Children's Unit.

It is a sad fact that even though child abusive images on the Internet have been in focus by international and national police authorities and by governments for some time now, they appear to become more and more numerous. As the flow of pictures of sexual abuse of children appears on the Internet, it becomes painfully clear that more and more children are involved in having experiences of sexual abuse, sexual exploitation and abuse documented by a camera.

On a regional level in the Baltic Sea area, the eleven member countries of the CBSS have decided to put an effort into fighting child sexual abuse and the sexual exploitation of children by joining the professional forces in place through a collaborative exercise. The collaboration in the region consists of exchange of experiences between professionals actively working with rehabilitation of abused and exploited children, researchers and policy makers. All these stakeholders are brought into the network of co-operation via the implementation of conferences, seminars, expert meetings and programmes aiming at shedding more light on the issue of abuse and exploitation of children in the Baltic Sea region. The governments in the region, through senior officials in the respective ministry responsible for children's issues have decisive influence over the precise issues that the co-operation should include and also ascertains that the results of the co-operation are brought to the attention of the governments. This close link with the decision makers actually constitutes the reason for several of the NGOs to participate in the networking. Connecting NGOs and governments in the area of protection of children at risk is a good way of establishing and maintaining a solid relationship between civil society and governments, especially important in countries that until recently lived under totalitarian regimes.

The Working Group for Co-operation on Children at Risk has put five issues as priorities:

1. The protection of children from all forms of sexual exploitation abuse and trafficking.
2. Unaccompanied and trafficked children.
3. Street children and children without a family.
4. The rights of children in institutions and in other forms of protection.
5. Young offenders and self-destructive behaviour in children.

The issue of sexual exploitation of children is a topic of major concern to all parties involved in the co-operation and it is also the topic where the network of professionals in the region is best developed. In all countries, knowledge of how children are affected by sexual abuse exist and professionals have developed methods on how best to assist children victimised by abuse. Some of the children that professionals meet with have also been sexually exploited, either in prostitution, through trafficking or in a few cases, through appearing in child pornography. The added difficulties facing the child survivor of exploitation is not an area where expertise is much developed. Not in this region, nor anywhere else. It is fair to assume that exploitation adds to the difficulties the child may experience, but how these express themselves and how a child is best assisted to assume control of them is not known.

An important aspect of the regional work is to try to develop expertise in areas where not enough knowledge exists in the region. Preventing child sexual abuse by preventing young persons turning into abusers, prevention on the so-called 'demand side' is certainly an area where gaps exist. What is it that turns a young boy into a man that may consider sexually abusing a child? Which attitudes can you find in young persons around these issues? We know little of adolescents' attitudes to and experiences of sexual exploitation and commercial sex. In order to have more knowledge on this, a group of researchers under the leadership of Dr Svein Mossige from NOVA Social Research Institute in Oslo, have started a joint research project where these questions are put to a group of young persons in seven countries. The study is conducted in the form of a questionnaire being distributed to a big group of young persons in the participating countries. The group needs to be large since many of the experiences that are asked about are expected to be low frequency phenomena and a big group of respondents may give enough material to draw conclusions from. The respondents are also asked about their use of pornography and about their attitudes to commercial sex. The research is up until now only finished in some countries but interesting results can already be seen. One result that is consistent with the few research attempts that exist in this area is that more boys than girls have experience of selling sex (Svedin and Priebe, 2004). The results will be used in the co-operation as we continue to think of ways to implement programmes that may target groups more likely to commit crimes against children. The results of the research will be published in the near future.

A child that is sexually abused, and where there is a depiction of the abuse, is faced with a number of considerations. Some of these are well known to the clinician but some are not. The abuse of a child thus covers five different but certainly related aspects:

1. The sexual abuse of the child.
2. The documentation; the photography, the video or the audiotape. That is the act of documenting the sexual abuse and violence.

3. The distribution of the images or the documents in a wider circle via use of the Internet or other electronic media distribution form.
4. The access to the abusive images, i.e. the person looking at the document of the abuse.
5. The downloading of the document.

Certainly all of the above acts are criminalised in most countries of the world with the exception of point 4. which is criminalised in some countries but not in others.

The police authorities investigate the crime and do as best they can to apprehend the offender. In doing this, the police have always been in need of assistance from the child clinicians since the investigation of the crimes need to be carried out in a child friendly manner in order to get as good an interview with the child as possible. If the interviews with the child are not carried out in child friendly ways, the acts committed by the abuser may continue to harm the child also in the investigative phase and the wise policeman and investigative officer understands that the more secure a child is when interviewed the better the evidence received. This makes knowledge on children and children's reactions to all of the above crimes important to understand for the police and for the prosecution. As with all other aspects of knowledge, this is something that comes with time and with experience and the more experiences that are accumulated, the better investigations will be performed by the individual investigating officer.

Police investigations on child sexual abuse are difficult to perform. In many cases it is a person very close to the child that is the suspected abuser and the child may well be reluctant to reveal much about what has occurred. The police investigations have become more and more sophisticated and expertise is being gathered as all countries' police forces gain increasing experience on how to carry out these interviews with children, and the police and child protection services also get more knowledge on how best to co-operate in order for the child to be kept safe and protected. However, the fact that an increasing number of cases of sexual abuse seem to involve a camera has not made a great impact in the forensic interviews of children, as the suspected victims of sexual abuse. Questions about the presence of a camera are rarely put to the child. Digital cameras are becoming common all over the world and the fact that pictures do not have to be processed makes it easy for the abuser to depict his victim. The knowledge of this comes from the fact that among the new child abusive pictures that appear, more and more seem to originate from home settings. Several cases where perpetrators have been apprehended and convicted for the production of child abuse images have involved children that are close to the perpetrator, living in their family or close by.

Child clinicians find themselves in a difficult area when it comes to the treatment and rehabilitation of a child who has been victimised by sexual abuse, photographing of the abuse, distribution of the images of the abuse, the accessing of the abuse by numerous strangers and the downloading and further distribution of the abusive images by uncounted numbers of 'anonymous' perpetrators. Children who have experienced the above crimes to their person and who have been identified are still few. Child clinicians with experiences of assisting these children in making sense of their experiences are also few in number, and this is why the sharing of experiences in this area, as in other areas of children at risk, is essential. So far, the knowledge on how children react to these experiences are only anecdotal and there is no research yet in place. Some descriptions and interviews have been made though and existing knowledge indicates some diverging strands:

1. **Peel an onion**. This is the expression used by Carl-Göran Svedin and Christina Back in their interviews with children who were part of a child pornography case pre Internet. The children would not disclose that they had been photographed, sometimes not even when the picture was

presented to them. In interviews with sexually abused children, the thing that is the most difficult to come to grips with is the issue that they will disclose last, leading to the metaphor of 'peeling an onion'. The thing that hurts the most is what abused boys and girls are the least likely to disclose to anyone. This also sheds some light on what other clinicians will tell you: If you don't specifically ask if there was a camera present during the abuse, the child will not disclose this, even if they will tell you other details.

2. **The abuse in itself overshadows the photography and the distribution of pictures**. This is a theory where the experience of the abuse would be so difficult to handle that the child does not consider the presence of a camera important.

3. '**Soft abuse**'. The unaware victim. In some cases, we know that the child has not been aware of the fact that they are being photographed. Maybe they have been secretly photographed on a beach or in a dressing room in a situation that is not abusive. These are the cases where there is evidence of exploitation but no abuse has taken place. The presence of the pictures naturally poses a severe exploitation of the child but the effects of the exploitation would be expected to be different than if the exploitation also includes abuse.

If we look at the impact that the presence of abusive images of the child has on the victimised child, we can, in my opinion, discern four levels that are of importance to the child and that should also be of importance both to professionals working with the rehabilitation of children and to law enforcement efforts, aiming at stopping the distribution of abusive images:

1. Global issues and global responses:

   - Finding the material through international co-operation.
   - Identifying children in the images. The international co-operation has this as an identified focus. Databases of pictures through which police authorities may receive information on seized pictures have been established in order for national police forces to be able to receive information on the child in the picture. A 'new' picture of what seems to be ongoing abuse can thus be prioritised so the police may find the child and stop the abuse. A 'new' picture from an old series may also prove important as it may add information to another investigation.
   - If we recognise the impact that distribution has on the individual child, a recognition that it may be of importance to the child eventually to know how widespread the distribution of the images are may arise. As the child becomes older, he or she may find some level of control over the experience through the knowledge that the images were found in distribution for three years, but that they seem no longer to be much distributed, provided this is the case.
   - Stopping distribution. Arresting distributors and closing down servers and networks used to distribute pictures has an impact on the individual child.

2. Regional co-operation.

   - Competence of assistance. Regional co-operation has its place in child protection and child rehabilitation especially when professionals in the field deal with protecting children from the effects of cross border phenomena like:
     (a) Distribution of child abuse images.
     (b) The trafficking of children.
     (c) Unaccompanied or separated children.

(d) Protection of children from domestic neglect and abuse when families move across national borders.

- Regional co-operation is also an invaluable tool when expertise and experience is scarce within the national setting. Many of the threats to children's safety when first recognised, are considered as minor threats on a national level. This first reaction is often due to the fact that when instruments to deal with them are not in place society will not be aware of them. One such historical phenomenon is the treatment and reintegration of young perpetrators of child sexual abuse. When young offenders were first recognised as a problem, they were considered to be so few in each country, that co-operation between professionals from different countries was absolutely vital as it was impossible for any professional to gather enough experience in the area. We now know that a large number of adult perpetrators admit to having committed their first offence when young making it inevitable that professionals everywhere meet with young offenders and that they all rise to the challenge of establishing services for them. The issue of rehabilitation of children that have been abused and photographed during the abuse and who experience these images to be distributed over the Internet is also such a phenomenon. The number of identified victims around the world is low and the experience professionals have is still scarce. The regional level should therefore at this point in time be used to establish contact channels and support systems for professionals who find themselves dealing with cases they so far have little experience in.

3. National responses. A number of specific challenges that have an impact on the ability for the individual victimised child to receive proper assistance are dealt with on a national level:

- Compensation. In a recent case in Sweden, the level of the financial compensation to the child victim of abuse and of having the pictures of the abuse distributed over the Internet was raised with a reference to the distribution. Since abusive images in Sweden are crimes against the state, not crimes against the individual child, this is an interesting change in thinking and may lead to courts taking a stand that all possession of child abusive images are violations against the child in the image thus opening the way for victimised children to be eligible for financial compensation.

- Court proceedings are obviously dealt with on a national level. How the court deals with the victimised child is crucial for the ongoing healing process. Many aspects play into this: time between disclosure and trial, appearance in court or ability to have video interviews with the child, etc.

- Sentencing may be another issue. In some countries the levels of sentencing are high, in others low. This plays into the recovery of the affected child in a number of different ways: it may affect the child's disclosure, especially if the perpetrator is a family member. It may also play into the possibility for the child protection agencies to protect the child from further harm if the sentencing is low, meaning that the suspected perpetrator will not be in custody prior to the trial and may have access to the child.

- Codes of conduct for the media. One important aspect for the recovery of the child is the control over the experience. Often the media attention may go counter to this as the child may become identified or feel as if he or she is identified by the intensity of the media coverage. In many countries the media have a code of conduct in cases concerning reporting on crimes against children. This code may need to be updated regularly in order for the media and others involved finding good working relationships. In the recent Swedish case, the media respected the need for the children to remain anonymous thus assisting in the recovery of the affected girls.

- Available assistance. Access to expert professional assistance for all affected children is an issue of importance that must be dealt with on a national basis. This concerns both access in different parts of the country and affordability of the assistance for all affected children.

4. Local accountability

- Protection and other child welfare policies are commonly the responsibility of the local community. How the local community manages its resources and finds room to assist affected children and their families is vital in the recovery process. In some communities it has not been possible for the child and the family to remain since the support level was so low. In other areas the local community has managed to pool its resources in order for the entire family to receive assistance and support 24 hrs a day.
- On the local level the access to qualified staff for assistance is of vital importance.

Case study

Drawing on the experiences from a recent Swedish case of victimised children I will present to you some of the lessons learned when dealing with exploited and victimised children. The case is one that dealt with the production, distribution and possession of large amounts of child abusive images over a long period of time. The number of victims was exceptionally high. The solutions found in the work around this case were adapted to the conditions that were present in the community.

The support to the affected children consisted of:

1. Crisis support. In the local community there existed a crisis plan. Law mandates each local council in Sweden to have such a crisis plan. The plan is there to be activated in any kind of crisis situation and points among other things to how the different local actors should co-ordinate their activities. The plan proved to be a solid foundation in the present case.
2. Support from day one. No part of the operation was hierarchically superior to any other part. This meant that the social support was as important as the police investigation and the psychiatric support to involved adults. All aspects of support were activated at the same time as the police made the first arrest. The involved authorities and agencies received information on the operation at the same time and could thus from the start be informed on the operation.
3. Support to parents and families. The involved families of the children were targeted alongside with the children. The involvement of adult psychiatric services from the onset proved to be extremely valuable as the adults needed a lot of support.
4. Highly organised. From the start the organisation of both the support and the police investigation were equally well-organised and timed in relation to each other. One example of this is how the different children were interviewed. These interviews were made in the presence of a supportive social worker. The social workers time for the interview needed to be co-ordinated with his/her other duties.
5. High availability. A 24 hr support telephone line was established.
6. Child friendly investigation. The interviewers were well acquainted with child friendly interview techniques.

Some of the prerequisites for a well functioning support structure that was identified by the professionals working on the case:

1. Strong and recognised leadership. The local police took charge of the whole operation from the start and remained the undisputed node.
2. Timing of the information. For the mobilisation of all resources to be really effective it was paramount that all agencies were given equal opportunities to plan their staff in order to meet the demands of the situation. Information was therefore not given only on a need to know basis since one part of the investigation/support team may be needed in a part of the operation that wasn't considered in the first place. This made unexpected turns in the developments possible to handle efficiently.
3. Involvement of operational staff within involved authorities and organisations leading to non-competitive co-operation. The fact that the operational staff, not the heads of the authorities were the ones that were involved from the onset made the co-operation develop without inter-agency competition or time-consuming discussions about mandates or boundaries.
4. The information strategy was mandated by the leadership.
5. Dealing with the media. Through the well designed information strategy to all involved it was possible to remain united in what should be said to the media and what should be kept out of public view.
6. Calling on the codes of conduct for the media regarding criminal cases involving children and regarding publishing names of suspects. The co-operation of the media was important. The media recognised the need to keep details from the public in order for the children to be given the best possible opportunity to heal.
7. Parental education/supervision. It took most of the involved professionals by surprise that parents needed so much information and time in order to be able to remain stable in relation to the involved children.

Lessons learned:

- Children need stable parents.
- Parents need information, information and more information to be able to remain stable.
- Parents need help to understand the child's reactions and the lack of visible reactions.
- Parents need to consider possible long-term reactions in their children.

Important aspects of online victimisation

Coming out of my own clinical experience and from discussions with colleagues working in the field I have come to think of the themes involved in the rehabilitation of exploited children as 'The four Cs':

- Complicity.
- Control.
- Closure.
- Compensation.

Complicity

In most cases of sexual abuse of children there is an element of complicity. Why did he abuse me? Is there something about me that made him choose me? In the abused child there is often a thought that it is their secret, the secret that sets them apart from other children that the abuser knows and has found. The fact that there are pictures of the abuse makes this feeling of complicity even more intense: maybe there are smiles in the pictures. The child may think that it looks like they are consenting to the abuse. The feeling of complicity is one that needs to be well considered in the rehabilitation of a child that is in this way publicly victimised. Several new issues may need to be dealt with in the course of treatment.

Control

The issue of control is one of the utmost importance to all of us. Growing up means gaining control over more and more of our immediate surroundings. When I was part of the team working to improve the identification of children appearing in abusive images on the Internet the team was once contacted by a woman. She stated that she thought there were pictures of her abuse on the Internet since she knew that the abuse had been photographed. She stated very clearly that she did not want to talk about it or to have anything to do with it – it had taken her years to come to some closure on this, she did not want to risk losing control of her experience by talking about it with some researcher. This to us was a very convincing testimony of how an abused and exploited woman considers her control over the event to be so fragile that a reminder, however small, jeopardised it. When assisting children in coming to grips with the aggressor and the violence, the issue of control fantasised or real, is essential. The loss of control over the situation seems to be one of the most disturbing memories of all kinds of violence that a child experiences. Regaining control is therefore a priority in all work to rehabilitate children that have been abused, and in the case of children that have been abused and exploited, it seems professionals need to maintain an extra battery of resources in order to assist the child in finding control. In the clinical setting this may include a small detail like controlling the door lock to the therapist's office.

Closure

Closure is the point where the boy or girl finds some kind of peace and may leave the experiences of the abusive situation behind them. Recognising that it has happened but that it is over is one element of this. Understanding that it cannot hurt them any more. Some authors argue that closure is impossible to find in cases where the evidence of the abuse, the abusive images, are out there and will circulate forever. Some professionals have even gone so far as to say that the child should not be told about the presence of abusive images that are in circulation. There may however be closure even when the images are in circulation, but it will probably need some thinking as to how it should be achieved. The pictures certainly will remain a scar each time a new paedophile ring is uncovered, with the thought that the abusive images may turn up. The fact that the images exist will need to be processed and each individual child will need to find a way to integrate this. In the few known cases where children have been identified and assisted the fact that the child's appearance will change is comforting to the exploited child. The person accessing the pictures of abuse on the Internet may thus not be able to recognise who the child is.

Compensation

Compensation may be one way of admitting to the affected child that what happened was wrong, illegal and should not have been allowed to happen. The compensation can come in many forms. One is through the legislation, insisting that the child and all affected children will be fully compensated through the incarceration of the perpetrators. Financial compensation is also an issue. We have all been saying that each person that looks at an abusive image commits an offence to the child in the picture. The child should therefore be liable for financial compensation from those accessing the picture on the Internet. In the latest Swedish case with identified victims of sexual abuse and of exploitation via distribution of abusive images on the Internet, the fact that the pictures where in distribution augmented the compensation for damages paid. Since possession of child pornography in Sweden is a crime against the state, this was new and possibly groundbreaking.

Some thoughts on systems involved in the struggle against child abusive images on the Internet

It is true and has many times been reiterated that child abusive images did not surface with the Internet. Long before this, child abusive images were sold and distributed in paper copies and on films and videocassettes. In several countries these magazines and films were legal and were sold quite openly in adult bookstores. Since the arrival of the Internet, the number of pictures available has grown and even though substantial efforts have been made to limit the distribution and to regulate the access to the Internet by those that produce and distribute pictures, the number of pictures keeps growing. The strategy recognised by everyone has been one of co-operation: co-ordinated actions between the police, the civil society, the regional organisations, the child protection services and the Internet Service Providers has been the modus operandi for a number of years. The fact is, however, that this co-operation hasn't provided the results hoped for. The Internet harbours more abusive images than before and new technological inventions and improvements have come in place, seemingly without considerations of how these may affect or put at higher risk children using the Internet or children at risk of being victimised via the Internet. This in my view makes it important to step back and reflect upon the path chosen. The partnership between all involved systems came about historically at a time when many decision makers on a European and national level were considering if it would be possible to enforce some form of regulations on the Internet industry. The industry responded with a strong lobby surge that included support for all forms of self-regulatory measures from their side of the industry. Disney Corporation produced safety awareness features that were available at their web site in which one of the three little pigs chatted with someone he thought was another little pig and gave the other little pig his home address. The other little pig turned out to be . . . the big bad wolf. As you can see the safety tips haven't changed much since the early days.

The EU eventually invested a lot of effort in the co-operation with the Internet Industry and has since the start of the Internet action plan programme invested large sums in projects where the Internet Service Providers and other parts of the Internet industry were to be natural partners in all endeavours. Development of filtering programmes, rating programmes, awareness raising programmes and hotlines for reporting of illegal material are some of the actions to protect children online that have been supported via this programme. All of these have had the positive aspect of raising the level of awareness regarding some of the dangers of the Internet. The fact that so much of that which we are still fighting has been there all along and has not been lessened by the joint efforts of the ISPs, the governments, the EU and the NGOs make it obvious to me that we may need to reconsider. I would claim that the wheel, contrary to what is regularly stated at meetings and conferences, has not been invented. The recirculation of ideas, the production of even more colourful mouse mats does not stop online child sexual victimisation. Maybe we are not doing the right thing? In my view the co-operation has at times clouded the view and impeded progress. The NGOs have been concentrating on what the police are doing and the international nature has made local actors passive. It is time for each agency to independently assess their ability and to find their specific input. The co-ordination may then be added once all actors are prepared to contribute with that which they do best, putting the protection of children before the protection of specific forms of co-operation or involvement of specific actors.

Governments find themselves in a rapidly changing environment when trying to respond to online victimisation of children. Governmental responses need to be influenced by the global discussion and practice in the areas, at the same time as the local, national and regional specificities need to be addressed. The regional co-operation enables ministries responsible for children's issues to have easy access to colleagues and professional expertise to make informed decisions on both the formulation of directives and on how best to formulate new laws. In my view it is time to put the victimised child at the centre of activities aiming at reducing and stopping the use of online technologies to abuse children. The perspective of the victimised child will assist us in making more informed decisions on how to proceed in this struggle. The lesson we have learnt from other areas of child abuse and violence against children is that it is more important to assist children at risk of becoming victimised through learning from the experiences of those that have already been abused. This has a bearing on how programmes are developed and how partnerships are formed.

Reference

Svedin, C.G. and Priebe, G. (2004) Ungdomars sexualitet – attityder och erfarenheter. Avsnitt sexuell exploatering. Att sälja sex mot ersättning/pengar. Bilaga 3. *Sexuell exploatering av barn i Sverige*. SOU:71.

Child sexual abuse and the Internet: tackling the new frontier

Edited by Martin C. Calder

"A high quality handbook." *Community Safety Journal*

"An accessible and useful reader." *Care & Health*

"Internet related sexual offending will soon be growing exponentially. This means it will figure largely in all our projects and all our caseloads...offending in this way is at least as complex a process as that which is involved in hands-on offending. As such it requires a tailored approach for assessment and treatment, an essential part of which is an understanding of the relationship between the Internet and its users...This book is a small but very useful handbook for us in our efforts to develop an understanding of the 'lie of the land', some pathways into it and how we can deal more effectively with those who use this frontier for the sexual abuse of children." *NOTA News*

"Informative and relevant to the daily work of professionals who deal with sexual offenders...I would strongly recommend this book to practicing professionals who wish to acquire basic and more advanced knowledge of assessing and managing individuals convicted of internet-related sexual offences." *Journal of Sexual Aggression*

CONTENTS

Introduction *Martin C Calder, Team Manager*

Understanding sexual offenders who use the Internet

The Internet: potential, problems and pathways to hands-on sexual offending *Martin C Calder*

The impact of viewing on offending behaviour *Dr Ethel Quayle*

From fixed to mobile internet: the morphing of criminal activity online *Rachel O'Connell*

Young people with sexual behaviour problems and the Internet *Robert E Longo*

Assessment and treatment issues

Assessing internet sex offenders *Joe Sullivan and Anthony Beech*

The challenge of sex offender assessment: the case of internet offenders *Sean Hammond*

Current treatment approaches *David Middleton*

Virtual offenders: the other side of internet allegations *Bill Thompson and Andy Williams*

Available now from Russell House Publishing Ltd. 144 pages   1-903855-35-7   £16.95

Russell House Publishing Ltd, 4 St. George's House, Uplyme Road, Lyme Regis, Dorset, DT7 3LS, UK.
Tel: 01297 443948 Fax: 01297 442722
Email: help@russellhouse.co.uk. Website www.russellhouse.co.uk

Prices are subject to change without notice. Registered Company Number: 2881219

Only pictures?
Therapeutic work with internet sex offenders
By Ethel Quayle, Marcus Erooga, Louise Wright, Max Taylor, & Dawn Harbinson

In recent years there has been a dramatic increase in the number of convictions for offences related to the use of child pornography. From the amount of child pornography available in public channels on the Internet, it would be safe to assume that this is mirrored by an increase in the numbers of people accessing such material, but who have not been caught.

Many practitioners are now confronted with the need to provide either therapy or effective management of this problem. This **timely and practical** book will help them do this well, by enabling more focused intervention with those who are seeking help as well as those who have committed offences. It arose out of significant collaborative work with those engaged in research and treatment provision to people who are accessing the Internet material.

Invaluable to anyone working in: child protection, social work, psychology, policing, probation, criminology; and including anyone working with those who self-refer or are referred by the courts. Readers will learn about: • sexual offences and the Internet • cognitive behaviour therapy approaches • how these approaches might be applied to the specific population. Practitioners will be helped to: • discriminate between different client presentations • assess the problem target • **draw up an appropriate intervention programme** • evaluate the effects of the implemented programme.

CONTENTS
Child pornography and the internet. Theories of child sexual abuse and the role of cognitive behaviour therapy. Process and problematic internet use. Images ARE children. Fantasy and its escalation. Emotional avoidance. Social activity and internet images. Collecting images. Future stumbling blocks.

Available now from Russell House Publishing Ltd. 176 pages   1-903855-68-3   £21.95

Russell House Publishing Ltd, 4 St. George's House, Uplyme Road, Lyme Regis, Dorset, DT7 3LS, UK.
Tel: 01297 443948 Fax: 01297 442722
Email: help@russellhouse.co.uk. Website www.russellhouse.co.uk
Prices are subject to change without notice. Registered Company Number: 2881219